African American Golfers During the Jim Crow Era

African American Golfers During the Jim Crow Era

MARVIN P. DAWKINS

AND

GRAHAM C. KINLOCH

Westport, Connecticut
London

Library of Congress Cataloging-in-Publication Data

Dawkins, Marvin P.
    African American golfers during the Jim Crow era / Marvin P.
Dawkins and Graham C. Kinloch.
        p.   cm.
    Includes bibliographical references (p.) and index.
    ISBN 0–275–95940–6 (alk. paper)
    1. Afro-American golfers—History.   2. Discrimination in sports—
United States—History.   3. Golf—Social aspects—United States—
History.   I. Kinloch, Graham Charles.   II. Title.
    GV981.D39   2000
    796.352'089'96073—dc21   99–34486

British Library Cataloguing in Publication Data is available.

Library of Congress Catalog Card Number: 99–34486
ISBN: 0–275–95940–6

First published in 2000

Praeger Publishers, 88 Post Road West, Westport, CT 06881
An imprint of Greenwood Publishing Group, Inc.
www.praeger.com

Printed in the United States of America

The paper used in this book complies with the
Permanent Paper Standard issued by the National
Information Standards Organization (Z39.48–1984).

10 9 8 7 6 5 4 3 2 1

Dedicated to
Ralph Dawkins, Sr.,
Professional Golfer
and
Altamese Dawkins
for her support and understanding

Contents

PART FOUR   DESEGREGATION BATTLES

PART FIVE   CONCLUSIONS

Preface

This book focuses on African American golfers and institutionalized racism in the United States during the period of racial segregation commonly referred to as the Jim Crow era. The impetus for this project was twofold: first, the book emerged out of a desire to learn more about the experiences of the first author's father, now eighty-nine years old, and other black golfers of the same generation. Second, both authors share a long-standing interest in more fully understanding the dynamics of institutionalized racism in the United States. Sport is a major type of social activity that offers important insight into discrimination processes. Also, golf is a relatively neglected area of serious analysis.

The earliest black golfers were largely introduced to the sport as young caddies for whites at exclusive, segregated country clubs. Shortly prior to the 1920s, the first author's father began caddying and became a serious golfer later that decade. By the late 1920s, he was convinced that he could pursue this sport as a professional career. However, like others of his generation, his golfing activity, especially in the following three decades, was restricted to settings provided by blacks themselves to offer opportunities for general play and avenues for the development of pro golfers.

A number of childhood golfing experiences stimulated the first author's interest in developing this project. As a youth growing up in the 1950s, I often went with my father to the black-owned golf course in my hometown but never developed an interest in the sport, which stood little chance of competing with my love for baseball. However, there was one short-lived occasion on which I thought I might become interested in this activity. My father would practice hitting balls at certain distances and I was required to stand in the vicinity where they would land, retrieving each and placing it in a canvas bag I carried. When the bag was filled, I returned the balls to him and he would again pour them out on the ground and usually instruct me to go a little further so he could practice longer drives. This process of "picking up balls" while he worked on his golf swing would go on for hours. Despite the consolation of earning money for this task, I found golf lacking in the excitement I derived from hitting, throwing, and catching a baseball until a particular day when I decided to combine the two sports. Unknown to my father, I brought my baseball glove along as I ventured out to await the sound of his hitting the balls that I could then catch like a fly ball in the outfield of a baseball park. Instead of picking up balls after they landed, I practiced chasing long fly balls. If I could catch golf balls on the fly, surely this would improve my ability to catch much larger baseballs! This was the most enjoyable golfing experience I had as a youth, but it ended immediately as my father calmly told me to leave the glove with him after I came in from retrieving a full bag of golf balls. I remember his exact words as he explained to me that "a golfer watches his ball until it stops rolling."

My father often told stories about the great golfers of the past and his own golf experiences. However, my brothers and sisters and I usually did all we could to keep from becoming "trapped" as his captive audience in one of his two-hour stories that traced the history of golf in America. When he got to the part about black pro golfers in the 1920s and 1930s, I was always convinced that he was really moving into the area of fantasy. Figuring out a way to distract him long enough to slip away became a family art. My best move was asking to be excused to use the bathroom. However, he would patiently wait until I returned and by that time he would have all of his golf clubs spread out in the living room and would proceed to give demonstrations to go along with the stories. I would remain in the bathroom as long as possible, until I heard someone else come into the house and get trapped by my father as his new audience. Then I would quietly slip out the back door, freed from these tales about black pro golfers. Even more incredible, my Dad said that *he* was a professional golfer. There was no question that he practiced and played enough golf out at the Lincoln Golf Course to be a pro golfer and occasionally went out of town to play in tournaments. However, since he did not really make any money from playing golf and always encouraged his children to aspire to other professions, I always figured this was something he *wanted* to be called because he loved the game so much. The only money I saw coming from his involvement in golf came from people who paid him to teach them how to play the game. There was also a little hustle I remember him playing, in which he would guarantee that he could straighten out someone's slice or hook for five dollars. He would say that if he could not get them to hit the ball straight in one lesson they did not have to pay him. He was usually successful but would laughingly explain to me that he would be able to make another five dollars from the same person next week because the person would drift back into the same mistake because of not practicing. He said *that* was one of the important distinctions between a leisurely golfer and a professional. By the time I reached adolescence in the early 1960s, I became more aware of the restrictions placed on black golfers and developed greater respect for their efforts to play the game on a wider scale. However, it would be many years later, well into my career as a sociologist specializing in race relations, before I developed an interest in examining the experiences of African American golfers in the context of racial segregation.

In the summer of 1991, I participated in a National Endowment for the Humanities–sponsored institute at Duke University entitled "Behind the Veil: African American Life in the Jim Crow South." The institute, which was conducted at Duke's Center for Documentary Studies and the Department of History, brought together a group of scholars, primarily from historically black colleges and universities, who were committed to documenting and preserving aspects of the lives of African Americans during the Jim Crow era. This unique and highly stimulating experience provided me with an enriching scholarly exchange and exposure to experts on the Jim Crow South who convinced me that despite not having formal training as a documentary specialist, I should dig deeper into exploring the topic of black golfers during the Jim Crow era. However, it was not until I organized a session at the Southern Conference on Afro-American Studies several years later that the idea for this book emerged. The theme for the conference focused on the years between the *Plessy* and *Brown* Supreme Court rulings and the session I organized was entitled "The Wide World of Segregated Sport." My co-author participated in this session and the response to the presentation of the experiences of Jim Crow era golfers, along with our long-standing mutual interest in institutionalized racism in America, led to this project.

The co-author was raised in the country of (what was then) Rhodesia, presently Zimbabwe. This setting was a rigid, caste-like colonial society in which the indigenous population was segregated from whites in every possible way. Needless to say, blacks were excluded from most sports, particularly golf, except for athletic activities available in their own schools and residential areas. However, I well recall sitting on my grandfather's porch, watching crowds of young black caddies practicing shots in a limited area on the golf course across the street, hoping to be employed by white golfers that day. Although these kinds of scenes have changed with independence, back then the "colonial" nature of the scene was clear, reflecting strict exclusion and subordination.

While the United States is typically depicted as "colonial" in a different way, this country nevertheless exhibits similarities to more traditional examples. I am constantly struck by the glaringly rigid nature of race relations in society, as well as parallels with my youthful experiences in Africa. Consequently, I have been keenly interested in the nature of institutionalized racism in American society for some decades. I was very excited when Marvin invited me to join him in developing this book, for the detailed insight into this kind of discrimination that the project clearly offered. Sports are depicted as one of the most "open" arenas in race relations, but are they in reality? Golf has also been relatively neglected in the research literature and media when it comes to monitoring the degrees and types of integration within it. The chapters that follow reveal in fascinating detail the widespread operation of institutionalized racism as reflected in black golf during the Jim Crow era of U.S. history. As a case study, this book reveals the dynamics of black sports activity, organization, and battles against segregation in the face of white racism's attempts to maintain its dominance despite these challenges, through a wide variety of techniques, including professional control of the sport. A number of changes need to be made if true equality and integration are to be achieved. I am very thankful for the opportunity I have been given to participate in this undertaking, and the insight it has provided into this important topic.

Acknowledgments

The authors would like to express their gratitude to a number of people who have contributed significantly to this enterprise. Sincere thanks for the stimulating discussions of the Jim Crow South are extended to Raymond Gavins and William Cafe, co-directors of the 1991 "Behind the Veil" summer institute along with the participants: Willie Fluker, James Eaton, Michael Hoffmann, Carolyn Denard, Henry Whelchel, Alma Williams, David Young, Florence Borders, the memory of Charles Frye (now deceased), Mary Nell Morgan, Dorothy Smith, Mary Coleman, Cynthia Lewis, Robert Jenkins, Marianne Bumgarner-Davis, T. Jesse Dent, Mack Staton, Freddie Parker, Alice Jones, Margaret Dwight, Lenwood Davis, Willie Legette, Ibiyinka Solarin, Howard Beeth, Lena Boyd-Brown, Lloyd Thompson, and Reginald Kearney. We would like to express our gratitude to students, especially Jacob Morton, who assisted at the early stages of the project. Special appreciation is also noted for work performed by Rosalie Roberts and Moneque Walker, who assisted by searching, retrieving, and reviewing information on golf-course discrimination suits. They were supported by the minority (undergraduate) summer scholarship program sponsored by the University of Miami's College of Arts and Sciences and eventually obtained law degrees and continue to hold interests related to racial discrimination and sports. Special thanks to Dori Powell, Shana Keller, and Shelby Gilbert who assisted in various ways, such as conducting searches of newspaper archives, meticulously transcribing hours of taped interviews, preparing the many drafts of the manuscript, and searching for people, places, and other little known information often with few if any leads. Thanks are due to Ken Shropshire for useful insights on the legal rights and protections of private organizations and for sharing his work in this area as it pertains to golf discrimination. We are indebted to Drs. Calvin and Elinor Sinnette. Calvin graciously shared his wealth of knowledge about African American golfers and provided access to other individuals and resources. Elinor offered insights related to her interview in 1986 with Ethel Williams of the Wake Robin Golf Club, the first independent black women's golf club in the United States. Several colleagues at the University of Miami, including Drs. Jomills Braddock, Don Spivey, Whittington Johnson, and Steve Sapp, were helpful and offered advice for which we are grateful. The Center for Research on Sport in Society at the University of Miami, under Dr. Braddock's directorship, supported the completion of work on the final drafts of the manuscript. Simone O'Bryan, CRSS graduate assistant, was especially helpful. We are also indebted to Dr. Kumble Subbaswamy, Dean of the College of Arts and Sciences at the University of Miami, for support that facilitated the completion of several rounds of interviews.

The first author's late wife and his present wife were the inspiration behind this book. Over two decades ago Willie Mae Leach Dawkins constantly asked the question of why sociologists seldom speak to issues of racism in ways that have meaning and significance beyond a small circle of scholars who spend most of their time writing and talking to each other rather than to the general public. Although you left us too soon, your wisdom continues to inspire. For Kim Elizabeth Dawkins, life itself is a treasure and opportunity to serve and share. Her life is an inspiration for those of us who, without her example, would be inclined to let life go by without doing our best to make a lasting contribution. We would also like to thank the following people who have provided advice and encouragement throughout the years: Dr. Marva Dawkins, Dr. Cecilia Dawkins, Dr. Donna Dawkins Baytop, Mattie Leach, Bettie Leach, Janet Leach, Lucy Leach, Thomas Leach, Richard Leach, and the late Thelma Commodore. Many years of "sports talk" with Jomills Braddock, Vincent Dawkins, Ralph Dawkins, Jr., and James Dawkins along with self-proclaimed experts from the North Dade (Miami) tennis team (Curtis Jackson, Joe Walker, Larry Pye, James Mahone, Nate Johnson, Robert Wilson, Tony Tynes, Dr. John Johnson, and Lonzo Williams) helped to keep the issue of racism in sports in constant focus. Thanks are extended to the following persons who offered encouragement at various stages in the development of this project: Bob Crain, Abel Bartley, Wornie Reed, Wayne Sifford, and Jeff Sammons. Bernard O'Dell shared personal insights related to his roles as tournament director of several of the tournaments sponsored by Joe Louis and as president of the Cosmopolitan Golf Association during the legal battle to desegregate the Miami Springs golf course.

We gratefully acknowledge the courtesy extended by various individuals and groups who granted permission to include material in the book. Sincere thanks to: JoEllen El Bashir and the Howard University Moorland-Spingarn Research Center, which granted permission to include quotes from a 1986 taped interview with Wake Robin member Ethel Williams contained in the Wake Robin Golf Club Papers; Donald Bradsher and the F. D. Bluford Library at North Carolina A & T University, which granted permission to include information from material contained in the Dr. George Simkins Papers; Saundra Sheffer and the Ralph W. Miller Golf Library, which granted permission to reprint the two photographs in Chapter 6 and for assistance in locating information related to activities of the PGA and other organizations; *The Western Journal of Black Studies*, which granted permission to reprint and modify Table 4.1 that is based on a table originally appearing in *The Western Journal*; the *Baltimore Afro-American Newspapers*, Inc., which granted permission to reprint the cartoon drawing of Joe Louis in Chapter 5 and selected photo clippings from the *Richmond Afro-American* newspaper contained in Chapter 6; and the *Chicago Defender* newspaper, which granted permission to reprint the photo clipping in Chapter 4 and selected photo clippings in Chapter 6. We are especially indebted to the following golfers who graciously recounted their experiences through taped interviews, provided photographs and other materials, and granted permission for us to include this documentary data in the book: Joe "Roach" Delancey, Ralph Dawkins, Sr., Everett Payne, Timothy Thomas, and Clarence Boyce.

Finally, our families were supportive throughout this undertaking, especially our wives, Kim and Beverley, who deserve special praise for tolerating months of our fun-filled preoccupation with golf courses, country clubs, and golf tournaments rather than work.

PART ONE
INTRODUCTION

CHAPTER 1

Sports and Discrimination

Professional sports have clearly become a major part of American popular culture, particularly its media and economy. On the surface, these activities may appear relatively equalitarian, meritocratic, and free of discrimination; closer examination, however, reveals the significant extent to which they reflect the larger society, particularly its racist stereotypes and discrimination. This book examines the historical operation of such inequality in a particular sport, focusing on historical periods of minority exclusion, segregation, and limited integration in the golfing arena.

American society has been racist since its colonial foundation. This has involved the subordination of Native Americans, expropriation of much of their land, forced importation of slaves, immigration of racially based contract labor, significant arrival of a wide range of ethnic groups, and continuing influx of refugees (cf. Kinloch, 1974). Within this context, a variety of racial and ethnic minorities have experienced prejudice and discriminatory treatment. Many have been differentially treated economically, politically, and socially—suffering significant levels of continuing deprivation.

Racism involves societal views of particular group members as presumably different and inferior on the basis of some identifiable physical characteristic, subjecting them to discrimination and exploitation. Race relations operate on at least three levels: individual, group, and institutional. The first involves individual prejudice, bias, and stereotyping, perpetrated and reinforced through socialization from early childhood. Attitudes also affect intergroup dynamics in the manner in which they function as the basis of group identity, particularly in competitive economic and political situations. Institutionalized racism, on the other hand, represents the manner in which inequality is *arranged* in the society at large with respect to organizational structures in the political, economic, and social spheres. Minorities may be excluded from full participation, subject to segregation with separate, unequal, and parallel types of arrangements, or eventually experience limited integration in the face of ongoing majority resistance. Regardless of the specific situation, minorities tend to experience unequal treatment, are assigned highly limited resources, and are continually subject to negative stereotypes regarding their assumed inferior traits (Kinloch, 1974). Throughout American history, they have experienced political exclusion and subordination, limited labor roles, and social stereotypes rationalizing their subordinate status.

This was particularly the case with Jim Crow laws that ensured that blacks were rigidly segregated, eventually in every sphere of American life. The term apparently originated in a song, "Jump Jim Crow," performed and popularized by a white minstrel performer, T. D. Rice, appearing in blackface depicting Jim Crow, a stereotypical black man (Jordan & Litwack, 1987), yet it also referred to legislation that goes back to the Reconstruction era in which a number of southern states passed laws excluding blacks from white transportation facilities (Woodward, 1957). This kind of segregation eventually extended to virtually every part of society, far beyond political rights and access to public transportation. Louisiana specifically enacted an 1890 law demanding separate train facilities for whites and blacks. This was challenged in 1896 in the well-known "separate but equal" case in *Plessy v. Ferguson*. The Court upheld the notion of "separate but equal" by majority vote, resulting in rigid types of racial segregation, not only in the South but in most parts of the country. As a result, segregation gained constitutional "respectability" and was consequently used to legitimize a wide variety of types of racial discrimination for many decades. Nowhere was this more applicable than at the golf course, a major social setting of white privilege and status. As we shall find, challenges to this particular kind of segregation were defended by the courts using the "separate but equal" interpretation of the Constitution for a significant period of time.

Professional golf, like many sports, has been subject to similar discriminatory practices. Except for a brief appearance by a limited number of individuals during golf's earliest days in the United States, African Americans were initially excluded from the game entirely, then permitted to assume the caddie role, established their own organizations and tournaments during segregation, and eventually experienced very limited acceptance into the sport, subject largely to continuing exclusion through stringent eligibility requirements imposed by professional elites. Recently, many sponsors reacted to the outrage of explicit racial exclusion in particular country clubs, reducing general levels of minority inclusion but with limited results.

This book represents a case study of the golfing experiences of African Americans particularly during the Jim Crow era. The Professional Golfers Association (PGA), largely unaffected by the 1954 *Brown* decision since it was a private organization, maintained a "Caucasian only" membership clause in its constitution until 1961. All-white private clubs continued racial exclusion also until the PGA Championship Shoal Creek Club Affair in Alabama during 1990. This book aims to correct the historical misconception that African American participation in the sport was extremely limited or largely nonexistent by examining their golfing experiences during the Jim Crow era. A variety of sources, including black newspapers, archival and museum data, in-depth interviews, and black club records will be assessed. This introductory chapter discusses the sociological significance of sports—the relationship between race and sports generally, the connection between race and golf specifically—and draws some preliminary conclusions.

SPORTS AND SOCIETY

The sports arena provides the observer with important insight into society generally. Sports activities involve all the relevant elements of social structure—individual, group, and institutional—and reflect the larger society as a whole (cf. Coakley, 1990). The behavior of individual players reveals their abilities, attitudes, and personalities and is defined by particular roles. Some are viewed as heroic "stars" while others may become vilified for their "unsportsmanlike" or "unpatriotic" behavior. Team dynamics are also involved, reflected in group norms, fierce intergroup competition, fan behavior, community support, business sponsorship, and organizational structures. Some sports are more typical of particular social classes (e.g., boxing versus golf, cf. Riess, 1994), while professional athletes experience limited mobility opportunities depending on their backgrounds (cf. Coakley, 1990; Melnick & Sabo, 1994). Sports are also a major factor in the institutional sphere, reflecting nationalistic attitudes (e.g., world league competitions), political symbols and speech, media programming, and corporate interests (e.g., team owners, commercial advertising, marketing of team logos).

All these factors highlight the manner in which sports reflect the larger society, particularly its social arrangements, types of inequality, and social dynamics. In a sense, athletic rituals may be viewed as *social dramas* in which social roles, norms, intergroup dynamics, organizational processes, institutional arrangements, and the dynamics of social change are all "played out" as "spectator sport." While such "dramas" may appear open and democratic, they clearly reflect the types of *inequality* predominant in the larger society, whether racial, ethnic, gender-based, class-oriented, or age-defined. We turn to examine the relationship between sports and racism in more detail.

SPORTS AND RACISM

Professional sports, particularly in the past, have been organized in a manner that maintains racial inequality and the exploitation of minorities. Historically, such institutionalized racism has proceeded through four general stages: (1) minority exclusion and/or exploitation; (2) segregation of and discrimination against minorities; (3) the beginnings of limited desegregation; and, (4) limited minority integration in the face of majority resistance to such changes.

During this society's plantation era, African American slaves were excluded from participation in white-controlled sports except in the case of a few owners who may have exploited some of them for betting purposes in sports such as boxing and horse racing (cf. Gilmore, 1995; Wiggins, 1980b, 1986). This is not to suggest that the "slave community" did not engage in its own play activities; indeed, there is evidence that both adults and children did so in significant ways (cf. Wiggins, 1977, 1980b). For the most part, however, organized sports were confined to the white elite.

During the centuries that followed and through World War II, blacks remained largely excluded from professional sports and white colleges, and were subject to formal discrimination, exclusion, and discrimination in most activities except for boxing (Eitzen & Sage, 1986). This included their nonparticipation in the National Football League (NFL) from 1934 through 1946 (Smith, 1988). In response, minorities organized their own teams and leagues, or "parallel structures" (Blackwell, 1991), particularly in the case of basketball in major cities such as Chicago (Gems, 1955), and their own baseball leagues (Jable, 1994; Peterson, 1984). Minority communities provided their own role models, gender ideals, and civic organizations (Captain, 1991) designed to inspire and facilitate their players and families. Whites responded by stereotyping black players as physiologically rather than intellectually endowed (Wiggins, 1989), demeaned them with Sambo-like cartoons in the press (Wiggins, 1988a), and have recently overemphasized the drug problems some players appear to experience relative to their white counterparts (Lapchick, 1991). Racial discrimination in sports, as in other areas of society, is rationalized by elites by highlighting the assumed uniqueness and inferiority of minority participants.

Desegregation began and accelerated in all major sports after World War II. These included football, basketball, and intercollegiate athletics (Eitzen & Sage, 1986). Such developments, of course, did not signal the end of prejudice and discrimination: black players have experienced white rejection and abuse throughout the contemporary scene (cf. Sifford, 1992); those less provocative and more temperate in their behavior, such as Joe

Louis and Jackie Robinson, have received more white acceptance and acclaim (Capeci and Wilkerson, 1983; Smith, 1979); while others more nationalistic and critical, such as Paul Robeson (Duberman, 1988), Muhammad Ali (Hauser, 1991), and Jack Johnson (Gilmore, 1975), have more often been treated as villains and potential outcasts (cf. Jaher, 1985). Black newspapers, for their part, played a significant symbolic role in demanding the complete desegregation of baseball (Wiggins, 1983). Minority athletes also engaged in protests against racial discrimination on student campuses from the 1940s on (Spivey, 1988; Wiggins, 1988b) and during the 1968 Olympic Games in Mexico City (Edwards, 1969; Wiggins, 1994). As both athletes and racial role models, however, these protestors experienced high levels of role conflict and external pressure, with limited success in effecting general social change (Wiggins, 1994). Minority demands were met by majority resistance during these early days of desegregation.

During recent decades, black athletes have been subject to limited integration in the sports arena, reflecting white adaptation to social change in a manner designed to maintain racial dominance. This is evident in "stacking" or the utilization of minority players largely in nonleadership sports roles, particularly in football and baseball (cf. Bivens & Leonard, 1994; Eitzen & Sage, 1986). Recruitment of black team managers and coaches has also been extremely limited (Braddock, 1989), while salary arbitration appears to reflect racial inequalities (Leonard & Ellman, 1994), as do actual salary levels in some cases (Lapchick, 1991). Minority after-sports mobility levels also appear limited (Coakley, 1990), and black players have often been subject to higher performance demands than their white counterparts (Lapchick, 1991). These trends illustrate the extent to which sports integration is racially defined and operates in a manner designed to maintain racial exploitation. Although significant social changes in professional sports have clearly taken place, these activities continue to reflect inequalities underlying the larger society. This is particularly so in the case of golf, as we shall see.

GOLF AND RACISM

Golf, in its typical country-club setting, tends to be more elitist, individualistic, and community-based than many other sports. In the past, many participants have come from professional backgrounds, players are evaluated predominantly as individuals and compete as such, while many courses are located in restrictive, "members-only" club environments. Nevertheless, the sport plainly reflects the historical racial trends defining professional sports previously discussed. As with other recreational activities, African Americans were initially excluded from golf. Eventually, they were assigned the subordinate caddie role and exploited as such (Ashe, 1988a). Exclusion and exploitation constituted their initial exposure to the game.

Formal discrimination and segregation ensued, epitomized in the 1943 PGA amended constitutional "Caucasian only" clause (McRae, 1991). Although conflicting information is presented by different authors on the exact date the organization inserted this particular clause (1916 is a year used by some), 1943 is the actual year it formally became part of their constitution. Responding to this development, Robert H. Hawkins and others founded the United Golfers Association in 1926 (McRae, 1991) to facilitate black golf. African American professional golfers became more visible, particularly such early players as John Shippen, Robert "Pat" Ball, and Howard Wheeler, and later golfers such as Teddy Rhodes, Bill Spiller, and Charlie Sifford, who was labeled by many as the "Jackie Robinson of golf" (Reed, 1991). Like Sifford, most blacks who became serious golfers began caddying as children, successfully participated in caddie tournaments, became teaching professionals largely restricted to black communities, and held a number of other jobs to support themselves (Reed, 1991). While highly successful, Sifford experienced blatant white ridicule and resistance to his participation in the sport (Sifford, 1992). Other major developments during the segregation era included Joe Louis's sponsorship of the "Joe Louis Open" in Detroit, supporting then well-known black players such as Clyde Martin and Ted Rhodes (McRae, 1991). Nevertheless, discrimination against black players continued largely unabated.

During 1945, in an instance of rare interracial tournament play, Calvin Searles's performance against top PGA golfers drew national attention; however, when Rhodes and Bill Spiller automatically qualified for tournament entry in 1948, they were rejected by the organization, which claimed they could exercise their own preference in the matter (McRae, 1991, p. 28). In response, a number of black suits were filed and temporarily settled, but with significant integration avoided by the PGA in its distinction between "invitational" (i.e., exclusionary) and "open" tournaments (McRae, 1991). Some courts reacted to these suits in the 1950s by invoking the "separate but equal" clause, others denied monetary damages, and still others supported the practice of part-time playing opportunities for blacks at white-controlled courses (Ashe, 1986b). Further outcries forced the PGA, to permit greater minority participation during the 1950s. Responding to ongoing legal pressure, the association finally dropped the controversial policy in 1961 (Reed, 1991).

Recent decades have highlighted a number of African American golf champions such as Pete Brown, Lee Elder, Calvin Peete, and Jim Thorpe (Reed, 1991). However, restrictive tournament eligibility criteria continued to be used against players such as Charlie Sifford and Pete Brown, reversing the tradition of automatically inviting the previous year's PGA winners to current tournaments (Reed, 1991). By limiting tournament invitations, the association managed to exclude significant numbers of well-known black players, maintaining its "private" privileges. More recently, the beginning of the 1990s brought an admission of discrimination against black golfers by the founder of the Shoal Creek Country Club in Alabama. The outcry of the Southern Christian Leadership Conference and corporate sponsors forced the PGA to require clubs hosting tournaments to implement a non-discriminatory policy regarding member background (McRae, 1991). Despite these advances, however, recent numbers of PGA black players have not significantly increased, and the golf cart has largely eliminated the caddie role as a potential career path for minority players (Reed, 1991). Finally, Eldrick "Tiger" Woods, a spectacularly successful young golfer, has been portrayed by the media as racially mixed, "more Asian than black," and reflecting "multiculturalism." According to one commentator, this represents a way of denying the reality of white racism in professional golf by highlighting a player's achievements despite his multiple-minority background (Yu, 1996). Supposedly, the champion reflects the larger society in a positive light!

CONCLUSION

In this introductory chapter, we have examined the degree to which racial discrimination has been a major part of America's colonial foundation and subsequent history. Focusing on how these have affected sports generally in the society, we delineated a number of typical historical stages moving from exclusion and exploitation through segregation, discrimination, and parallel structures to the beginnings of desegregation and eventually limited integration in the context of white resistance. Concentrating on professional golf, we found that these historical stages operated also in the manner in which this sport has been controlled by the white majority. Added to this has been the sophisticated and varying way in which racial exclusion has been maintained and "professionally" elaborated by the PGA in its manipulation of tournament eligibility requirements.

This book represents a case study of how these racial factors have affected the African American golfer largely during the segregated Jim Crow era. The chapters that follow examine the experience of golf caddies at the turn of the century, the founding of black golf clubs and associations, major sponsors of black players, legal challenges to the "Caucasian only" PGA clause, and major desegregation efforts. A crucial part of the text involves profiles of and interviews with major Jim Crow era golfers, providing fascinating insight into their backgrounds, golfing experiences, tournament play, and interracial contacts. Using these materials, we draw detailed analytical and policy conclusions regarding the continuing nature of American racism generally and its sophisticated, multifaceted exclusionary nature in the case of professional golf. While clearly *not* an exhaustive historical account of African American golf, the information in these data offers fascinating insight into the dynamics of institutionalized racism operating in this kind of social activity.

After completing this introductory discussion, Part Two outlines the development of black golf as revealed in the "caddie-to-professional" careers of players, sponsorship of the sport by the black elite, the organization of the United Golfers Association (UGA), and Joe Louis's major contribution as one of the sport's major ambassadors. The next section presents profiles of Jim Crow era players presented in black newspapers and personal interviews. Part Four describes the push to desegregate public courses, leaders of such movements, and white resistance. The final section brings together the project's major conclusions regarding black golf and white racism.

PART TWO

THE DEVELOPMENT OF BLACK GOLF

_____ CHAPTER 2 _____

From Caddie to Professional: The Making of a Black Golf Pro

The earliest African American golfers were active when the sport was introduced during the late nineteenth century. The first notable black golfer, John Shippen, participated in mid-1890s tournaments organized by the United States Golf Association (USGA). One of the earliest innovations, the golf tee, was patented by a prominent black dentist in 1899. For the most part, however, African Americans were relegated to subservient roles as the sport became a major amateur and professional pastime in the first quarter of the twentieth century. Most blacks served as caddies for wealthy white golfers at newly developed, exclusive country clubs. Many white caddies also aspired to become professionals. At the turn of the century, the caddying role was a major springboard to the professional ranks for many successful white players. Black players, on the other hand, facing current Jim Crow policies, found it increasingly difficult to move beyond the available roles of caddie, greenkeeper, or pro shop attendant. Nevertheless, this experience served as a catalyst for some of the more serious competitors in gaining important knowledge and skill and preparing them to assume roles as "black pro golfers" in their own communities.

JOHN SHIPPEN: FIRST "COLORED GOLF PRO"

American golf's foundation is popularly traced to Shinnecock Hills, Long Island, New York, in the early 1890s. Most accounts tend to overlook the major roles played by the Shinnecock Indians and John Shippen, described as part-Indian and part-black (Graffis, 1975). Shippen was actually born in Washington, D.C., of African American parentage, but lived for a time among Shinnecock Indians (Sinnette, 1998). The Shinnecock Hills Golf Course, built in 1891, is widely recognized as one of the first and most significant of the courses that sprung up when the game finally reached America in the 1880s. Willie Dunn, Jr., a member of a well-established family of Scottish golf professionals, was hired by W. K. Vanderbilt, the wealthy American industrialist, to design and build a course in a traditionally Scottish layout (Barkow, 1974). He employed a crew of Shinnecock Indians to construct the 18-hole course on a former Indian reservation under his supervision. Shippen was a member of this crew who, along with some of the Indians, received golf lessons and training to be caddies after the course's completion. Dunn became the club professional and, although Shippen was a caddie, he took him under his wing and trained him to be a player and teacher of the sport (Graffis, 1975). After the USGA was established in 1894, Shippen competed in the 1896 National Open, the second to be held by the USGA, and several other USGA National Open Tournaments in the early years of the association. His performance during a period dominated by British professionals, including his mentor, Willie Dunn, Jr., is astonishing given the lack of experience and success of American golfers generally. Shippen appeared in the USGA National Open at least four times (1896, 1899, 1900, and 1913), yet many of the early records of the USGA are incomplete and, therefore, may not accurately reflect his total play.

In 1896, Shippen competed in his first USGA Open Championship, finishing tied for fifth place (McRae, 1991). Despite the absence of a policy restricting black participation, the climate of racial discrimination prevailing in 1896, the year of the *Plessy v. Ferguson* "separate-but-equal" ruling by the U.S. Supreme Court, involved objections by some white players to his participation. Whites who entered the tournament, the second to be held after the USGA was established in 1894, threatened to withdraw if Shippen and Oscar Bunn (a full-blooded Shinnecock Indian) were permitted to play. In response, Theodore Havemeyer, the first USGA president, insisted that their constitution did not discriminate and that if these whites refused to play, the Open would proceed without them (Barkow, 1974). Subsequently, none of them withdrew and the tournament continued without incident. Despite this potentially distracting controversy, Shippen's fifth-place finish was well ahead of twenty-two of the twenty-eight players who completed the 36-hole tournament. It should be noted that three of the top five players who finished with better scores were experienced British professionals: James Foulis, tournament winner, was a Scottish professional who was club pro at the Chicago Golf Club; Horace Rawlis, who finished second after winning the inaugural tournament in 1895, was a twenty-year-old English professional who had come to the United States to be an assistant pro at the Newport Golf Club in Rhode Island; and Joe Lloyd, who finished third, was an English professional associated with the Essex Country Club of Manchester, Massachusetts (Grimsley, 1966). Even more amazingly, this young black caddie at eighteen years old finished ahead of the three most outstanding British professional players in the United States at that time: Willie Dunn, Willie Davis, and Willie Campbell. Dunn was considered the leading Scottish professional to migrate to the United States. Davis was associated with the Newport Golf Club, and Campbell was with The Country Club in Brookline, Massachusetts. All three had been brought by wealthy white elites to teach golf to Americans and help build their courses (Sommers, 1996). Among the American golfers finishing well back in this tournament was John Reid, one of the founders of the famous St. Andrew's Golf Club of America. The skill level of American golfers tended to be extremely low, which was even more reason for Shippen's feat to be viewed as a cause for celebration among American golfers. However, his accomplishments as an American-born golfer in this early tournament, as well as others in the history of the USGA, were given little or no coverage (Sommers, 1996).

Instead of celebrating Shippen's success in his first appearance in the USGA National Open, one has to speculate why, as a black man at the height of the rising tide of segregation, he was even permitted to enter the tournament over the objections of several of the white entrants. Given prevailing Jim Crowism at that time, USGA President Havemeyer's bold stance might appear to reflect a desire to promote "openness" as a USGA principle. An alternative explanation, however, involves the president's personal funding of the tournament and desire to prevent the sport's becoming a target of social criticism. During these early years, in particular, golf's mostly wealthy participants were regarded as "gentlemen-players," above the "petty bickering" of the nation's masses. Havemeyer, described as a person of exceptional tact and charm, used his sugar industry wealth to cover the costs of the first 1895 USGA championship personally. This inaugural event was a carnival-like affair that attracted the "society" set (Grimsley, 1966). He went out of his way to make the event an unqualified success by sponsoring parties, a $1,000 trophy, and thirty-two white entrants, most of whom were only marginal players (Wind, 1956). He was not about to permit current racial conflict to tarnish the image of the sport he loved so dearly, nor were white objections powerful enough to dissuade other "gentlemen-golfers" from enjoying their subsidized participation in an increasingly popular activity among the elite. Although Shippen competed in four USGA championships between 1899 and 1913, he does not appear in the USGA records after finishing tied for forty-first place in the 1913 Brookline, Massachusetts, tournament (Graffis, 1975).

Shippen's second and third appearances in USGA national championships occurred in 1899 and 1900. In both events he entered as a nonaffiliated golfer, although officially he was a caddie at several different clubs

in the New York area. Although he made respectable showings in both
years (finishing among the top twenty scorers), these tournaments were
dominated by transplanted professionals from the "Old Country" (Grimsley, 1966). Not until shortly before Shippen's final listed appearance in a
USGA National Tournament in 1913 did a breakthrough occur when white
American-born golfers, who were mostly ex-caddies, began to finish among
the top players. Former Philadelphia caddie John McDermott, who represented the Atlantic City (New Jersey) Country Club, won back-to-back
championships in 1911 and 1912. Ex-caddy Walter Hagen, along with
McDermott and several other American golfers, were among the top finishers in 1913 when Shippen competed for the last time in this event. The
tournament was won by another ex-caddie, Francis Ouimet, who defeated
the two top British professionals in the world, Harry Vardon and Ted Ray
(Andrews, 1991), with Shippen finishing well behind the top competitors.
These white American-born golfers, who after rising from the ranks of
caddying, had finally demonstrated the skill to compete successfully against
the Scottish and English migrants, received wide acclaim from the American
public. Ouimet's victory, for example, given front-page coverage throughout the nation, was described as showing that you did not have to be British
to win a major golf tournament (Andrews, 1991). In contrast, Shippen,
who had earlier demonstrated that he could compete with the top Scottish
and English professionals in the 1890s when golf was first introduced to
Americans, was not similarly recognized.

The strengthening of Jim Crow laws at the turn of the century intensified
this exclusionary climate, even though no formal USGA policy of discrimination existed (Reed, 1991). Likewise, when the PGA was established in
1916, no formal racial membership restrictions were evident (Ashe, 1988a).
However, in his authoritative work, *The PGA: The Official History of the
Professional Golfer's Association of America*, Graffis notes that there is no
evidence of Shippen's ever having applied for membership in the organization (Graffis, 1975). Instead, Dewey Brown, a black caddie in the New
Jersey and Philadelphia area, is on record as the first black member. Unlike
Shippen, records of Brown's tournament participation, including the pretournament-circuit days, are scarce (Sinnette, 1998). He was, however,
known as a pro shop attendant at the Buckwood Inn course in Delaware,
recognized as one of the most attractive in the nation (Graffis, 1975). Recent evidence suggests that the PGA withdrew Brown's membership shortly
after discovering that the fair-skinned African American was not Caucasian
(Sinnette, 1998). It is unlikely, however, that Shippen simply lost interest
in the game with the PGA's establishment in 1916. He had successfully
competed in USGA tournaments, playing with some of the best golfers over
a period of seventeen years, extending back to the origin of American golf.
If the PGA had extended him a membership invitation, there is little doubt
he would have joined. It should be noted that he competed in the earliest

days of American golf in tournaments played on courses that were confined primarily to the Northeast and Midwest rather than the South. The establishment of the PGA during a period of increasingly hostile anti-black sentiment throughout the country may have contributed to a mutual understanding on the part of both Shippen and the PGA of the undesirability of either a membership request from him or an invitation by the PGA.

RACIAL DIFFERENCES IN THE "CADDIE-TO-PRO" CAREER PATH

The caddie-to-professional career path can be traced to Scotland, the country where golf originated. In fact, an old caddie adage, "Caddying in early life, professional golf later, bring a man into good company" (Mackenzie, 1997), expressed the aspirations held by many young boys whose earliest exposure to golf came through this activity. Most white Americans who became golf professionals during the first quarter of the twentieth century, in fact, began in this manner, learning the game "from the ground up" (Graffis, 1975). The caddie status was a major avenue for many poor youth aspiring to club professional careers at elite clubs. Walter Hagen, for example, a player in the first PGA tournament in 1916 and the only golfer to win this championship four years running (1924–1927), was introduced to the game at eight years old by caddying for ten cents an hour (Alliss & Hobbs, 1986). Despite his German immigrant parents' disapproval of his new career, the nineteen year old was appointed club pro at Rochester, New York, at a salary of $1,200 per season. He was also able to obtain his blacksmith father a job as greenkeeper despite his lack of experience (Alliss & Hobbs, 1986). Similarly, Gene Sarazen, another of the great early-twentieth-century champions, caddied at the age of eight. Because his family was poor, Gene gave all his earnings to his father. Around the age of seventeen, he began to sweep out the pro shop and clean clubs for eight dollars a week. He moved to Florida in 1919, where he earned some tournament prize money, but continued to work in a railroad yard and at other odd jobs. His early golfing success resulted in a job offer as assistant pro at Fort Wayne Country Club, Indiana, and later, at age nineteen, a pro position in Titusville, Florida. At twenty, he set the record as the youngest winner of the U.S. PGA championship, as the match-play format was called in 1922 (Allis & Hobbs, 1986). Although the caddie-to-pro route was not the only career mobility avenue, it represented an important opportunity for poor youth who would not otherwise have gained such valuable playing experience.

Although this career path was open to young whites, it was largely closed to aspiring blacks who, in contrast, were viewed as occupying the "natural" position of caddie. Historically, this role emerged in Scotland out of players' needs to have their clubs carried by others (Mackenzie, 1997). Consequently, caddies were established prior to the development of club manufacturers, pros, and greenkeepers (Editors of *Golf Magazine*, 1970). However, the positive image and invaluable role of the caddie in Scotland were not immediately transferred to the American golfing scene at the turn of the twentieth century. Reviewing the past decade of progress in the development of American golf, one USGA official (Van Tassel Sutphen) observed in 1906 that the chief annoyance was the caddie, who was characterized as the worst club carrier in the world and literally a poisoner of a golfer's game by his laziness, ignorance, and insolence (Shapiro, Dohn, & Berger, 1986). While not referring to blacks specifically, this stereotypical view of the caddie emerged at a time when the image of black inferiority predominated in America, reinforcing the prevailing notion that the proper place for blacks on the golf course was in a position of servitude. In characterizing the relationship between the golfer and his caddie, Sutphen noted that the latter was largely ignored, treated like a "mere machine," and spoken to only when wrong, resulting in minimal attention to the work at hand (Shapiro, Dohn, & Berger, 1986). This view of the passive, docile caddie contrasts sharply with those expressed by black golfers who were introduced to golf while caddying and were perceptive observers, as we shall see in later chapters. A plan was formulated to develop a decent caddie, even out of unpromising material, by dividing them into two divisions: Class A and Class B. The former would be distinguished by their higher level of efficiency and better behavior, and would, therefore, receive a slightly higher wage. Clubs would guarantee all caddies a minimum wage for the week and players would be allowed to choose their own caddies, paying the caddie an extra compensation of five cents for this privilege. If ten cents were paid, the caddie would be expected to clean the player's golf clubs without further charge. This would replace the rule that prevailed at nearly every club where caddies were sent out in rotation with players required to accept any assigned to them, thus making it impracticable for golfers to train thirty or forty caddies to meet their requirements (Shapiro, Dohn, & Berger, 1986). While not referring to black caddies specifically, this idea of hiring and training golf course *servants* fitted well with Jim Crow America at the turn of the century. This image of blacks was consistent with the stereotypical white view of their subordinate role in the society generally. Thus, black caddies were perceived in a similar light as the ubiquitous Pullman porters in passenger trains. Whites could think of blacks as "caddie Willie," their personal golf course servant, just as all porters were expected to respond to "George," as if all white passengers received personal attention from George Pullman, the wealthy white owner of the Pullman Coach Company. Even the idea of classifying caddies according to training and efficiency of service was consistent with the well-established system of classification for porters in which the four categories of porters—busboy, sleeping car, food service, and private car—assured wealthy white passengers of the highest quality of service by choosing porters with the most expertise (Perata, 1996).

Although some clubs may have considered classifying caddies by skill level and others adopted the practice of selecting "regular" caddies each time they played, many clubs hired caddie masters (usually whites) to supervise the process of caddying assignments. However, the black caddie was as vulnerable to insults and abuse on the golf course as Pullman porters received at the hands of white passengers. In 1927, for example, a twenty-four-year-old black caddie, Eugene Harris, was shot and killed in Birmingham, Alabama, by a white caddie master who claimed Harris was caddying out of turn. The caddie master followed him to the first green and ordered him to the clubhouse, shooting him after claiming that he drew a golf club. The player, however, claimed that he had called Harris at the first tee and denied that Harris had drawn a club on the caddie master (*Pittsburgh Courier*, June 11, 1927, p. 1).

After the 1920s, when golf had become more popular, caddies were granted more respect, particularly at black tournaments. A highly select group of caddies was assembled for a major black tournament during 1941, referred to as "the smartest looking fellows on the golf course" in "blue and white jerseys" (*Baltimore Afro-American*, August 2, 1941). Many of the better black caddies also began playing competitively in caddie tournaments organized by their white club pro employers. Some white courses, especially in the South, permitted them to play on Mondays, the day traditionally set aside for them. In actuality, Mondays were also the days for preparing the course for the week's activities. Black caddies outside the country were also recognized for their professional golfing potential: many of them in South Africa during the 1920s demonstrated exceptional playing skills despite similar racial restrictions and limited equipment. Some used improvised clubs made of heavy iron wire bent at the end. The club head was a short piece of iron pipe with a rag or cloth grip wrapped with wire. Joseph Kuzwayo used such a crude club to win a club tournament at a resort in Bloemfontein. Some observers noted that many of the "native caddies" played better than those with more regular equipment (*Pittsburgh Courier*, June 4, 1927).

BLACK PRO GOLFERS AS CATALYSTS FOR THE SPREAD OF BLACK GOLF

Black caddies assumed the role of promoting golf in the African American community and also found that this provided an alternative avenue to achieving the status of golf "professionals." John Shippen was among a small group of black golfers who were the first to assume this role. He continued to hold caddie, greenkeeper, and pro shop attendant positions at exclusive white clubs in the New York area, simultaneously becoming recognized as a "pro golfer" in his own community in response to white exclusion. When one of the first black golf clubs was established during the 1920s in Washington, D.C., he was hired as greenkeeper and instructor, and began to promote African American tournaments. As with white pros in the 1890s, Shippen staged exhibition matches initially in the Washington, D.C., area (Dawkins, 1996). Shippen went on to become widely recognized as the first "colored pro golfer" in the United States, spending thirty years as a club professional at the Shady Rest Club of New Jersey, one of the earliest black golf clubs in America, although in reality he can be considered "America's" first golf professional. Despite his passage to this status, most black caddies who showed promise and determination as players in the earliest years of American golf did not reach the same heights. However, many of those who started out as caddies became experts as both teachers and players in their own communities throughout the country.

CONCLUSION

This chapter has examined the early golfing involvement of African Americans as caddies and their attempts to develop as players. Unlike their white counterparts, these players were largely prevented from moving up to the professional ranks. The overwhelmingly restrictive racial climate in America, accelerating at the turn of the century, prevented them from getting beyond the status of caddie or the equally restrictive positions of greenkeeper and pro shop attendant. As an example, the experiences of John Shippen, one of the earliest black caddies, are highlighted, focusing on his introduction to golf as a caddie and involvement in tournaments held by the USGA from the 1890s through 1913. The racially restrictive environment in which the PGA was founded in 1916 ensured the exclusion of Shippen and other black caddies from rising through the career path of caddie to pro that was open to white caddies who aspired to become professional golfers and gain employment as golf pros at exclusive, all-white country clubs. Although the original PGA constitution did not include language that specifically restricted membership based on race, African Americans were customarily excluded from organizations clearly intended for whites during this period of heightened Jim Crowism. In reaction, some aspiring black caddies began to promote the sport in their own communities. However, it was not until middle-class blacks were attracted to the sport and began to form their own clubs on a more widespread basis in the 1920s that opportunities increased for blacks to play as professional, amateur, and recreational golfers.

We turn next to black elites and their role in establishing clubs and professional players of their own.

CHAPTER 3

Golf and the Black Elite

In the early 1920s, baseball was by far the most popular sport among most African Americans. However, golf also had a particular appeal to the small but rising black middle class. In 1921, for example, the year that Rube Foster's Chicago American Giants won the championship of the Negro National Baseball League, E. L. Renip wrote a regular column in the *Chicago Defender* educating blacks about the game of golf, encouraging them to join the newly established Windy City Golf Club. He began with the basics and covered a particular aspect of the sport on a weekly basis. He also provided updated reports on the performance of well-known white players such as Walter Hagen, Chick Evans, and others. He admonished African American players to obtain "competent and conscious" instruction before venturing out onto the links (*Chicago Defender*, April 16, 1921, p. 10). During the Jim Crow era, country clubs established by wealthy whites were closed to African Americans regardless of their standing; consequently, as in other areas of their lives, members of the black middle class, including business and civic leaders, established their own facilities to promote the sport and their own social activities.

Aspiring black golfers faced playing barriers more than the purely racial; however, the game's popularity increased significantly among them, leading to the establishment of their own national organization in 1926, the United Golfers Association (UGA). This was a "parallel" structure formed partially in response to the exclusionary practices of the elite-controlled PGA established ten years earlier. The UGA promoted the sport among both professionals and amateurs. By the mid-1930s, black golf associations existed in major regions of the country with tournaments organized at these levels as well. The UGA also staged the annual Negro National Open Tournament. These clubs and playing opportunities provided avenues for a small but growing number of serious black players who emerged from the caddying ranks at white clubs to gain recognition as "professionals" in the black community.

In this chapter we describe the founding and early activities of some of these black clubs before focusing specifically on UGA activities in the next chapter. Particular attention is accorded the black elite's role in increasing the game's popularity as well as the visibility of black professionals in the press.

ESTABLISHMENT OF BLACK GOLF CLUBS

Black golf clubs were first established primarily on the East Coast and in the Midwest. Although most were founded outside of the South, a few were formed by prominent African Americans in southern cities. Black interest in the sport was particularly strong in the Washington, D.C.–Boston corridor and the Chicago area. Table 3.1 presents the names and locations of selected black clubs founded during the Jim Crow era based on descriptions of club activities in such newspapers as the *Chicago Defender* and *Baltimore Afro-American*. Except for Chicago's Windy City Golf Club in the Midwest, Richmond's Acorn Country Club, and Jacksonville's Lincoln Golf Club in the South, most golf clubs established during the 1920s were located in or near the cities of Boston (Mapledale Golf Club in Stow), New York (Saint Nicholas Golf Club), Philadelphia (Fairview Golf Club; Shady Rest Golf Club of Westfield, New Jersey), Baltimore (Wilson Park Golf Club), and Washington, D.C. (Riverside, Citizens, Capital City-Royal, and National Capital Golf Clubs). Pittsburgh's Bunker Club was also an early eastern golf club. During the 1930s, other significant clubs were established in the East and Midwest, with one major club also formed in the West. In the Midwest, Detroit's Rackham and Motor City Golf Clubs, Chicago's Pioneer and Sunset Hills Golf Clubs, Indianapolis's Douglass Golf Club, and Cleveland's Forest City Golf Association were among the most prominent. In the West, the popular Cosmopolitan Golf Club of Los Angeles appeared during this decade. The Lincoln Golf Club of Atlanta, which became a major catalyst for black golf in the South, was also established at this time. After 1940, new black golf clubs continued to be formed throughout the country, extending to the farthest points west (Fox Hills and Riviera Golf Clubs in Los Angeles) and south (Cosmopolitan Golf Association in Miami).

Leading black citizens were usually club sponsors and officers. The Windy City Golf Association's membership in 1922, for example, included locally established golfers Walter Speedy, Robert Ball, Henry Johnson, Ty-

Table 3.1
Selected Golf Clubs Established by African Americans During the Jim Crow Era

Decade Founded	Name of Club	Location
1920 – 1929	Acorn Country Club	Richmond, VA
	Alpha Golf Club	Chicago, IL
	Citizens Golf Club	Washington, DC
	Capital City Golf Club	Washington, DC
	Riverside Golf Club	Washington, DC
	Shady Rest Golf and Country Club	Westfield, NJ
	Saint Nicholas Golf Club	New York City, NY
	National Capital Country Club	Laurel, MD
	Mapledale Golf Club	Stow, MA
	Bunker Golf Club	Pittsburgh, PA
	Windy City Golf Club	Chicago, IL
	Fairview Golf Club	Philadelphia, PA
	Lincoln Golf and Country Club	Jacksonville, FL
	Wilson Golf Park Club	Baltimore, MD
1930 – 1939	Pioneer Golf Club	Chicago, IL
	Wake Robin Golf Club	Washington, DC
	Chicago Women's Golf Club	Chicago, IL
	Royal Golf Club	Washington, DC
	Sunset Hills Country Club	Kankakee, IL
	Motor City Golf Club	Detroit, MI
	Lincoln Golf and Country Club	Atlanta, GA
	Douglass Park Golf Club	Indianapolis, IN
	Ansley Park Golf Club	Atlanta, GA
	Rackham Park Golf Club	Detroit, MI
	Heart of America Golf Club	Kansas City, MO
	Forest City Golf Association	Cleveland, OH
	Greater Pittsburgh Elks	Pittsburgh, PA
	Monumental Golf Club	Baltimore, MD
1940—	Cosmopolitan Golf Club	Los Angeles, CA
	Detroit Golf Club	Detroit, MI
	Stanton Heights Golf Club	Pittsburgh, PA
	Sixth City Golf Club	Cleveland, OH
	Fairway Golf Club	Dayton, OH
	Par Makers Golf Club	Gary, IN
	Forest Hills Golf Club	Indianapolis, IN
	Druid Hills Country Club	Chicago, IL
	Lone Star Negro Golf Association	Houston, TX
	Vernondale Golf Club	Los Angeles, CA
	Paramount Golf Club	St. Louis, MO
	Yorkshire Golf Club	Pittsburgh, PA
	New Castle Elks	Detroit, MI
	Twin City Golf Club	Minneapolis, MN
	Detroit Amateur Golf Club	Detroit, MI
	Cosmopolitan Golf Association	Miami, FL
	Lake Shore Golf Club	Cleveland, OH
	Apex Golf and Country Club	Atlanta, GA

ler Dixon, Horace McDougal, and Carter Hayes (*Chicago Defender*, August 19, 1922, p. 10). The 1925 founders of the Riverside Golf Club in Washington, D.C., included Victor R. Daly (a real-estate dealer), S. W. Rutherford (president of the National Benefit Life Insurance Company), as well as Charles E. Burch and Clarence H. Mills (Howard University professors). The Citizens Golf Club, also founded in Washington, D.C., in 1925, included among its officers Dr. M.L.T. Grant (a physician), Dr. A. T. Price (a pharmacist), John R. Hawkins (bank president and financial secretary of the A.M.E. Church), and John R. Langford (architect for the A.M.E. Church). The National Capitol Country Club located near Laurel, Maryland, in the Washington, D.C.–Baltimore corridor included among its officers in 1926 Dr. E. J. Scott of Howard University, president, Dr. A. M. Curtiss, first vice president, Dr. Harry S. McCard, second vice president, Thomas H. R. Clarke, third vice president, and Judge James A. Cobb, chairman of the membership committee (*New York Age*, August 19, 1926, p. 7). The Shady Rest Country Club of Westfield, New Jersey, was headed by a leading businessman, H. C. Parker, who served as president in 1927 (*Pittsburgh Courier*, August 13, 1927, p. 4). However, later in that same year (October) the club was reorganized with the following officers: Dr. William H. Washington, president, J. V. Peeples, vice president, C. Lansing Nevius, secretary, Dr. W. G. Alexander, treasurer, and Dr. R. H. Thompson, chairman of entertainment (*Pittsburgh Courier*, October 19, 1927, p. 6).

A few of the earliest black clubs were established in the Deep South. One of the first was the Acorn Country Club of Richmond, Virginia, founded in 1924. The city's black elite built a private course and club facility, attracting hundreds of new members to an exhibition match organized by two businessmen, Russell Banks and Samuel Cullens (*Baltimore Afro-American*, December 13, 1924, p. 5). The Lincoln Golf and Country Club, developed in Jacksonville, Florida, in 1927, became the pride and showcase of southern black golf from the 1920s through the 1950s. The clubhouse and land were purchased by A. L. Lewis, president of the Afro-American Life Insurance Company of Jacksonville, who served as the club's treasurer. Other prominent officers included A. J. Joyner, president, D. D. Powell, first vice-president, Dr. S. P. Livingston, second vice-president, E. D. Ballard, third vice-president and Lawton L. Pratt, secretary (*Chicago Defender*, September 22, 1928, p. 10). The similarly named Lincoln Country Club of Atlanta, Georgia, became the major staging ground for black golf in that state after its 1932 establishment. Members included a broad range of professionals, educators, businessmen, and other executives. A 1934 membership drive added a long list of new members, including the noted Atlanta University intellectuals, Drs. W.E.B. Du Bois and S. Nabrit (*Atlanta Daily World*, August 12, 1934, p. 5).

These southern private courses were vital to the promotion of black golf in the context of prevailing Jim Crow laws excluding African Americans from "whites only" public courses. In some cities, members of the black elite pushed successfully for the opening of segregated, "blacks only" facilities under the principle of "separate but equal." One of these was the Lincoln Memorial Golf Course founded in Washington, D.C., in 1925. Although there were six public courses in Washington, this course was the only one reserved for "colored" persons. Some middle-class blacks who supported these arrangements were occasionally criticized for fostering

"Jim Crow golf" rather than fighting to end discrimination in all public facilities (*Baltimore Afro-American*, June 8, 1925, p. 8). However, it is clear that status-conscious black professionals wanted to emulate the white elite in this way. This is evident in the inaugural address of Dr. Grant, president of the Citizens Golf Club, who pointed with pride to the accomplishments of white champions such as Bobby Jones and Walter Hagen, expressing the belief that the club would become the wealthiest colored club in the world, producing its own champions (*Baltimore Afro-American*, June 8, 1925, p. 8). Likewise, the *Pittsburgh Courier* noted that golf was followed closely by a significant proportion of the white population (*Pittsburgh Courier*, August 8, 1927, p. 4) and endorsed the 1927 formation of the first black club in Pittsburgh (the Bunker Club) by admonishing young professionals to compete with other races in all endeavors, particularly sports (*Pittsburgh Courier*, July 16, 1927, p. 6).

BLACK GOLF PROS AND THE BLACK ELITE

While the black elite was successful in organizing golf in their own communities, most of them pursued the game strictly as a leisure activity. However, these clubs were major factors behind the 1926 establishment of the UGA, referred to previously. This local network and the UGA provided a staging ground for the emergence of "recognized" professional black golfers. When the Citizens Golf Club was established in Washington, D.C., in 1925, John Shippen was hired as greenkeeper and instructor. Already well known as the first "colored golf professional," he had held a number of positions at white country clubs in the New York area since 1900. Despite his recognized role as one of the pioneers of American golf (Graffis, 1975), he never had the opportunity to rise to the professional ranks when the PGA was founded in 1916. However, he quickly became one of the prime movers in the Washington, D.C., black community and other cities by organizing local tournaments and staging exhibitions.

Other lesser known but talented players, some of whom would become widely recognized professionals, appeared during this period: during the First International Golf Championship Tournament (a forerunner of the UGA's National Open), held in Westfield, New Jersey, in 1925, Harry Jackson of Washington, D.C., won the tournament, followed by Shippen (Washington, D.C.), C. E. Brice (Darby, Pennsylvania), L. Martin (Washington, D.C.), Wallace Braxton (Darby, Pennsylvania), Robert E. Lee (Plainfield, New Jersey), Ira Herrington (New York, New York), R. Harvey (Mt. Vernon, New York), Elmer Brent (New York, New York), and Reggie Lewis (Mt. Vernon, New York). The tournament's great success stimulated further developments in the sport, culminating in the 1926 establishment of the UGA by golfing doctors George Adams and Albert Harris from Washington, D.C., with Robert Hawkins as its first president. When the

inaugural tournament was held at Stow, Massachusetts, Harry Jackson became the organizations's first "official" National Open Champion.

Other early UGA champions included Robert "Pat" Ball, Edison Marshall, John Dendy, Howard Wheeler, Solomon Hughes, and Cliff Strickland
(Ashe, 1988a). UGA National Open winners during the Jim Crow era (pre-
1962) also included Hugh Smith, Ted Rhodes, Charles Sifford, Richard
Thomas, and Pete Brown. The black elite was proud to showcase the talents
of these professional players in their membership promotions. Early professionals John Shippen and Harry Jackson, for example, celebrated the
opening of the new 9-hole course at the National Capital Country Club in
1927 by playing an 18-hole exhibition to the delight of the club president
Dr. Emmett J. Scott of Howard University and Judge James A. Cobb, chairman of the executive committee (*Pittsburgh Courier*, July 30, 1927, p. 4).

The black press also promoted golf among business and civic leaders by
following the tournament play of the leading black pros in major cities.
Robert "Pat" Ball, originally from Georgia, became a household name in
golfing circles, particularly after winning UGA titles in 1927, 1929, and
1934. Likewise, Howard Wheeler of Atlanta, who was to become the only
UGA professional to win titles spanning three decades (1933, 1938, 1946,
1947, 1948, and 1958), became a widely recognized golf professional,
known particularly for his unorthodox cross-handed grip. John Dendy,
originally from Asheville, North Carolina, also became a three-time UGA
National Open Champion while attending Atlanta's Morehouse College,
and Ted Rhodes and Charlie Sifford dominated UGA championships from
the late 1940s throughout the 1950s.

GOLF AND SOCIAL ACTIVITIES AMONG THE
BLACK ELITE

While the black middle class was highly successful at spreading the sport
throughout the African American community, the game's elitist image was
also useful in facilitating social interaction in exclusive voluntary associations, including fraternities, lodges, and country clubs. As early as 1934 in
Atlanta, for example, golf teams from the four major black fraternities
(Omega Psi Phi, Alpha Phi Alpha, Phi Beta Sigma, and Kappa Alpha Psi)
held head-to-head matches for individual and team champions. The Greater
Pittsburgh Elks Lodge began attracting members to its tournament in the
1930s. By the 1950s, the Elks' J. Finley Wilson Golf Tournament in Pittsburgh was one of the most recognized amateur events of the year (*Pittsburgh Courier*, June 8, 1957, p. 23). Leading black golf and country clubs
were also the prime movers and shakers of the "society set" in the cities in
which these clubs were established.

Black colleges became another setting for introducing golf into elite society. During the 1930s, golf and tennis teams were formed in elite black

colleges, becoming part of traditional intercollegiate rivalries that had already been established in football and other sports. The Southern Intercollegiate Athletic Conference (SIAC), which included black colleges such as Morehouse, Tuskegee, Morris Brown, and Fort Valley, was one of the earliest to promote competitive golf among black colleges. Tuskegee Institute took the lead as students initially played in large open areas on campus. In 1926, under the leadership of its famed athletic director, Cleve L. "Major" Abbott, it became the first black college to build a 9-hole golf course. The course was a 3,400 yard, par-35 facility located about three miles from campus on a plot of ground near a greenhouse (*New York Age*, September 13, 1930, p. 6). Students caught on quickly: golf became part of the regular activities of Tuskegee students and was included in the annual Tuskegee Relays athletic event (Hawkins, 1994). In 1938, the SIAC held the first intercollegiate golf tournament among black colleges with teams fielded by Alabama State, Florida Agricultural & Mechanical, Fort Valley Normal & Industrial, Morehouse, Morris Brown, and Tuskegee. As expected, Tuskegee golfers excelled, with Alfred Holmes and Maxwell Vails medalists for the men's division and Cora Lee McClinick winner of the women's division. However, by 1940, other black colleges had increased their golf play dramatically, as reflected in the last place finish of the Tuskegee men's team in the 1940 Tuskegee Golf Tournament, in which Morehouse finished first followed by Morris Brown and Florida A & M (Hawkins, 1994). Since the 1940s, golf has been a regular part of athletic competition in black college sports. Ironically, some of the best black golfers who attended college during the Jim Crow era did not participate on their college golf teams. John Dendy, for example, who won several UGA National Open titles while attending Morehouse College in the 1930s, earned letters in football and basketball but never played on the Morehouse golf team (Hawkins, 1994). However, some college teams did arrange matches with black golf clubs on a limited basis.

SOCIAL PROTEST AND BLACK GOLF CLUBS

While golf provided an avenue for the black elite to promote their values and social interaction through the creation of their own organizations, the black middle class also became heavily involved in efforts to build golf courses and secure access for African American golfers to play beyond the traditional caddie role. These efforts included protests to gain access to racially restricted, "whites only" public golf courses as well as the push for better facilities at courses designated for black play. Prior to the more widespread impetus to desegregate public golf courses during the civil rights period of the late 1940s and 1950s, which we will cover in greater detail in Chapter 8, the earliest sustained protests were carried out by some of the first golf clubs organized by elite blacks. A brief look at the early experiences, especially social protest activities, of two well-known black golf clubs—the Royal and the Wake Robin Golf Clubs of Washington, D.C.—well illustrate the role of black elites in resisting Jim Crow treatment of African American golfers.

The Royal Golf Club

Although the Royal Golf Club (originally called the Capital City Golf Club), formally established in Washington, D.C., in the early 1930s, is considered by some the first golf club organized by blacks in America, the Windy City Golf Club in Chicago held meetings in the early 1920s in the home of its organizer, Walter Speedy. Even before that, Speedy had been a part of Chicago's Alpha Golf Club, which sponsored a tournament in 1915 described as "the first golf tournament ever pulled off in America by expert colored golfers" (*New York Age*, October 14, 1915, p. 6). Even in Washington, D.C., the Capital City Golf Club, which evolved into the Royal Golf Club, was not the first club to formally organize. The short-lived Riverside Golf Club was founded by Victor R. Daly in 1925, just after the 9-hole Lincoln Memorial Golf Course was established restricting black play to that course. Daly was a real-estate dealer whose business office was located in the heart of the black business district on Florida Avenue. His visibility and initiative in establishing a golf club for blacks immediately attracted the interest of leading citizens in Washington's black elite, with approximately 100 of them joining at a membership fee of two dollars. However, in less than six months after the Riverside Club was established, some of the members became dissatisfied with how Daly conducted club business, specifically charging that he never gave an accounting of the money collected from membership fees. Consequently, a group of members split from the Riverside Golf Club, which apparently dissolved in 1925, to form a new club called the Citizens Golf Club (*Baltimore Afro-American*, June 8, 1925, p. 8). The name was changed in 1927 to the Capital City Golf Club and again in 1933 to the Royal Golf Club.

From its outset, the Royal Golf Club was serious about promoting golf play, both for its members and the larger African American public. On the local scene, a major obstacle was the lack of adequate, accessible facilities. Among its founders were prominent and leading citizens of Washington, D.C., who possessed the knowledge, determination, and resources to push for change. As the participation by blacks in golfing activities increased, it became clear that the Lincoln Memorial course would not meet the demand. Two alternatives were presented: (1) push for access to one of the other five public golf courses in the area where blacks were not permitted to play or (2) seek the construction of a new course for blacks. The five courses for whites only that were maintained by the federal government included an 18-hole course in East Potomac Park, a 9-hole course in Rock Creek Park, and two 9-hole courses in West Potomac Park.

The second alternative was chosen, and John Langford, a prominent architect and member of the Capital City Golf Club (forerunner to the Royal Club), wrote a letter to the Department of the Navy in 1927 requesting that a public facility for black golfers be included in plans then underway for recreational development in the Anacostia River area of the city. Over the next twelve years, black players mounted a campaign, ranging from writing letters and attending meetings to staging demonstrations culminating in the opening of a new black course—the Langston Golf Course. Based on records of the National Register of Historic Places, the official response to the letter sent by Langford apparently did not arrive until 1934, when a delegation from the Royal Golf Club was invited to meet with officials from Public Buildings and Grounds at the Department of the Navy. The Royal delegation included Langford, Dr. George Adams, Dr. Albert Harris, and James N. Saunders, who was a Dunbar High School teacher. After a site was selected, the actual work was carried out by the Civilian Conservation Corps (CCC) and Works Project Administration (WPA). Both the CCC and WPA were part of the New Deal program developed by President Franklin D. Roosevelt during the Great Depression of the 1930s. The John Mercer Langston Golf Course, named for the first black Virginian to represent his state in the U.S. House of Representatives, opened on June 11, 1939. Although the Royal Golf Club was proud of the victory it achieved in pressuring the Department of the Interior and National Park Service to construct this modern golf course for blacks in Washington, it was recognized that the government had not fully lived up to its promises. Instead of an 18-hole course as agreed to, the hurriedly constructed Langston course only contained 9 (the same as the Lincoln Memorial course) and some of the greens did not have grass. Although the Royal Golf Club had a "home" course in Langston, it was inadequate to meet the needs for interstate tournament play and other expanded golfing activities. Despite these shortcomings, the opening of Langston increased the accessibility of golf to growing numbers of black golfers. This rising interest in the sport, coupled with the clearly inadequate facilities at Langston, led to a renewal of efforts by the Royal Club to consider alternatives in meeting black golfing demands. This time, however, the club decided not only to push for an expansion of Langston to 18 holes but also gain access to other segregated golf courses in the city. Accordingly, in July 1941, only two years after Langston opened, Dr. George Adams and fellow Royal Club member and community activist Edgar Brown led a group of black golfers to the East Potomac Park Golf Course with the intention of playing at this segregated course. Hostile whites prevented them from doing so by throwing rocks and taunting them with threats of physical violence. Later, black golfers petitioned Secretary of the Interior Harold Ickes, requesting access to the East Potomac course. He granted their request, taking the position that as taxpaying citizens, blacks had the right to play on the city's public courses. Despite finding an ally in Ickes, African Americans who ventured to the East Potomac, Rock Creek, or other public golf courses in the city after 1941 did so at great risk, sometimes requiring police escorts to ensure that they were not attacked by resentful whites. Black golfers often found that their cars were tampered with when they were out on the course; while playing on the East Potomac course, for example, Jasper Smith had sand poured into his gas tank on one occasion and sugar and coffee grounds dumped into his carburetor and oil pump on another (*Baltimore Afro-American*, August 9, 1941, p. 21). Washington's public golf courses were not formally desegregated until 1955, after the U.S. Supreme Court's 1954 ruling in *Brown v. Board of Education of Topeka* banned segregation of public facilities. Finally, in 1955, the Langston course was expanded to 18 holes. The Royal Golf Club, which spearheaded the push to desegregate courses, was now able to center its golfing activities at Langston because its expansion could more fully accommodate the club's tournament and related needs.

The Royal Golf Club also played a major role in the promotion of black golfing beyond the local scene, especially the early development of the UGA and other black golf associations. Some Royal Golf Club members were among the prime movers of black golf nationally: John Shippen, for example, played in the earliest tournaments of the USGA in the 1890s and was recognized as the first black professional golfer. His brother Cyrus Shippen became the golf coach in 1928 at Washington's famed Dunbar High School. Dr. George Adams and Dr. Albert Harris were founding members of the UGA in 1926. Edgar Brown, president of United Government Employees, was also a golf enthusiast who lent his organizing skills to the fight for black equality on the golfing front and in other areas. His wife, Paris Brown, became tournament director of the UGA and was succeeded by Timothy Thomas, thus providing a stabilizing force for the organization's major national event for several decades.

While the Royal Golf Club was initiated by prominent members of the black elite, its membership increasingly drew from a wider and more diverse population. Many of the better players came up through the caddying ranks, but from lower socioeconomic stations. As the club became more involved in intercity team matches, strong players from all social classes were welcomed to join and contribute to the team. Intercity rivalries developed as the Royals traveled to Baltimore, Philadelphia, New York, and cities in the New Jersey area to engage in informal golf matches with clubs in those areas. As a result of these matches, the Eastern Golf Association (EGA) was formed in the 1930s with the Royal Golf Club as its backbone. The Royals also joined the UGA in the early thirties and maintained its

Group photo of Royal and Monumental Golf Clubs at the Carroll Park clubhouse in Baltimore, Maryland about 1938. Courtesy of Everett Payne.

membership continuously, becoming the oldest club in active UGA participation.

The Wake Robin Golf Club

The Wake Robin Golf Club was initiated in 1936 by thirteen women
who met at the home of Helen Webb Harris, educator and wife of prominent Washington, D.C., physician, Dr. Albert Harris, the co-founder of
the Royal Golf Club. In fact, the club was formed largely by wives of the
men who were members of the Royal Club because of their own desire to
become involved in golf. The aims of the Wake Robin club were "to perpetuate golf among Negro Women, to make potential players into champions and to make a permanent place for Negro Women in the world of
golf" (Wake Robin Papers, 1986; Courtesy of Moorland-Spingarn Research Center, Howard University). However, these African American
women encountered the same racial barriers as men and consequently became active in battles to gain access to golf play for blacks generally. Mrs.
Harris served as the club's first president and under her leadership the Wake
Robins joined the UGA and the EGA. In 1947, Helen Webb Harris was
elected President of the EGA, the first woman to hold that position, which
she held for two terms. Although they encountered initial resistance from
exclusively male Royal Golf Club members, the women of the Wake Robin
Golf Club soon became highly respected for their accomplishments as players, activities pushing for the integration of public golf courses in Washington, D.C., and promotion of black women's participation in the sport
regionally and nationally.

The initial involvement of African American women in golf during the
Jim Crow era differed from men in how they were introduced to the sport
and their opportunities to play on a regular basis. Unlike black men, many
of whom learned to golf in their youth as caddies, black women did not
become caddies and, therefore, were introduced to golf later as adults. As
Ethel Williams, who at ninety-five years old is the only surviving member
of the "original thirteen" Wake Robins, describes her introduction to golf,
"Men could play on white-only public courses on Mondays as caddies but
the women could not play because we were not caddies. [Black] men also
played on a course between Washington and Baltimore . . . My husband
and I used to play tennis and he had a condition with his legs that prevented
him from jumping. So the doctor recommended that he take up walking.
So we started playing golf. He was working at night and it was very difficult
for him to get anybody who could play with him in the morning. That's
when I came with him to the course with a 5 iron and a putter so that he
could have someone to play with. . . . I started playing in 1936 with my
husband but I had no formal lessons. I had two young children so I didn't
have much time. I got very interested in golf when we had meetings. I could

hardly wait to get out to play, especially with the women. . . . We use to wear hats and dresses but no spikes because the greens were sand greens. My first golf shoes were Girl Scout oxfords" (Wake Robin Papers, 1986).

The Wake Robins stimulated interest in golf among black women in other cities, leading to the establishment of golf clubs by African American women in such cities as Baltimore, Atlantic City, Philadelphia, and New York. The women golf clubs were particularly active in promoting social activities, contributing to charities, and engaging in fund-raising events to help send members to golf tournaments in other cities. These women were also involved with Royal Golf Club members in pushing for the desegregation of the Washington, D.C., public golf courses and establishment of the Langston course, which was set aside for blacks. They started playing at the segregated Lincoln Memorial Golf Course and, just as the men, were dissatisfied with the inadequate facilities offered there. As Mrs. Williams points out in her description of the Lincoln Memorial course, "All you needed was a 5 iron and a putter to play the course. You had to walk across streets to go from one hole to another hole. . . . When we wanted to play golf where we would use more than an iron and a putter, we had to go to Baltimore because courses were segregated in Washington" (Wake Robin Papers, 1986). Consequently, the Wake Robin Club joined the Royal Club in protests to desegregate Washington's public courses in 1938, which eventually led to the opening of the Langston Golf Course. As Ethel Williams recalls, "One of the charter members of Wake Robin, Adelaide Adams, was the first woman to tee off at Langston and I was playing with her so I was the second" (Wake Robin Papers, 1986). Similar to the experiences of their male counterparts, these women also encountered white resistance to their attempts to play on public courses after they joined the Royal Club in successfully petitioning Interior Secretary Ickes to integrate the courses in 1941. These pioneering efforts of the Wake Robin women to fight for access and equity in golf (McDaniel, 1994; *Washington Post*, April 26, 1987, p. B3; May 28, 1997, p. A1, A10) earned great respect for them from black male golfers and led to the assumption of leadership positions by women in some of the associations in which men were in the majority. During the 1940s, for example, Wake Robin founder Helen Webb Harris was elected to the presidency of the EGA and fellow Wake Robin, Paris Brown, assumed the tournament directorship of the UGA, becoming the first women to hold such positions.

CONCLUSION

In this chapter, we have examined the role of the black elite in the establishment of black golf clubs and the promotion of the sport generally throughout the African American community. Golf had a particular appeal to middle-class blacks, given the prestige and elite values associated with a sport that was first introduced to America through the country clubs of wealthy whites. However, in the racially discriminatory climate of the Jim Crow era, elite blacks were barred from these clubs and their facilities. They were also permitted limited access to golf courses in the North and almost totally excluded from playing on courses in the South, except for the conditional provisions accorded black caddies as previously discussed. In response to such exclusion, African Americans established their own golfing organizations and activities and fought for the creation of public courses designated for them and, subsequently, gained access to white, segregated golf courses. African American women were also major participants in this important social movement, as we have shown, supporting the efforts of their male counterparts as well as becoming champion players in their own right.

A critically held view of elite blacks' interest in sports during the Jim Crow era suggests that this was part of the general "preoccupation of Negro 'society' with sports" (Frazier, 1962). According to Frazier, this preoccupation of the black bourgeoisie was a phony identification with sport to gain status rather than a genuine interest in pursuing sport through serious participation. Our examination reveals that, in the case of golf, black elites had more than a superficial identification with and demonstrated their interest in this sport as a serious pursuit in two primary ways: first, the organizations that they established encouraged broad-based involvement and were more open to black participation across social class lines than the largely exclusive white country clubs. While being promoted as recreational activity for the business and professional class, golf was also viewed as a sport that should appeal to blacks generally. In addition, most of the more experienced golfers came from the ranks of caddies, who were from poor economic circumstances but were heavily relied upon by middle-class blacks to become teaching and playing professionals in their organized clubs and associations. Second, black elites demonstrated their seriousness about increasing the opportunities for blacks to play by assuming a major role in pushing for an end to racial discrimination in golf, manifested through the denial of black access to public courses. These struggles began with the early establishment of black golf clubs in the 1920s, continued throughout the civil rights period of the late 1940s and 1950s, and not only focused on the desegregation of public golf courses but also targeted racially discriminatory policies and practices of the PGA and other established golfing organizations. Despite assuming the role of pushing for change on the racial front, however, middle-class blacks devoted much of their energies toward promoting their own organizational activities at both local and national levels.

We turn next to examine, in greater detail, the early activities of the UGA, the national organization established by blacks during the Jim Crow era to expand African American golf.

CHAPTER 4

The Organization of Black Golf: The United Golfers Association

Completing a detailed study of the United Golfers Association's (UGA) activities during the Jim Crow era is difficult because there are no definitive works documenting its history during this crucial period in the growth of black golf. The need for a comprehensive UGA source is particularly evident in the inconsistencies reflected in existing sources (cf. Ashe, 1988a; Barkow, 1974, 1989; Dawkins, 1996; McRae, 1991; Reed, 1991; Rust, 1985). Some accounts, for example, claim that the organization was formed in 1928, with "Pat" Ball as the first National Open champion (Barkow, 1974; 1989), while others point to 1926 as the UGA's founding year, with Harry Jackson as its first national tournament winner (Ashe, 1988a; McRae, 1991; Reed, 1991). However, a closer examination of UGA activities reported in the black press during the Jim Crow era reveals insights that cannot be gained by relying solely on existing accounts. Thus, it is significant to note that a 1925 black golf tournament reported in the *Baltimore Afro-American* as being the first "International Golf Championship Tournament" was played at the Shady Rest Country Club in Westfield, New Jersey, and won by Harry Jackson the year *before* most existing sources report that the first UGA championship was held (*Baltimore Afro-American*, July 18, 1925, p. 6). The success of the 1925 tournament contributed to the idea of staging an annual national tournament beginning in 1926, with what has been regarded by most accounts as the first UGA national championship tournament actually being played under the auspices of the "Colored Golfers Association of America" that later evolved into the UGA (*Baltimore Afro-American*, May 22, 1926, p. 8). Additionally,

while the UGA's origin has been attributed to two Washington, D.C., golfing doctors (George Adams and Albert Harris) responding to their racial
exclusion from the sport (Ashe, 1988a), African American women in Washington, D.C., who later formed the Wake Robin Golf Club, the first
independent African American women's golf organization, played a significant role. Helen Harris and Adelaide Adams, who were the wives of Drs.
Harris and Adams, along with several other women, were active in the
early development of the UGA, with one of its members, Paris Brown,
rising to the powerful position of UGA national tournament director. Even
the first presidency of the UGA, which has sometimes been the source of
some confusion, can be better understood by examining newspaper accounts of UGA activities. Although by most accounts this honor is be-
stowed on Robert Hawkins, the president of the Mapledale Golf Club, in
Stow, Massachusetts, where the organization was formed (Ashe, 1988a;
Black Enterprise, 1997; McRae, 1991; Reed, 1991), Dr. George Adams
was later honored as the first official UGA president, since his presidency,
beginning in 1927, came when the organization was first recognized as a
legally constituted body (*Florida Star*, 1959, September 5, p. 7). Despite
these inconsistencies, it is clear that the kind of Jim Crowism prevailing in
the 1920s gave rise to the UGA's foundation and emergence as a major
force in black golf.

   The following discussion examines the UGA based primarily on its activities reported in some of the leading black newspapers of the 1920s
through the early 1960s to gain insight into its role in promoting African
American golf in the face of PGA exclusion and related barriers. While not
claiming to be exhaustive, this chapter looks through the lenses of the black
press to develop a more detailed account of UGA activities than is typical
of previous accounts (cf. Ashe, 1988a, b; McRae, 1991; Reed, 1991). We
focus particularly on the organization's earliest years in promoting black
golf at the national, regional and local levels.

   Some of the UGA's outstanding early male golfers included Harry Jack-
son and John Shippen of Washington, D.C., Robert "Pat" Ball of Chicago,
Edison Marshall and John Roux of New Orleans, Frank Gaskin of Phila-
delphia, George Aaron and Cliff Taylor of New York, Howard Wheeler of
Atlanta and Philadelphia, Bob Seymour and Eddie Jackson of Detroit,
Clyde Martin of Washington and Detroit, John Dendy of Asheville, North
Carolina, and Landy Taylor of Norfolk, Virginia. Later stars to emerge in
the 1940s through the 1950s, to name a few, included such players as
William Spiller, Eural Clark, Joe Roach, Ted Rhodes, Charles Sifford, Pete
Brown, and Lee Elder. Some prominent women included Marie Thompson,
Laura Osgood, Julia Siler, Ella Able, Melanie Moye, Cleo Ball, Lucy Wil-
liams, Thelma Cowan, Ann Gregory, and Ethel Funches. Although previous
accounts suggest that a few players dominated black golf tournaments during various periods of the Jim Crow age (Ashe, 1988a, b), many compet-

itive black players participated in tournaments sponsored by the UGA and other black groups. Among the top golfers in tournaments over the first two decades of major black golf activity are not only those who were more highly publicized like Howard Wheeler, Clyde Martin, Robert Ball, Edison Marshall, John Dendy, Zeke Hartsfield, and Ted Rhodes, but others who became champions such as George Aaron, Elmer Stout, Porter Washington, Bob Seymour, Joe Roach, Solomon Hughes, Ben Davis, Hugh Smith, Cecil Shamwell, Everett Payne, John Thompson, Ralph Dawkins, Howard Pitts, Sanders Mason, Eddie Roby, Willie Mosley, Preston Knowles, Frank Calhoun, and many, many more. Some were among the top finishers in selected tournaments between 1925 and 1946 presented in Table 4.1. A few of the early African American golfers later received national acclaim, yet most remain virtually unknown today outside of informed golf circles. Although we will take a closer look at the coverage of such players in the black press (Chapter 6) and firsthand accounts of some of their experiences based on personal interviews with some of them (Chapter 7), it is clear that popular historical accounts of the sport tend to obscure the wide variety of its successful participants.

ROBERT H. HAWKINS: THE "FATHER OF NEGRO GOLF"

One of the central figures in the establishment of the UGA and the development of a golf course that became the site of the first three UGA national championship tournaments was Robert H. Hawkins. Hawkins started as a caddie at all-white, exclusive country clubs in New England. He first caddied at the Forest Park Club in Adams, Massachusetts, in 1897. When his family moved to Vermont in 1902, he caddied at the Waubanakee Club in Burlington, where he rose to the position of caddie master. By the time he graduated from high school in 1907, he was working in the clubhouses of other exclusive country clubs in Vermont and gained the respect of his employers, leading to an appointment as general manager of the Sandy Burr Country Club in Wayland, Massachusetts. He was the first black to rise to this level in New England. Hawkins was keenly aware that African Americans did not have access to these clubs and became interested in developing a country club for blacks in New England. Accordingly, in 1926 he purchased a 196-acre country estate in Stow, Massachusetts, which is about twenty-five miles outside of Boston, for the purpose of establishing a private country club for blacks. The estate included a large twenty-room mansion and Hawkins built a 9-hole golf course along with facilities for other sports, including tennis and horseback riding. The estate became known as the Mapledale Country Club. He served as its first president and, when the UGA was organized during the national tournament held there in September 1926, he was elected first UGA president. Although some accounts list Dr. George Adams of Washington, D.C., as the first

Table 4.1
Top Finishers in Selected African American Golf Tournaments over Two Decades
(1925–1946) During the Jim Crow Era as Reported in Black Newspapers

Ranking	Tournament/ Players	Year
First International Golf Championship, Shady Rest Country Club Westfield, New Jersey		1925
1	Harry Jackson (Washington, DC)	
2	John Shippen (Washington, DC)	
3	C. E. Brice (Darby, PA)	
4	L. Martin (Washington, DC)	
5	Wallace Braxton (Darby, PA)	
6	Robert E. Lee (Plainfield, NJ)	
7	Ira Herrington (New York City)	
8	R. Harvey (Mt. Vernon, NY)	
9	Elmer Brent (New York City)	
10	Reggie Lewis (Mt. Vernon, NY)	
United Golfers Association (UGA) National Open Championship, Mapledale Country Club Stow, Massachusetts		1927
1	Robert "Pat" Ball (Chicago, IL)	
2	John Shippen (Washington, DC)	
3	Harry Jackson (Washington, DC)	
4	Elmer Stout (Westfield, NJ)	
5	Landy Taylor (Norfolk, VA)	
UGA National Open Championship, Sunset Hills Country Club Chicago, Illinois		1933
1	Howard Wheeler (Atlanta, GA)	
2	Edison Marshall (New Orleans, LA)	
3	Robert "Pat" Ball (Chicago, IL)	
Southern Open Championship, Lincoln Country Club Atlanta, Georgia		1934
1	John Dendy (Asheville, NC)	
2	Hugh Smith (Thomaston, GA)	
3	"Honey" Smith (Atlanta, GA)	
4	Zeke Hartsfield (Decatur, GA)	
5	Howard Wheeler (Atlanta, GA)	
6	Joseph Henderson (Birmingham, AL)	
7	Howard Pitts (Columbus, GA)	
8	A. D. V. Crosby (Atlanta, GA)	
9	Ben Redd (Athens, GA)	
10	Elijah Green (Savannah, GA)	
11	Clarence Chandler (Atlanta, GA)	
12	Charles Jones (Atlanta, GA)	
13	Hicks Broughton (LaGrange, GA)	
14	Ben Philpot (LaGrange, GA)	
15	Wiley Jordan (Thomaston, GA)	
UGA National Open Championship, Palos Park Chicago, IL		1937
1	Howard Wheeler (Atlanta, GA)	
2	John Roux (New Orleans, LA)	
3	Ben Green (New Orleans, LA)	
4	John Dendy (Asheville, NC)	
5	Robert "Pat" Ball (Chicago, IL)	

Ranking	Tournament/ Players	Year
First Annual Joe Louis Open, Rackham Course		1941
Detroit, Michigan		
1	Clyde Martin (Detroit, MI)	
2 (tie)	Calvin Searles (New Orleans, LA)	
2 (tie)	Zeke Hartsfield (Atlanta, GA)	
3 (tie)	Ben Davis (Detroit, MI)	
3 (tie)	Ben Green (New Orleans, LA)	
3 (tie)	Bob Seymour (Fort Custer, MI)	
3 (tie)	Theodore Rhodes (Nashville, TN)	
8	Howard Wheeler (Los Angeles, CA)	
9	Solomon Hughes (Gadsden, AL)	
10	Eddie Jackson (Detroit, MI)	
UGA National Open Championship, Ponkapoag Golf Club		1941
Canton, Massachusetts		
1	Robert "Pat" Ball (Chicago, IL)	
2	Clyde Martin (Detroit, MI)	
3	Zeke Hartsfield (Atlanta, GA)	
4	Solomon Hughes (Gadsden, GA)	
5	James Clark (Hartford, CT)	
6	Eddie Jackson (Detroit, MI)	
7	Calvin Searles (New Orleans, LA)	
8	Hugh Smith (Thomaston, GA)	
9	Ed Roby (Atlanta, GA)	
10	Joe "Roach" Delancey (New York City)	
11	Cecil Shamwell (Washington, DC)	
12	Edison Marshall (Indianapolis, IN)	
13	James Adams (Hartford, CT)	
14	P. Washington (Boston, MA)	
15	Ralph Dawkins (Jacksonville, FL)	
16	Oscar Clisby (Pasadena, CA)	
17	Hugh Shippen (Washington, DC)	
18	Beltran Barker (Washington, DC)	
19	Ted Jones (New York City)	
20	J. Thompson (Washington, DC)	
21	Preston Knowledges (New York City)	
22	Ernest Hill (Boston, MA)	
23	Tom Pearson (New York City)	
24	Benny Robinson (VA)	
25	Rudolph Johnson (New York City)	
26	C. R. Clark (Chicago, IL)	
UGA National Open Championship, South Park Golf Course		1946
Pittsburgh, Pennsylvania		
1	Howard Wheeler (Los Angeles, CA)	
2	Theodore Rhodes (Nashville, TN)	
3	Solomon Hughes (Minneapolis, MN)	
4	Zeke Hartsfield (Birmingham, AL)	
5	Myron Coleman	
6	Warren Sharrock (Ossining, NY)	
7	Robert "Pat" Ball (Chicago, IL)	
8	C. Stewart	
9	Frank Radcliffe (New York City)	
10	Willie Mosely (Detroit, MI)	
11	Preston Knowledges (New York City)	
12	Charles McCauley (Cleveland, OH)	
13	Alton Smith (Indianapolis, IN)	
14	Marcus King (Detroit, MI)	
15	John Skelton (Philadelphia, PA)	
16	Clyde Martin (Detroit, MI)	
17	Vance Watts (New York City)	
18	John Green (Indianapolis, IN)	
19	Joe "Roach" Delancey (New York City)	
20	Herbert Howard (Washington, DC)	
21	Sgt. Ernest Wilson (Lockbourne Air Base, OH)	
22	Jacob Mallory	
23	Estell Satchell (New York City)	
24	John Tatum (Washington, DC)	
25	Beltran Barker (Washington, DC)	

Note: Adapted by permission from Dawkins, M. P. (1996). "African American Golfers in the Age of Jim Crow." *Western Journal of Black Studies*, 20:39–47.

UGA president because he was elected to this position when the organization was formally constituted in 1927 (*Florida Star*, September 5, 1959, p. 7) for his pioneering role in facilitating the establishment of the UGA and the Negro National Open Championship, Hawkins became known as the "Father of Negro Golf" (*The Courier*, February 2, 1952, p. 20).

EARLY UGA NATIONAL OPEN CHAMPIONSHIPS

From its outset, the UGA (originally called the United States Colored Golfers Association) staged a national tournament to provide black golfers with an experience that paralleled the excitement the USGA and PGA championship tournaments offered white golfers. The UGA Negro National Open Championship was an annual affair, with the winners laying claim to the title of "national champion" in both professional and amateur divisions. Table 4.2 shows the UGA championship winners among both men and women golfers (1926–1962) during the Jim Crow era. One of the most successful UGA champions, Charlie Sifford, who won six National Open championships between 1952 and 1960 before becoming the first black golfer to win a major PGA tournament after breaking through golf's racial barrier, recently referred to the UGA National Open as the "Masters" tournament for black golfers, which carried with it bragging rights for its winners (*Black Enterprise*, 1997).

The first official National Open championship was scheduled for Sunday and Monday, September 5 and 6, 1926, at Stow, Massachusetts, sponsored by the Mapledale Country Club with Robert H. Hawkins as its major planner. Participating clubs on the East Coast included the Mapledale Country Club (Boston), the Shady Rest Club (Westfield, New Jersey), the Citizens Golf Club (Washington, D.C.), and the Wilson Park Club (Baltimore) (*Baltimore Afro-American*, May 22, 1926, p. 8). There was also a contingent of Midwestern golfers from the Windy City Golf Club of Chicago (*Chicago Defender*, August 28, 1926, p. 6). As the tournament drew near, enthusiasm began to mount and efforts were made to attract participants from more clubs in the East, a challenging task given competing interests. In July, the Shady Rest Club in New Jersey held a two-day tournament to generate interest among New Yorkers in the upcoming UGA championship. Twenty-four players qualified, many from New York. John Shippen, the club professional at Washington, D.C.'s Citizens Golf Club, won the event over George Aaron of the St. Nicholas Golf Club in New York (*Pittsburgh Courier*, July 10, 1926, p. 15). Shippen, who had long competed against the strongest white players, was highly instrumental in promoting black golf in the Washington, D.C., area in the face of racial segregation. Aaron belonged to a group composed of black players who competed against whites in citywide public tournaments and had his sights on the National Public Links Championship Tournament—an opportunity

Table 4.2
National UGA Tournaments and Winners (1926–1962)

Year	Location	Amateur Men's	Amateur Women's	Professional
1926	Stow, Massachusetts			Harry Jackson
1927	Stow, Massachusetts			Pat Ball
1928	Stow, Massachusetts			Porter Washington
1929	Westfield (Scotch Plains), NJ	Frank Gaskin		Pat Ball
1930	Casa Loma, Wisconsin	George Roddy	Marie Thompson	Edison Marshall
1931	Kankakee, Illinois	Jay McCoy	Marie Thompson	Edison Marshall
1932	Indianapolis, Indiana	Frank Gaskin	Lucy Williams	John Dendy
1933	Kankakee, Illinois	Isaac Ellis	Julia Siler	Howard Wheeler
1934	Detroit, Michigan	Percy Jones	Ella C. Able	Pat Ball
1935	Yorktown Heights, NY	Frank Radcliffe	Ella C. Able	Solomon Hughes
1936	Philadelphia, Pennsylvania	Clifford Taylor	Lucy Williams	John Dendy
1937	Cleveland, Ohio	George Roddy	Lucy Williams	John Dendy
1938	Kankakee, Illinois	Dr. Remus Robinson	Melnee Moye	Howard Wheeler
1939	Los Angeles, California	Gus Price	Geneva Wilson	Cliff Strickland
1940	Chicago, Illinois	Dr. Remus Robinson	Melnee Moye	Hugh Smith
1941	Boston, Massachusetts	Clifford Taylor	Cleo Ball	Pat Ball
1942-45	No Competition	War Years	No Competition	War Years
1946	Pittsburgh, Pennsylvania	Bill Brown	Lucy Mitchum	Howard Wheeler
1947	Philadelphia, Pennsylvania	Alfred "Tup" Holmes	Thelma Cowan	Howard Wheeler
1948	Indianapolis, Indiana	Gordon Goodson	Mary Brown	Howard Wheeler
1949	Detroit, Michigan	Barther Cooper	Thelma Cowan	Ted Rhodes
1950	Washington, D.C.	"Tex" Guillory	Ann Gregory	Ted Rhodes
1951	Cleveland, Ohio	Joe Louis	Edline Thornton	Ted Rhodes
1952	Pittsburgh, Pennsylvania	Gordon Goodson	Alice Stewart	Charles Sifford
1953	Kansas City, Missouri	Joe "Roach" Delancey	Ann Gregory	Charles Sifford
1954	Dallas, Texas	Joe "Roach" Delancey	Thelma Cowan	Charles Sifford
1955	Detroit, Michigan	Joe "Roach" Delancey	Thelma Cowan	Charles Sifford
1956	Philadelphia, Pennsylvania	Gordon Goodson	No Competition	Charles Sifford
1957	Washington, D.C.	Howard Brown	Ann Gregory	Ted Rhodes
1958	Pittsburgh, Pennsylvania	Alfred "Tup" Holmes	Vernice Turner	Howard Wheeler
1959	Washington, D.C.	Rafe Botts	Ethel Funches	Richard Thomas
1960	Chicago, Illinois	Calvin Tanner	Ethel Funches	Charles Sifford
1961	Boston, Massachusetts	Willie Green	Vernice Turner	Pete Brown
1962	Memphis, Tennessee	Calvin Tanner	Carrie Jones	Pete Brown

to play against a group of the country's strongest white players, some of whom belonged to the exclusive PGA. Recognized as one of the leading "colored" players in New York, Aaron had recently won the right to play in the finals of the Public Links Championship in New York City and was probably more interested in representing the city at the National Public Links Championship tournament than gearing up for the UGA tournament (*Pittsburgh Courier*, June 19, 1926, p. 15). However, more enthusiasm among club members prevailed in Boston, New Jersey, Washington, D.C., Baltimore, and Chicago, which increased general interest in the upcoming UGA tournament. William Brice of the Citizens Golf Club in Washington, D.C., and Walter S. Savoy, for example, prepared for the event by playing a round at the West Potomac Park public links, with the former shooting a hole in one, only the sixth recorded in the course's history (*Pittsburgh Courier*, August 28, 1926, p. 15). The Shady Rest Club in New Jersey held a preparatory tournament for both professional and amateur players in July and later staged an open tournament for the general public on September 5 and 6 to coincide with the UGA championship for those who would not be traveling to the event in Stow (*Pittsburgh Courier*, August 21, 1926, p. 14). Chicago's highly organized Windy City Golf Club was also preparing for this major event, which promised to secure for its winners bragging rights relating to which region of the country produced the best black golfers. Led by club president Walter Speedy, the Chicago hopefuls included the increasingly recognized Robert "Pat" Ball. Speedy and Ball, along with another Windy City golfer, Henry B. Johnson, had entered the officially nonsegregated Chicago city championship tournament several years earlier and when Ball made it to the semifinal round against some of the best golfers in the city, including recognized pros, it created such a furor among white golfers that by some subterfuge blacks had been effectively excluded from the city's public links championship but eventually succeeded in regaining the right to play in this event several years later (*Chicago Defender*, August 28, 1926, p. 6). Consequently, Ball's reputation earned him the respect of other black golfers throughout the country and made him one of the favorites to win the inaugural UGA national championship. The entry fee was set at four dollars with a September 1 deadline. By August 26, entries indicated that this tournament would attract the largest number of black players to any golf event to date. Elegant social activities were planned, including a formal associational meeting, a testimonial dinner in honor of the Mapledale club founder Robert Hawkins, who would be elected first UGA president, and a formal presentation of the prizes on September 6 by the Honorable J. W. Schenck of Boston (*Pittsburgh Courier*, August 28, 1926, p. 14). Thirty-eight players from ten states and the District of Columbia entered the tournament, held on the newly constructed course at Mapledale, which was not particularly appealing to players since such courses usually took time to learn and be "broken in." The tournament lived up to its billing and provided exciting events both on and off the course. Harry Jackson of Washington, D.C., won the championship by completing the 72 holes with a score of 295. Two Chicagoans, Robert "Pat" Ball and Porter W. Washington, finished tied for second with a 299 score, while John Shippen of Washington, D.C., came in fourth at 304 and Elmer Stout of Shady Rest, New Jersey, finished fifth at 310. Washington and Ball played an extra hole to break the second-place tie, with Washington coming out on top by taking in a four, while Ball required five strokes to complete the hole. Championship cups to be retained for one year were awarded to the top finishers, along with prize money: $100 for first place, $75 for second place, $50 for third place, $25 for fourth place, and $15 for fifth place. The awards were formally presented at a ball held for golfers and their guests the night of the final day (September 6) at the clubhouse. Other golfers who were top competitors in the first UGA national championship tournament and their scores included Landy Taylor (Virginia) 316, Frank Calhoun (Chicago) 334, Howard Hill (New Jersey) 339, Beltran Barker (Washington, D.C.) 341, Lawrence Fryerson (Chicago) 346, Bertram Coombs (Massachusetts) 352, Clifford Edmunds (Rhode Island) 359, George McPherson (New Jersey) 380, Dr. E. J. Ricks (Chicago) 389, and Elmer Young (New Jersey) 390 (*Chicago Defender*, September 11, 1926, p. 8).

The next UGA National Open Golf Championship was also held at the Mapledale Country Club on September 5 and 6, 1927. In addition to clubs in the area, entries were received from New Orleans, North Carolina, and Virginia. Again participating was a strong contingent of eight players from Chicago, including Robert "Pat" Ball, Walter Speedy, and Henry Johnson (*Pittsburgh Courier*, September 3, 1927, p. 5). Despite fierce competition from defending UGA champion Harry Jackson and the well-known John Shippen, Chicago's Ball was the overwhelming winner this time with a score of 293—twenty points better than Shippen's performance. He was awarded custody of the championship cup and $100 first prize. Second-place winner Shippen received $75 and Jackson received $50 for third place. The remaining prize money was distributed among the other top finishers ($5 each), which included Elmer Stout of New Jersey and Landy Taylor of Virginia, finishing in fourth and fifth place, respectively (*Pittsburgh Courier*, September 17, 1927, p. 4). Although Shippen and Jackson were well known in the Washington, D.C., area, Ball was probably the most recognized black player in the Midwest at this time. With roots in Georgia, he moved to Chicago and was among the prime movers of the game in that city. He was secretary of the Windy City Golf Club, one of Chicago's earliest black golf clubs. Members played on other public courses while awaiting construction of a new course, the Sunset Hills Golf Club at a nearby resort. Ball was among a small group of African American golfers who continued to enter citywide, public links tournaments at which racial restrictions did not always apply. In fact, prior to winning the 1927 UGA National Open, Ball also won the Cook County Open Championship in Chicago in August of that year (*Pittsburgh Courier*, August 13, 1927, p. 4).

As with the previous events, the 1928 Third Annual UGA National Open Championship was scheduled for the Mapledale course. Planning committee members included well-known black golf promoters such as Walter Speedy (Chicago), Robert H. Hawkins (Stow), George W. Adams (Washington), Landy Taylor (Norfolk), George Aaron (New York), and A. Tanksley (Philadelphia). Added tournament features were designed to attract more players, including an amateur championship, expansion of the tournament to three days, qualifying rounds, exhibition matches among professionals for a $200 purse, and special prizes for the best-dressed golfer, best-looking club set, and the longest drive. The $300 prize for professionals was retained, as was the winner's custody of the championship cup. The entrance fee was increased to five dollars and amateur prizes included gold, silver, and bronze medals as well as silver cups (*Pittsburgh Courier*, August 11, 1928, p. 4). The event also received elite endorsement on the "society page" of black newspapers that emphasized the sport's aristocratic and dignified nature and its appeal to all ages (*Pittsburgh Courier*, August 4, 1928, p. 4).

Porter Washington, who had moved from Chicago to become club pro at Mapledale, won the 1928 UGA championship in the professional division by defeating Robert Ball, his long-time fellow Windy City teammate. The amateur championship was won by Frank Gaskin of Philadelphia with Beltran Barker of Washington, D.C., finishing second. The scores for the top finishers among the pros were as follows: P. Washington (Mapledale) 285, R. Ball (Chicago) 290, H. Jackson (Washington) 294, J. Shippen (Washington) 295, L. Taylor (Norfolk, Virginia) 306, G. Aaron (New York) 318, T. Persons (New York) 327, R. Harris (New York) 336, G. Edmund (Providence) 338, R. Peddy (Montclair, New Jersey) 345, and A. Hunter (Norfolk, Virginia) 359. Among the added features of the tournament, the exhibition match by professionals was by far the biggest attraction. The 1927 UGA champion, Robert "Pat" Ball was teamed with the newly crowned UGA winner, Porter Washington, against a team of white professionals, who included George Aulbach, the New England PGA champion, and Jack Curley, pro at the Stone Brae Club. The Aulbach–Curley combination won the spirited exhibition match as a huge gallery watched them play (*Chicago Defender*, September 8, 1928, p. 7).

In 1929, the UGA National Open moved for the first time away from Stow, Massachusetts, to the well-known Shady Rest Golf Club of Westfield, New Jersey, that served as host for the event. Clubs represented at the tournament included Lincoln of Jacksonville, Florida, Big Walnut of Columbus, Ohio, Casa Loma of southern Wisconsin near Chicago, Sunset

Hills of Chicago, Citizens of Washington, D.C., Fairview of Philadelphia, Mapledale of Stow, Massachusetts, and St. Nicholas of New York City. The biggest threat to dethrone Porter Washington of Mapledale, the 1928 winner, was Robert "Pat" Ball, who was trying to regain the championship title he held in 1927. Other outstanding professionals in the tournament included Washington's Harry Jackson and John Shippen, Norfolk's Landy Taylor, and Bermuda's Louis Corbin, while the defending amateur champion was Frank Gaskin of the Fairview Golf Club in Philadelphia (*Pittsburgh Courier*, August 24, 1929, p. 5). An exhibition match was once again scheduled, pitting the Robert Ball–Porter Washington pair against two leading white pros in the area. The championship of the 1929 UGA National Open was captured by Robert Ball, who set a new course record at Shady Rest in the process of regaining the title, with a total of 284 strokes for the 72 holes. His nearest opponent was Elmer Stout of Newark (290) followed by Louis Corbin of Bermuda (294), Beltran Barker of Washington, D.C. (299), and Robert Peddy of Montclair (303). Gaskin repeated as amateur champion defeating Elmer Brent of New York (*Pittsburgh Courier*, September 7, 1929, p. 5).

By the close of the 1920s, the annual UGA national championship tournament, the "Negro National Open," was well established as the elite event among African American golfers and the "society set." These early tournaments stimulated the formation of local and regional play throughout the country, even in the rigidly segregated South, providing opportunities for young black golfers coming up through the caddying ranks to compete at the tournament level against the best black golfers in the country. In 1928, for example, one of the few private, black-owned clubs in the deep South, the recently established Lincoln Country Club in Jacksonville, Florida, held the first Florida Junior Golf and Tennis Tournament in that state's history. Eighteen-year-old Ralph Dawkins, a caddie at exclusive white golf clubs in the area, won the golf event and, along with other youths who primarily made up the field of fifty-eight entrants, was one of the future hopefuls who would one day travel north to represent the state of Florida at the national UGA tournament (*Chicago Defender*, September 22, 1928, p. 10). Most aspiring black golfers in the South during this period, however, including such notable players as Robert Ball, found it necessary to leave the South to realize their desire to participate in golf on a wider scale. Ball began in golf as a caddie for the white golf champion, Bobby Jones, at the East Lake Country Club in Atlanta, Georgia. While caddying for Jones, he also worked as a club maker at the Druid Hills Country Club golf shop before moving to Chicago at age sixteen (*Pittsburgh Courier*, August 30, 1941, p. 17). With the growth of the black golfing community in the 1930s, UGA champions increasingly came from southern cities such as Atlanta and New Orleans, as well as transplanted southerners, like Ball, who moved to other regions of the country.

THE UGA IN THE 1930s

As interest in golf attracted greater numbers of African Americans during the 1930s, the UGA assumed a leading role by promoting greater participation in its activities, especially the now well-established National Open championship tournament. It has been estimated that some 50,000 blacks participated in golf during this decade (Ashe, 1988a; Reed, 1991). The UGA expanded its activities in the 1930s by shifting the site of the National Open tournaments from the East to the Midwest and West, stimulating public interest in rivalries among leading players and, in the process, generating greater coverage of golf in leading black newspapers. Although all four UGA national tournaments in the 1920s were held in the East, eight of the eleven tournaments between 1930 and 1940 took place in the Midwest, one in the West, and only two in the East (see Table 4.2). The first UGA National Open to be staged in the Midwest was held at the Casa Loma Country Club in southeastern Wisconsin in 1930 and hosted by the Pioneer Golf Club of Chicago (*Pittsburgh Courier*, August 9, 1930, p. 4). The success of this tournament, won by Edison Marshall of New Orleans, led the UGA tournament committee to decide to keep the National Open in Chicago the following year (1931). Extensive coverage by the *Chicago Defender* ensured broad-based publicity for the event and increased the visibility of black golfers among national audiences. Headlines appearing on the sports page of the *Defender* rivaled the usually greater coverage given to baseball, boxing, and other sports, as illustrated in the following, which appeared between August 22 and September 5, the first day of the tournament: NATION'S GOLF STARS EYE CHICAGO (*Chicago Defender*, August 22, 1931, p. 11), EDISON MARSHALL, GOLF CHAMP, HERE SEPTEMBER 5TH FOR MEET (*Chicago Defender*, August 29, 1931, p. 9), and CHICAGO WELCOMES GOLF KINGS (*Chicago Defender*, September 5, 1931, p. 8). The latter story included an accompanying photo with the caption "The Champion and His Companions" depicting defending champion Edison Marshall with fellow golfers newly arrived from New Orleans standing alongside the automobile they drove from Louisiana, each with a bag of golf clubs at his side. The arrival of Marshall and his entourage was significant because the promotional buildup depended heavily on his returning to Chicago to defend his championship against such formidable opponents as Chicago's Robert Ball, who held the UGA title in 1929 before Marshall wrestled it away from him in 1930, Washington, D.C.'s Harry Jackson, who won the first UGA National Open championship in 1926, and others. There was an earlier fear that Marshall might not make the trip. It was not unusual during this early period of the economic depression in the United States for an element of uncertainty to prevail in such planning. However, this concern was allayed when Walter Speedy, president of the Pioneer Golf Club, the tournament's sponsor, received a telegram from Marshall about two

The 1930 UGA defending Negro National Open Golf Champion, Edison Marshall (far right), arrives in Chicago in 1931 after driving from New Orleans with several of his golfing companions (from left: Joseph Burfect, Berganie Green, Charles Harris and John Roux) to defend his title (*Chicago Defender*, September 5, 1931, p. 8). Courtesy of the *Chicago Defender*.

weeks before the event confirming that he would positively be in Chicago to defend his title (*Pittsburgh Courier*, August 22, 1931, p. 11). The enthusiasm and interest generated by this publicity kept a national black audience fully informed and able to follow the performance of the star participants over the three days of the tournament. Although originally scheduled for the course at the Casa Loma Country Club, the site of the previous year's UGA championship, the tournament was switched to the 9-hole course at Sunset Hills Country Club in Kankakee, Illinois (near Chicago), when Casa Loma failed to open for 1931. The tournament included forty-eight amateurs, twenty-three pros, and twelve women and was highlighted by Edison Marshall's successful defense of his title in the pro division holding off the challenges of former UGA champion, Robert Ball, who finished second and fellow New Orleans golf mate, John Roux, who finished third (*Pittsburgh Courier*, September 12, 1931, p. 4). As expected, the *Chicago Defender* gave extensive coverage to the tournament's outcome that matched its pre-tournament promotion. Although the September 12 edition of the paper, the first to appear after the tournament was over, carried articles on baseball, tennis, football, and golf on the front page of the sports section, the lead article with the bold headline MARSHALL DRUBS BALL AT GOLF overshadowed other sports stories (*Chicago Defender*, September 12, 1931, p. 8). In providing details of the performances of key players, the "rivalry" between Marshall and Ball was particularly played up, as well as the unexpectedly strong challenges by New Orleans's John Roux, a teammate of Marshall, and Newark's Elmer Stout, who finished a close fourth, only one stroke behind Roux (*Chicago Defender*, September 12, 1931, p. 8). This rivalry generated so much public attention that a head-to-head match between Edison Marshall and Robert Ball was scheduled for the Douglass Park Golf Course in Indianapolis one week after the UGA tournament ended. Marshall teamed with John Roux, and Ball was joined by Porter Washington, formerly of Chicago, not only to create a Ball–Marshall match-up but a Chicago–New Orleans challenge match. The best-ball match produced exciting action as it ended up even after a dramatic comeback by Marshall and Roux who scored birdies on the 17th hole to tie the game (*Chicago Defender*, September 19, 1931, p. 8). The match was also seen as a way of generating interest in the next year's UGA championship tournament (1932) that was scheduled for Indianapolis. Other highlights of the 1931 UGA National Open included the women's division championship won by Marie Thompson of Chicago, with Lucy Williams of Indianapolis and Elizabeth Groves of New York finishing second and third, respectively; a driving contest in which Porter Washington of Boston tied with John Hodge of Nashville; and at the business meeting, the election of Chicago's Dr. E. J. Ricks as the new UGA president (*Pittsburgh Courier*, September 12, 1931, p. 4).

The 1932 UGA National Open in Indianapolis, along with five of the next six UGA championships between 1933 and 1938, were won by golfers from the South. John Dendy, originally from Asheville, North Carolina, won titles in 1932, 1936, and 1937; Howard Wheeler from Atlanta won in 1933 and 1938; and Solomon Hughes from Gadsden, Alabama, triumphed in 1935. In fact, except for Robert Ball, who won the 1934 UGA championship in Detroit, and Cliff Strickland, who won in 1939 on his home turf in Los Angeles, when the tournament was played on the West Coast for the first time, all the pro division championship titles during the 1930s were captured by southern golfers. This was ironic given that the South appeared to be more restrictive in terms of the accessibility of golf courses to blacks and the concentration of UGA activities outside the South. By the end of the 1930s, all the UGA National Open tournaments had been held in either the East or the Midwest and this would continue until 1954 when Dallas would become the first Deep South city to host a UGA National Open. One possible explanation for the success of the southerners is their early exposure to golf through caddying and experiences as youths playing on "caddie days" and participating in caddie tournaments before gaining wider exposure through the organized black golf clubs in some cities. However, probably the most activity among golfers in the South was concentrated in cities where African Americans established their own, private golf courses. Among the few cities in which this was the case were Atlanta, Georgia, and Jacksonville, Florida. Jacksonville's Lincoln golf course established in the late 1920s and Atlanta's course also named Lincoln established during the same period became the center of black golfing activity in the Southeast. After visiting Jacksonville's Lincoln Country Club course, Wendell "Smitty" Smith, sportswriter for the *Pittsburgh Courier*, rated it one of "the best links owned and operated by Negroes in the country" (*Pittsburgh Courier*, January 10, 1941, p. 16). Atlanta's Lincoln Country Club golf course was equally impressive and became the major site for golf activity in the Southeast. Except for Chicago's Robert Ball (whose earliest exposure to golf was actually gained through caddying as a Georgia youth), and New Orlean's Edison Marshall, the 1930s UGA champions, Dendy, Wheeler, and Hughes were all part of the Atlanta golf scene and participated regularly in that club's annual sponsorship of the Southern Open championship tournament. In fact, the winner of the Southern Open in both 1932 (Dendy) and 1933 (Wheeler) went on to win the UGA titles for those years (*Pittsburgh Courier*, June 16, 1934, p. 4). Although John Brooks Dendy was an Asheville, North Carolina, native, he was associated with the strong contingent of black golf pros in Atlanta, where he attended Morehouse College. After winning his first UGA championship in 1932 at the age of nineteen and his third UGA national title in 1937, he became only the second golfer to achieve this honor since the organization's beginning. Among his chief competitors was fellow Atlanta pro Howard Wheeler, who would go on to win the UGA national championship six times and become the only golfer to win a UGA title during the decades of the 1930s, 1940s, and 1950s. Wheeler would eventually leave the South for Philadelphia and reside for a period on the West Coast.

The success of the Atlanta area golfers in competing at the national level during this period may also be attributed to their serious preparation for the trip north to participate in the UGA National Open. After Howard Wheeler won the national championship in 1933, the Lincoln Golf Club began to hold elimination matches to select its representatives for the National Open. In preparation for the 1934 tournament at the Rackham Park course in Detroit, Michigan, A.D.V. Crosby, the club professional, devised a method to ensure every member an opportunity to compete (fourteen were involved), by pairing amateurs in a series of 18-hole matches with professionals grouped for 36-hole medal play. Competing professionals included "Smiling" Eddie Roby, Clarence Chandler, the reigning club champion, A.D.V. Crosby, former club and interfraternity champion, Zeke Hartsfield, and Stokes Stalmaker. Amateur participants included Theodore Goosby, Walter Parks, Johnnie Logan, Neal Smith, J. W. Smith, A. L. Miller, "Honey" Smith, and James Martin. Two club members, Howard

Wheeler and Teddy Grimes, due to their championship status, were exempt from elimination matches and awarded honorary playing slots. Wheeler was the defending UGA National Champion with Grimes the Southern Amateur Champion (*Atlanta Daily World*, August 19, 1934, p. 5). However, Wheeler decided to participate in elimination play to polish his game, providing exciting play as he tied for first place with Zeke Hartsfield. These players turned in a pair of sub-par 64s and par 66s for the 36 holes, setting a new club record. Eddie Roby captured the other professional slot by achieving two rounds of 68 and 67 to finish in second place. Grantland Copeland, a late entrant, won the amateur elimination match by defeating Joel Smith, Neal Smith, and Stokes Stalmaker (who competed as an amateur). Considering he had only been playing for a year, Copeland was considered one of Lincoln Club's greatest amateurs (*Atlanta Daily World*, August 21, 1934, p. 5).

An important highlight of the 1930s was the significant contribution of Robert "Pat" Ball to the emergence of organized black golf. Since Ball participated in the first UGA national tournament in 1926 and achieved the status of becoming the first professional to win the UGA National Open championship three times with his 1934 victory in Detroit (*Pittsburgh Courier*, September 15, 1934, p. 5), he was highly respected within UGA circles. However, his success against white competition as one of the few black golfers regularly engaged in such action during the 1930s, which required pressure to remove racial barriers in the sport, probably did more to legitimize organized black golf and gain respect for the UGA than his performance in UGA tournaments. Ball not only performed consistently well at UGA-sponsored tournaments, but was equally competitive against white golfers when he was able to gain access to often racially restrictive public links tournaments in Chicago and other cities. Initiated by the United States Golf Association (USGA) in 1922, the public links tournaments consisted of citywide championship tournaments open to the public and played on public golf courses, with winners advancing to the National Public Links championship tournament. Ball won the Cook County (Chicago) Open championship (in which he was often the only black contestant) in 1927, 1929, and 1934 and the Midwest Open in Des Moines, Iowa, in 1932 and 1934, as well as other tournaments against white competitors (*Pittsburgh Courier*, August 30, 1941, p. 17). In 1932, Ball attempted to enter the National Public Links tournament in Philadelphia. When he was denied entry, he continued to push for access, as he had done during the 1920s in Chicago, and sought an injunction in Common Pleas Court, where he won, thereby becoming the only black golfer in the tournament (African American Historical and Cultural Museum, 1996). He also operated his own private golf school and, in 1938, was named golf pro at Chicago's 18-hole Palos Park public golf course (serving about 50 percent white participants), becoming the first black person to serve in that capacity on any public course (*Pittsburgh Courier*, August 30, 1941, p. 17).

Another highlight of the 1930s was the inauguration of the *United Golfer*, the official magazine of the UGA, which reported organizational news items as well as articles relating to such issues as golf course discrimination. As an example of a typical edition, the *United Golfer*'s August 1938 issue reported on the activities of the Chicago Golfers' Trophy Club, where James Poythrees, chairman of the tournament committee, was thanked for his efforts in making that year's club tournament a success and Mrs. Cleo Ball was recognized as winner of the ladies handicap match, along with Mrs. Bowman and Mrs. Philpot, who finished second and third, respectively. The same issue includes an update on the suit filed by four members of the Heart of America Golf Club in Kansas City, Missouri, against the city for denying them the right to play on the segregated public golf courses at Swope Park. Blacks were not permitted to play on the No. 1 course and could use the No. 2 course only on Mondays and Tuesdays (*United Golfer and Other Sports*, August 1938, p. 11). Other highlights at the close of the decade included the historic West Coast debut of the UGA National Open tournament, when it was held in Los Angeles, California, in 1939 and hosted by the Cosmopolitan Golf Club. Cliff Strickland, a member of the host club won the pro division championship, with Gus Price and Geneva Wilson winning the amateur men's and women's titles, respectively. Finally, the decade ends as the attraction of world heavyweight boxing champion Joe Louis to golf brings greater exposure for the UGA and its activities.

THE UGA IN THE 1940s

In the early years of the 1940s, the UGA made significant strides toward greater visibility and participation in golf among African Americans compared to other more popular sports in the black community. This was due in large part to the lure of Joe Louis's name after he entered the UGA National Open in 1940 and established his own national tournament, the Joe Louis Open in Detroit. Although the UGA National Open was suspended during World War II, the postwar years saw the emergence of a number of new star performers, such as William Spiller, Ted Rhodes, and Charles Sifford who provided a formidable challenge to Marshall, Ball, Martin, Wheeler, and other champions of the previous decade. In particular, the rivalry between Howard Wheeler and Ted Rhodes became legendary in UGA and other tournaments in which both of them played. However, many lesser known but equally competitive golfers continued to labor behind the veil of segregation in the sport they loved with fading hopes of one day having the opportunity to play in PGA tournaments and other white-dominated golf events. This appeared to change toward the end of the 1940s as increased efforts on the part of some of these black golfers to exert more aggressive challenges to Jim Crow restrictions were initiated. Most notable was the 1948 legal challenge to the PGA "Caucasian only" rule by Ted Rhodes, William Spiller, and Madison Gunter. Optimism was enhanced by the racial breakthroughs occurring in other sports, particularly the heralded entry of Negro league player Jackie Robinson into the ranks of previously all-white major league baseball. Ironically, the less successful the push for similar actions in golf, the more the UGA would continue to thrive as a parallel structure providing opportunities for blacks to play in the face of continued racial exclusion.

Joe Louis's impact on the rise of black golf in the 1940s will be covered in greater detail in Chapter 5, yet it is important to note that the arrival of the popular champion on the scene of the 1940 UGA National Open in Chicago lured thousands of spectators to the galleries to watch him play despite his golf game being described as not "worthy of writing home about" (*Richmond Afro-American*, August 24, 1940, p. 8). Louis also contributed to the tournament's success by donating one of the trophies to be awarded to the winner of the amateur division championship. Although Dr. Remus Robinson of Detroit won the amateur championship in a closely contested finish against the popular "Tup" Holmes of Atlanta, the participation of Joe Louis was the tournament highlight. Media attention also provided greater visibility to the professional division UGA champion of 1940, Hugh Smith of Thomaston, Georgia, and runner-up Clyde Martin of Washington, D.C., who had been recently hired by Louis as his private teaching pro (*Richmond Afro-American*, August 31, 1940, p. 21). Louis's enthusiasm for golf led him to sponsor his own national tournament the following year. The 1941 inaugural Joe Louis Open Tournament would have the richest purse of any black golf event and would be held in Detroit, Louis's hometown. Another significant attraction for golfers was the strategic dates for the tournament, August 13, 14, and 15, which complemented rather than rivaled the well-established annual UGA National Open. The Louis Tournament was scheduled for the weekend prior to the UGA tournament, set for August 19 through the 22, to enable golfers to travel to and participate in both events within a ten-day period. The highly publicized and well-planned Louis Tournament stimulated greater interest in the UGA tournament among both golfers and spectators, particularly given the former's plans to enter both events playing as amateurs. More than 250 golfers, the most ever, were expected to compete at the 1941 UGA National Open, which would be held at the Ponkapoag (public) golf course in Canton, Massachusetts, near Boston. As the lure of Louis's avocation propelled golf to the top of the black sports agenda for 1941, second only to boxing, his vocation, the elite as well as the rank and file of black golf throughout the country made plans for the journey to Boston, many also traveling initially to Detroit for the Joe Louis Open. The Midwest group would be led by current UGA president, Ralph Chilton from Chicago, A.D.V. Crosby from Columbus, Ohio, and Dr. Remus Robinson, reigning UGA amateur champion from Detroit. Dr. George Adams from Washington, D.C., Joe Hudson from New Jersey, and New York's Frank Radcliffe and a host of other easterners headed north to the tournament. First vice president of the UGA, A. L. Miller from Atlanta, was expected to lead a large contingent of southerners, including three-time UGA national champion John Dendy from Asheville, North Carolina, and other former UGA champions from the South. More elaborate plans than in any previous year were made by the UGA committees in preparation for the record number of golfers expected. The *Chicago Defender*, reporting on the planning, noted that two new dressing rooms and shower rooms were being constructed, grooming of the fairways, greens, and tees had been completed, and Class A caddies were being recruited from nearby country clubs. During the tournament, the course would be reconditioned each morning before play began and men would be stationed at each green to rake the sand traps. Experienced state police would handle the gallery and other security needs, led by the captain of the state police who would personally oversee these measures, including twenty four-hour protection for trophies and clubs, where additional checking facilities to accommodate 300 bags of clubs were set up. A caterer would serve a la carte meals with an outdoor dining room facility also provided (*Chicago Defender*, August 9, 1941, p. 21).

Although slightly below expectations, the 1941 UGA National Open tournament attracted 200 golfers, which set a record for the event (*Pittsburgh Courier*, August 30, 1941, p. 17). Participants came from all regions of the country and, except for the conspicuous absence of Joe Louis and Howard Wheeler, they comprised a "star-studded" array of African American golfers, described by A. L. Miller, who covered the event for the *Atlanta Daily World* sports department, as the "fastest field of professionals ever assembled" (*Atlanta Daily World*, August 20, 1941, p. 5). Many golfers came directly from Detroit after competing in the first Joe Louis Open tournament, which finished only four days earlier. Even though Louis had already sent in his entry, made reservations, and asked for the assignment of a caddie, his recent reconciliation with his wife, Marva, led him to alter his plans by remaining in Michigan to spend a second honeymoon. However, he donated the leg trophy for the women's championship with the men's trophy provided by the *Chicago Defender* (*Chicago Defender*, August 30, 1941a, p. 20). Although the first day of the tournament was cut short by a huge rainstorm, which also made the Ponkapoag course much slower than usual for the three-day event, the spirited competition and enthusiasm were not dampened. Clyde Martin, who was the teaching pro to Louis and recent winner of the Joe Louis Open, was considered the favorite, along with Calvin Searles and Zeke Hartsfield who were co-runners-up in the Joe Louis Open. Top competitors in the professional and amateur (men's and women's) divisions of the tournament included many of the well-known performers of previous UGA national championships as well as less familiar golfers who were lured to this year's event by the greater than usual pre-tournament promotional build-up. In the professional division, Zeke Hartfield of Atlanta led by three strokes after the first 36 holes only to falter in the second round with a pair of 79s. The championship boiled down to a duel between Pat Ball, the veteran pro at the Palos Park golf course in Chicago, and Clyde Martin, a transplanted Washingtonian from Detroit and the first Joe Louis Open Champ, with Ball winning by one stroke for a total of 302 in the 72-hole event. Hartsfield, the powerful Atlanta pro and winner of the Southern Open in 1939 and 1941, finished third (*Atlanta Daily World*, August 23, 1941, p. 6). The approximately $1,000 purse was distributed as follows: Pat Ball (Chicago) $275; Clyde Martin (Detroit) $150; Zeke Hartfield (Atlanta) $110; Solomon Hughes (Gadsden, Alabama) $90; James Clark (Hartford, Connecticut) $75; Eddie Jackson (Detroit) $60; Calvin Searles (New Orleans) $45; Hugh Smith (Thomaston, Georgia) and Eddie Roby (Atlanta) $32.50 each; Joe Roach (New York) $20; Cecil Shamwell (Washington, D.C.) and Edison Marshall (Indianapolis) $15 each (*Chicago Defender*, August 30, 1941b, p. 21). The amateur men's title was won by Cliff Taylor of New York, who narrowly defeated Claude Ross of Washington, D.C.'s Royal Golf Club and former D.C. champion. This was Taylor's second UGA amateur championship title; his first was in 1934 (*Richmond Afro-American*, August 30, 1941, p. 22). The amateur women's championship was won by Chicago's Cleo Ball, the wife of Pat Ball, who defeated Geneva Wilson, the defending champion also from Chicago, in the semifinal round and Vivian Pitts, another Chicagoan, in the final (*Chicago Defender*, August 30, 1941a, p. 20).

The victory by Robert "Pat" Ball in the 1941 UGA National Open championship held personal significance for him and can also be viewed as a transition point in the historical development of black golf for several reasons. The forty-two-year-old Chicago pro, despite being considered by some to be past his prime, became the first person to win four UGA championships, even though this would be his last. Second, this tournament would also be the last time that the major pioneers of black golf dating back to the UGA's beginning would be as heavily represented, playing alongside some of the emerging star players of the later 1940s and 1950s. A complete listing of the top finishers in the historic 16th UGA National Open of 1941 is presented in Table 4.3. Among the participants are some who appeared in the earliest UGA National Open tournaments in the 1920s: Pat Ball, Porter Washington, Cliff Edmonds, Beltran Barker, and Dr. George Adams hold the distinction of having played in the first UGA

Table 4.3
UGA 16th National Open Golf Championship—1941

Professional

First 36 Holes		Scores
Zeke Hartfield	74	75— 149
Pat Ball	77	75— 152
Hugh Smith	73	81— 154
Clyde Martin	78	76— 154
Solomon Hughes	79	75— 154
Joe Roach	81	75— 156
James Clark	74	83— 157
Eddie Roby	82	75— 157
Ed Jackson	79	79— 158
James Adams	77	81— 158
Calvin Searles	78	81— 159
Porter Washington	84	76— 160
Ralph Dawkins	80	80— 160
Hugh Shippen	77	83— 160
Cecil Shamwell	77	83— 160
John Dendy	78	85— 163
Jack Bradley	85	79— 164
Pleasant Goodwin	85	79— 164
Everett Payne	77	88— 165
Edison Marshall	78	87— 165
A. D. V. Crosby	82	83— 165
Ted Jones	86	79— 165
Oscar Clisby	86	80— 165
Arthur Douglas	75	92— 167
Beltran Barker	82	85— 167
John Thompson	86	82— 168
Preston Knowles	83	89— 172
Benny Robinson	83	90— 173
Ernest Hill	93	80— 173
Tom Pearson	92	89— 181
Sam Jones	91	92— 183
B. H. Hughes	87	86— 183
Rudolph Johnson	94	94— 188
W. M. Jones	99	93— 192
C. R. Clark	92	100— 192
Noble Mitchell	86	no card

Final 36 Holes			
Pat Ball	152	76	74— 302
Clyde Martin	154	73	76— 303
Zeke Hartfield	149	79	79— 307
Solomon Hughes	154	80	75— 309
James Clark	157	73	80— 310
Ed Jackson	158	75	78— 311
Calvin Searles	159	73	80— 312
Hugh Smith	154	79	82— 315
Eddie Roby	157	80	78— 315
Joe Roach	156	79	81— 316
Cecil Shamwell	162	80	76— 318
Edison Marshall	165	75	78— 318
James Adams	158	81	81— 320
Porter Washington	160	82	82— 324

Professional (continued)

Ralph Dawkins	160	81	83— 324
Oscar Clisby	166	80	78— 324
Hugh Shippen	160	80	88— 328
Beltran Barker	167	82	81— 330
Ted Jones	165	87	85— 337
John Thompson	168	85	85— 338
Preston Knowles	172	83	87— 342
Ernest Hill	173	83	86— 342
Tom Pearson	181	80	81— 349
Benny Robinson	178	96	90— 359
Rudolph Johnson	188	87	96— 371
C. R. Clark	192	87	94— 373

Amateur

Qualifying		Scores
Cliff Taylor	40	39— 79
Claude Ross	38	41— 79
Vance Watts	41	38— 79
Clarence Chandler	41	43— 84
Oliver Holmes	44	41— 85
Lester Lewis	44	41— 85
Dr. L. S. Terry	45	40— 86
F. Wise	41	46— 87
Francis Alford	47	40— 87
Dr. Cortes A. English	45	43— 88
George Rivers	45	43— 88
George Harris	48	50— 88
Asa Williams	46	42— 88
Sam Stewart	44	45— 89
Roy Jones	46	44— 90
William Brooks	48	42— 90
Fred Lyles	46	44— 90
Martin Beleno	46	45— 91
Cliff Edmonds	44	47— 91
Dr. R. W. Brown	47	44— 91
C. A. Crawford	45	47— 92
Tim Thomas	49	43— 92
Wellington Young	49	43— 92
Isaac Brown	49	43— 92
Dave Strohman	46	46— 92
Hayden Hibbett	46	46— 92
James Parish	49	43— 92
Ben Ransom	48	44— 92
Carey Wimbish	49	43— 92
R. C. Chilton	47	45— 92

Second Flight		
T. R. Wall	48	45— 93
William Powell	46	47— 93
Dr. K. T. Brown	47	46— 93
E. T. Gibbs	47	46— 93
Ray Mitchell	48	47— 94
Ed Mallory	45	49— 95
John McGee	47	49— 96
John Mince	49	47— 96
James W. Scott	49	47— 96
Frank Caul	52	44— 96
Dr. George Adams	50	47— 97
Charles Martin	48	50— 98
Joe Hudson	51	47— 98
James Legon	51	47— 98
Dr. J. J. Peters	54	46— 100
Ernest Wood	53	47— 100

Table 4.3 (*continued*)

Amateur (continued)

Third Flight

Franklin Booker	52	48— 100
W. A. Tate	51	49— 100
Clarence Reese	51	50— 101
D. S. King	51	50— 101
E. E. Barlow	53	48— 191
Sea Ferguson	51	50— 101
William Carter	49	53— 102
Arthur Gatewood	54	48— 102
Al Simmons	51	51— 102
Andrew Sharpe	53	50— 103
Reed White	51	52— 103
M. H. Harper	52	51— 103
Vincent Johnson	53	50— 103
Dr. H. H. Holmes	52	51— 103
Otis Parham	50	55— 103
B. Dudley	52	53— 105

Fourth Flight

Dedrick Jones	54	51— 105
J. E. Miller	56	49— 105
Richard Smith	56	49— 105
S. Garland	56	50— 106
J. R. Russell	52	54— 106
J. H. Bowman	52	55— 107
Glen Williams	53	54— 107
Cliff Brock	55	53— 108
Ed Lumpkin	58	50— 108
Ralph McGuinn	59	50— 109
Howard Boardley	57	52— 109
James Dyke	55	54— 109
W. H. Childs	58	53— 111
Everett York	57	55— 112
Dr. F. A. Fisher	56	57— 113
Phil Snowden	55	59— 114

Women's

Qualifying

		Scores
Mrs. Sarah Smith	51	50— 101
Mrs. Lucy Williams	53	49— 102
Mrs. Vivian Pitts	52	50— 102
Mrs. Cleo Ball	51	52— 103
Mrs. Thelma McTyre	51	55— 106
Mrs. Geneva Wilson	55	54— 109
Mrs. Marguerite Brown	56	55— 111
Mrs. Ana Black	56	56— 112
Mrs. Rhoda Fowler	59	54— 113
Mrs. Marie Jones	60	58— 113
Mrs. Esther Wilson	55	58— 113
Mrs. Marie Long	64	51— 115
Mrs. Blanche Bowman	57	58— 115
Mrs. J. J. Peters	58	56— 116
Mrs. Ethel Terrell	60	58— 118
Mrs. Helen Harris	64	55— 119

Second Flight

Mrs. Ella Morphis	62	59— 121
Mrs. Sadie Caldwell	54	54__ 121
Mrs. Florence Coleman	58	67— 125
Mrs. Hazel Forman	64	61— 125
Mrs. Thomas Howell	67	58— 125
Mrs. Elizabeth Mitchell	60	67— 127
Mrs. Morphelis Winston	63	65— 128

Women's (continued)

Third Flight

Mrs. Minnie Miller	65	65— 130
Mrs. Grace Price	71	59— 130
Mrs. Clara Hudson	67	64— 131
Mrs. Neomi Brock	67	64— 131
Mrs. G. W. Adams	69	63— 132
Mrs. Marie Murphy	69	64— 133
Mrs. Vydie Carter	69	65— 134

Fourth Flight

Magnolia Gambrell	66	68— 134
Mrs. Amelia Lucas	69	65— 134
Mrs. Marion Hudson	70	65— 135
Mrs. Bonita Harvey	63	73— 136
Mrs. Mozelle Clark	65	73— 138
Mrs. George Evans	71	68— 139
Mrs. M. Etallings	72	72— 144
Mrs. Josephine Hughes	75	72— 147
Mrs. Rachel Flowers	76	73— 149

Fifth Flight

Mrs. Dorothea Hooks	69	80— 149
Mrs. Vivian Mitchell	79	76— 155
Catherine Weaver	81	74— 155
Mrs. Victoria Adams	80	84— 164
Mrs. Clara Jones	88	76— 164
Mrs. Sarah Payne	88	77— 165

championship in 1926. Also participating in the 1941 championship tournament were six of the nine UGA pro champions between 1926 and 1941, including Pat Ball (1927, 1929, 1934, 1941), Porter Washington (1928), Edison Marshall (1930, 1931), John Dendy (1932, 1936, 1937), Solomon Hughes (1935), and Hugh Smith (1940). Third, because this tournament would be the last UGA National Open to be played until World War II ended, a time transition created a significant change in the top stars of black golf. When the UGA National Open resumed in 1946, none of the UGA pro champions previously mentioned would ever ascend to that status again, with the exception of the seemingly ageless Howard Wheeler. Thus, the 1941 UGA championship represented a "changing of the guard" in black golf. In addition, the organizational structure of the UGA reflected a change toward the leadership of the past. At the 1941 UGA annual meeting held in conjunction with the national championship, the first two UGA presidents Dr. George Adams (1927) and Robert Hawkins (1926) were elected president and first vice president, respectively, along with second vice president, Sea Ferguson (Indianapolis), third vice president, Paris Brown (Washington, D.C.), and fourth vice president Anna Black (Chicago) (*Chicago Defender*, August 30, 1941a, p. 20).

Despite the enthusiasm generated by the highly successful 1941 UGA national tournament in Boston, a decision that the 1942 event be moved southward to Washington, D.C., was met with skepticism and reflected continued dissatisfaction with the progress made by black golfers in eradicating Jim Crow barriers in some regions of the country. Although Washington, D.C., was the hometown of the newly installed president, concern was expressed that the continued resistance by whites to blacks playing on previously segregated public courses in the nation's capital and the unsuitableness of the 9-hole, black patronized (public) Langston golf course as an alternative, would attract much fewer participants to the 1942 tournament than the record-setting number who had attended the 1941 event. As discussed in Chapter 3, African Americans were only recently permitted to play on the more attractive, 18-hole public courses in Washington, previously restricted to whites until U.S. Department of the Interior Secretary Harold Ickes ordered that the racial ban be lifted. The leaders of the UGA afiiliate, the Royal Golf Club of Washington, D.C., on receiving word of the decision to hold the UGA national championship tournament there, planned to ask Ickes to provide one of the "white" golf courses for the three-day event. However, most local blacks were becoming discouraged from playing on public golf courses in Washington, except for the Langston course, due to harassment. At one of these golf courses (East Potomac), park police officers guarded black golfers as they played around the course, leading sportswriter Ric Roberts to observe that "The part Washington golfers may play as hosts to the 1942 meet may be marred by Jim Crow tactics in the very shadow of the supposed world capital for democracy"

(*Richmond Afro-American*, September 13, 1941, p. 23). Brewing skepticism over Washington, D.C., as the site for the next year's meet became moot when the UGA National Open was canceled, as were many other sporting events, after the bombing of Pearl Harbor by the Japanese on December 7, 1941, and the U.S. declaration of war against Japan the following day. Although no UGA national tournaments were held between 1942 and 1945, a letter that was drafted by the president, Dr. George Adams, for circulation to UGA members in October 1945, after the executive committee met in July, called for the resumption of the National Open tournament, but did not indicate a resumption of plans to hold the tournament in Washington, D.C. (Letter to UGA members, October 1, 1945).

The 1946 UGA National Open tournament was held in Pittsburgh, hosted by the Yorkshire Golf Club, and began the rivalry between Howard Wheeler and Ted Rhodes, who were dominant black golfers in the latter half of the 1940s. Even though the wide field of entrants included such past UGA national champions as Pat Ball, John Dendy, and Solomon Hughes, the 1946 championship boiled down to Wheeler and Rhodes, with Howard Wheeler finishing with a one over par 73 score in the final round for a total of 293, two strokes better than runner-up Ted Rhodes, who finished at 295 for the 72-hole event. Robert Ball, who was the previous UGA national champion the last time the tournament was held in 1941, finished the last round with a two under par 70; however, he could only reach seventh place in the final standing behind Solomon Hughes, Zeke Hartsfield, and Myron Coleman, and tied with Warren Sharrock, after posting high scores in the earlier days of the tournament (*Pittsburgh Courier*, September 7, 1946, p. 27). Wheeler also defeated Rhodes the following year in the UGA National Open of 1947 at Philadelphia's Cobb's Creek course. As club pro at Philadelphia's Fairview Golf Club, Wheeler was playing in his own backyard on the Cobb's Creek course and outdistanced relative newcomers to the national golf scene, Charlie Sifford and Bill Spiller, who finished second and fourth, respectively. Rhodes finished in a tie with Spiller for fourth place, and golf veteran Zeke Hartsfield finished in third place (*Pittsburgh Courier*, September 6, 1947, p. 15). In 1948, Wheeler won his third consecutive professional division title when the UGA National Open was held in Indianapolis; however, the rivalry between the nation's top African American golfers was overshadowed in 1948 when Rhodes along with Bill Spiller and Madison Gunter attempted to exert legal pressure on the PGA to lift its racial ban that prohibited participation by black golfers in PGA-sponsored tournaments.

The incident involved a lawsuit filed by the three black golfers who qualified for the PGA-sponsored Richmond Open in California as a result of their performance in the Los Angeles Open the previous week (*Pittsburgh Courier*, January 24, 1948, p. 15; *Pittsburgh Courier*, March 6, 1948, p. 17; *Pittsburgh Courier*, July 24, 1948, p. 9). Although the UGA was not directly involved in these suits, this legal action was eagerly followed by black golfers who viewed the out-of-court settlement of the PGA's promise to end its "Caucasian only" clause in exchange for the suit's being dropped (Ashe, 1988b; McRae, 1991) as a significant step toward lifting the racial barriers to black participation in PGA tournaments. As a result of this action, both Rhodes and Spiller became highly visible at a time when the two, especially Rhodes, were at the top of their game. Although Wheeler won the UGA National Open championship titles in 1946, 1947, and 1948, Rhodes was the most successful of the two, winning or finishing near the top of all the tournaments he entered. Ted Rhodes won Joe Louis Open championships in 1946, 1947, and 1948, the same years that Wheeler won UGA titles. In 1949, when both the UGA National Open and the Joe Louis Open tournaments were held in Detroit, Rhodes became the first golfer to win both titles in the same year. The showdowns between Rhodes and Wheeler received wide publicity in the black press and earned great respect for both golfers. However, by the early 1950s, with Rhodes's ill health adversely affecting his performance, Charlie Sifford had become the premier UGA golfer and would dominate National Open championship tournaments throughout the decade.

THE UGA IN THE 1950s

By 1950, African Americans had broken through the racial barrier in professional baseball, football, and basketball. However, golf remained an exception. The PGA continued to resist popular protests against black exclusion from PGA-sponsored tournaments and full PGA membership, despite being pressured into an agreement in 1952 that facilitated participation on a limited basis in selected PGA co-sponsored tournaments. Given that only a few significant opportunities existed in which black golfers were welcome to compete on an interracial basis (e.g., the L.A. Open and Tam O'Shanter tournaments), the UGA and its network of affiliated clubs continued to be the "backbone" of black participation throughout the 1950s. Because UGA tournaments were less competitive and had smaller cash prizes than predominantly white events, serious-minded black professional golfers sought more expanded opportunities, some resulting from successful civil rights protests. By the end of the decade, significant pressure was once again applied to the PGA, resulting in the first African American golfer's gaining "approved tournament player" status and eventual removal of the "Caucasian only" clause in 1961.

In 1950, the UGA organized a full schedule, including fifteen approved tournaments, culminating in its annual national championship. These tournaments provided opportunities for pros and amateurs (both men and women) to play competitively throughout the summer months. UGA-sanctioned tournaments for 1950 included the following: the Garden State

Invitational (amateur), Westfield, New Jersey; Penn State Open and Amateur, Philadelphia; Sixth City amateur (pros invited), Cleveland; New Lincoln Open and Amateur, Atlanta; Ohio Amateur, Cleveland; Fairway Amateur (pros invited), Dayton, Ohio; Memorial Tourney (pros invited), Indianapolis, Indiana; Central States Amateur (closed), Omaha, Nebraska; Detroit Amateur (pros invited), Detroit; Chicago Women's Amateur (pros invited), Chicago; Ray Robinson Open and Amateur (including women), New York; Toledo Midwestern Amateur, Toledo, Ohio; Joe Louis Open and Amateur (including women), Detroit; Vehicle City Amateur (pros invited), Flint, Michigan; and the UGA National Open and Amateur, Washington, D.C. It should be noted that only one of the tournaments was played in the Deep South, the New Lincoln Open in Atlanta, with 1950 marking the beginning of the UGA Southern district. Along with affiliated golf clubs in the other three districts (Eastern, Midwest, and Central), the total number of UGA clubs stood at forty (*Pittsburgh Courier*, May 27, 1950, p. 23). As a promotional device, the *Pittsburgh Courier* initiated a system to rate the top professional and amateur players, a practice that potentially generated the kind of interest in black stars that many of the leading Negro baseball players of the 1940s received. For each of the UGA-sanctioned fifteen tournaments, individual golfers received points based on their final scores. A tournament winner received 20 points; the runner-up received 15 points, and the remaining eight finishers were awarded points in the following order: 12, 10, 8, 6, 4, 3, 2, and 1, respectively. No points were received beyond the tenth-place finisher. At the end of the summer schedule, the final ranking of the most outstanding male and female golfers was compiled (*Pittsburgh Courier*, June 17, 1950, p. 22). Much excitement was expected to develop as weekly rankings were released in the form of a "UGA Bulletin Board," which presented the latest standings separately for pros, amateurs, and women. The rankings after about one month into the 1950 tournament season as presented in Table 4.4 apparently did not attract sufficient popular interest to be continued. For the most part, no real surprises emerged, with the top performers, as expected, already the most well-known golfers such as pros Rhodes, Wheeler, Spiller, and Sifford, amateurs Joe Louis, Leonard Reed, and Eural Clark, and, among the top women, Ann Gregory, Lorraine Sawyer, and Eoline Thornton (*Pittsburgh Courier*, July 15, 1950, p. 24; *Pittsburgh Courier*, July 22, 1950, p. 24). Although other golfers making the list received greater exposure to a national black audience, they continued to be better known in their local settings.

Despite its highly organized tournaments, the UGA could not provide the monetary incentives for black pro golfers to engage in the sport full-time. The few attempting to participate regularly found it increasingly difficult to earn more than a subsistence income. Ted Rhodes, who in the best years of the late 1940s earned more than $4,800 by capturing the top prize

Table 4.4
UGA Bulletin Board—Rankings (1950)

JULY 15, 1950

Professional	Points	Amateur	Points	Women	Points
Ted Rhodes	20	Joe Louis	20	Lorraine Sawyer	24
Howard Wheeler	20	Ben Crisci	20	Ann Gregory	20
Charles Sifford	15	Leonard Reed	15	Hazel Foreman	15
Bill Spiller	15	Jerry Ruffo	15	Elsie Rice	15
Charles McCaulley	12	Ulysses Barrow	12	Alice Stewart	12
Josh Skelton	12	James Bailey	12	Viola Turner	12
Van Mims	10	B. Simone	10	Myrtice McIver	12
Doug Palmer	10	Robert Williams	10	Betty Groves	10
Bennie Philpot	8	Clarence Watson	8	Amelia Lucas	10
James Brown	8	Eural Clark	8	Ella Bishop	10
E. S. Satchel	6	Jerry Sumpter	6	Eoline Thornton	10
Lucius Mumford	4	Earl Dales	10	Clara Jackson	10
Marcus King	3	W. Williams	3	Alice Parrish	8
Jerry Hood	2	Richard Young	2	Ersie Anderson	6
		Robert Crawford	6	Ida Mason	6
		Tim Thomas	3	Hazel Bibbs	3
		Earl Combs	2	G. Britser	2
		Eugene Beatty	1	Ecee Richardson	1
		Dave Turner	1	Rhoda Flowers	1

JULY 22, 1950

Professional	Points	Amateur	Points	Women	Points
Ted Rhodes	40	Joe Louis	40	Ann Gregory	40
Howard Wheeler	40	Leonard Reed	30	Lorraine Sawyer	24
Bill Spiller	21	Eural Clark	22	Eoline Thornton	21
Charles Sifford	15	Ben Crisci	20	Myrtice McIver	20
Richard Terrell	15	John Brown	20	Hazel Foreman	15
Myron Coleman	15	Jerry Ruffo	15	Elsie Rice	15
E. S. Satchel	12	George Nelms	15	Alice Stewart	12
Charles McCaulley	12	Ulysses Barrow	12	Viola Turner	12
Ralph Alexander	12	James Bailey	12	Marjorie Cabbell	12
John Green	12	B. Simone	12	Betty Groves	10
Josh Skelton	12	Robert Williams	10	Estella Williams	8
Van Mims	10	Curtis Lloyd	10	Amelia Lucas	8
Zeke Hartsfield	10	Clarence Watson	10	Ella Bishop	8
B. J. Blair	10	Jerry Sumpter	10	Ecee Richardson	7
Doug Palmer	10	Earl Dales	10	Clara Jackson	6
Alton Smith	10	W. Williams	8		
James Brown	8	Chester Beatty	6		
William Butler	8	Robert Crawford	6		
Bennie Philpot	8	Clarence Webb	6		
Lucius Mumford	4	Lawrence Small	4		
Preston Allen	4				
George Roddy	4				
Marcus King	3				
James McClure	3				
William Johnson	3				
Jerry Hood	2				
William Hillman	2				
Hubert Dixon	2				

at major UGA tournaments, found that by the 1951 season the pickings for black pros were extremely slim (*Chicago Defender*, June 30, 1951, p. 13). Only four of the fourteen tournaments that year were open to professionals: the Southern in Atlanta, Joe Louis in Detroit, Fairway in Dayton, and the UGA National in Cleveland; and Rhodes, or any other pro, could expect to collect less than $3,000, even if they won all four of these tournaments (*Chicago Defender*, June 30, 1951, p. 13). By 1952, the outlook was even more dismal as the number of tournaments offering pro purses remained low and prize amounts declined. The UGA National Open slated for Pittsburgh, the Southeastern Open in Jacksonville, Florida, and the Houston Open in Houston, Texas, were the only tournaments to offer purses, with the total amount for winners if victorious in *all* of them only approximately $2,000 (*Chicago Defender*, July 19, 1952, p. 14). A particularly strong blow was dealt to the tournament circuit when the Joe Louis tournament ended. After becoming the richest tournament in black golf when initiated with prize money totaling $1,000, the purse swelled to $4,000 in 1949, only to be reduced to $1,500 in 1951, the last year the tournament was held. Ironically, in 1952, the Lone Star Golf Association's Houston Open, with a prize fund of $1,500, was expected to attract a large entry of pros precisely because of what was now viewed as a large cash award (*Chicago Defender*, August 30, 1952, p. 14).

Despite smaller cash prizes, the UGA continued to attract black pros such as Ted Rhodes, Bill Spiller, Zeke Hartsfield, and the seemingly ageless Howard Wheeler to its national tournaments during the 1950s. However, Charlie Sifford, Rhodes's protégé, became the leading UGA golfer as he captured consecutive UGA national championship titles in 1952, 1953, 1954, 1955, and 1956. By the end of 1956, the civil rights movement was in full swing, including efforts to desegregate public golf courses. Sifford had become the logical "path blazer" among "UGA circuit" players to compete in PGA-sponsored tournaments as targeted protests culminated in a partial lifting of the PGA ban on black participants. As a result of a historic protest by Joe Louis and Bill Spiller at the PGA co-sponsored San Diego Open, a committee consisting of Joe Louis, Ted Rhodes, Bill Spiller, Howard Wheeler, and Eural Clark was set up to screen black golfers for participation on a limited basis in PGA tournaments by invitation of local clubs and sponsors (*Chicago Defender*, January 26, 1952, p. 10). The immediate effect of this plan was that three black golfers qualified for the $10,000 Phoenix Open, the next tournament on the PGA tour; Ted Rhodes (at one under par 71) and Bill Spiller and Eural Clark (both shooting par 72) became the first African Americans to qualify for the Phoenix Open, with Charles Sifford (with a three over par 75) and Joe Louis (finishing with an 81 for the 18 qualifying holes) failing to qualify (*The Courier*, January 26, 1952, p. 20). Sifford would later describe an overtly discriminatory act that took place during this qualifying round that wrecked his

concentration (*Black Enterprise*, 1997). As the decade progressed, he became the most visible black professional from the UGA "circuit" to compete in tournaments open to African Americans. White tournaments offered
large monetary prizes, but sometimes in the face of subtle and even overt
white resistance. Consequently, Sifford continued to play in UGA-
sanctioned tournaments until 1960, when he recorded his sixth UGA National Open title (Sifford, 1992). This period produced mixed results for
the UGA. On the one hand, UGA members were able to derive a sense of
pride and legitimacy in producing players who could effectively compete
against white golfers and gain public recognition for their performance. On
the other, the removal of racial barriers to greater participation in PGA
events by black golfers would signal the beginning of the end for the UGA
insofar as a major facilitator of golfing activity for black pros. During the
1950s, this issue was largely moot because: (a) despite officially lifting its
rigid ban against black golfers, other forms of institutionalized racism remained and (b) most of the best black golfers were nearing or already past
their prime and the available pool of good black golfers was steadily declining. The UGA retained its status as the major focal point for black golf
during the 1950s, while also serving as a "launching pad" for the few black
golfers, such as Lee Elder and Pete Brown, coming out of UGA circles with
aspirations of PGA tournament entry. However, these golfers needed to be
prepared to overcome the obstacles, both social and financial, that limited
greater involvement beyond the UGA circuit.

CONCLUSION

This chapter has documented the significant extent, continuity, and organization of black golf, from the 1920s through the 1950s as documented
by the African American press. While an initial tournament was held in
1925, Robert H. Hawkins, known as the "Father of Negro Golf," organized one of the first championship events at his recently established Mapledale Country Club in Stow, Massachusetts, during 1926. From then on,
tournaments were held annually throughout this and the following decades.

Each period brought its particular kind of successes and golfing developments: (1) the 1920s involved significant numbers of players and regional
shifts in tournament sites; (2) the following decade saw the spectacular
achievements of southern players, emergence of "star" players, and establishment of an official magazine, the *United Golfer*; (3) during the 1940s
the sport received significant sponsorship from major sporting figures such
as Joe Louis, reached a peak of player numbers, and saw the filing of court
suits attacking black exclusion from white facilities; while, (5) the following
decade experienced continuing racial barriers to full black participation,
the UGA's economic and potential activity decline, and the emergence of
UGA players aspiring to PGA tournament admission.

In all these trends, black golf's continuing viability is evident from its foundation, revealed in its significant number of participants, regional spread, emergence of "star" players, establishment of official publications, player sponsorship, legal attacks on white racism, and professional aspirations of its champion players. Far from representing the isolated activities of a few, African American golf was a widespread, long-term, well-organized part of the black community throughout the country from the 1920s through the 1960s. Other views of the enterprise tend to be inaccurate, incomplete, and problematic portraits of this minority's significant contribution to the sport.

We turn to examine one of its major sponsors and ambassadors: Joe Louis, famous heavyweight boxing champion.

CHAPTER 5

Joe Louis: Black Golf Ambassador

Golf has always lured stars from the entertainment world, as well as major figures from other activities. The sport has a strong appeal to black celebrities, many of whom engage in it as a form of leisure. During the Jim Crow era, some of them became golf enthusiasts, not only pursuing it seriously, but also promoting the activity throughout the African American community. Perhaps the best known supporter among nationally recognized sports heroes of that period was world heavyweight boxing champion Joe Louis. During his reign as boxing champion (1937–1949), he assumed the role of black golf ambassador, attracting other black celebrities, increasing the visibility of the sport among the black masses, and fostering contact between black and white golfers. Furthermore, failing to make a significant dent in long-standing policies of black exclusion through his goodwill efforts, Louis became a leader in the fight to break down the institutional racial barriers in golf that continued to maintain discrimination throughout the Jim Crow era. Since the white media followed his every action, both inside and outside the boxing ring, he was able to call national attention to the PGA's policy of excluding blacks from participation in its tournaments, formally adopted in 1943. This role contrasts sharply with the widely held view of Louis as nonradical and accommodating on racial issues.

Despite the seriousness he attached to this aspect of his life, recent biographical accounts of his golfing activities are brief and provide anecdotal rather than serious examinations of his impact on the sport. In his battle with the PGA in 1952 to gain entry to a PGA-sponsored tournament in

San Diego as an amateur himself and Bill Spiller as a black professional, Louis termed this struggle the "biggest fight of his life" (*New York Times*, January 15, 1952, p. 31). He eventually won a partial victory by becoming the first black to play in a PGA-sponsored tournament. This triumph was incomplete because Spiller was not permitted to play in the San Diego tournament because the PGA steadfastly maintained its "Caucasian only" rule applied to black professionals. Louis vowed to continue to push for black access, as he had done before the 1952 incident. However, biographical accounts tend to focus only on his involvement in golf as a leisurely pursuit and possible distraction during his boxing career and as a form of recreation after he retired from the ring. Ashe (1988a), for example, noted that some observers claimed that Louis's loss to German boxer Max Schmeling in 1936 was due in part to his having played too much golf. Later in his boxing career Louis was criticized for using the time needed for fight preparation engaging in his golfing "hobby." After a lackluster performance against "Jersey" Joe Walcott in 1947, when he was knocked down twice by the challenger before winning in a disputed verdict, the nation's sports editors voted Louis the "biggest disappointment" of 1947 in the annual year-end poll conducted by the Associated Press (*New York Times*, January 17, 1948, p. 13).

Responding to the criticism that he was distracted by golf, Louis sought a return match against Walcott vowing that "golf is out and maybe that'll make a difference" (*New York Times*, January 24, 1948, p. 18). In reality, Louis's involvement in golf increased after the return match with Walcott and continued into his retirement shortly thereafter. Mead (1985) discussed Louis's involvement in golf as a recreational player during his boxing career and, in his later years, playing to satisfy a need for leisurely activity. However, in the earlier years of his retirement, especially in the 1950s, Louis participated more actively in golf than at any previous time. Between 1950 and 1952, he won numerous amateur events, including the coveted UGA National Open amateur championship in 1951. Therefore, although Mead's critically acclaimed biography of him as "black hero in white America" (Mead, 1985) provides a detailed account of Louis's boxing career, the "hero" status accorded Louis by African Americans should also be extended to golf, his avocation, by virtue of the role he played in promoting the sport and agitating for greater black access to segregated tournaments and facilities. Such anecdotal information is typical of existing biographies that ignore the deep commitment he displayed and the significance of his impact on the sport, indicating a need for reassessment. To be sure, relative to golf, Louis's career as a boxer deserves the major attention it receives. As the world heavyweight boxing champion, Louis's impact was felt by millions of African Americans who derived a sense of racial pride and uplift from his accomplishments. However, Louis was also a catalyst in furthering the development of black golf and using his national recognition to support efforts to end its Jim Crow treatment.

In this chapter, we provide insight into Joe Louis's impact on Jim Crow golf, especially in the 1940s and early 1950s, through an examination of his roles as player, promoter of his own tournaments, personal sponsor of black professional golfers, and proponent of equality, who used his fame to foster public debate over the need to change the discriminatory treatment of black golfers. His initial interest in the sport during the 1930s began a passion that lasted the rest of his life. He became friends with many black golfers, but was also able to venture to golf courses with white celebrities and players, especially at the height of his fame, at a time when other African Americans experienced very limited access to playing opportunities. Although members of black elites would certainly derive a measure of "status" by inviting him to play at their country clubs, he was also very much at ease playing golf with everyday players. In his travels around the country, he maintained an active involvement in golf. After gaining the world heavyweight boxing title in 1937, his involvement in golf increased the visibility of the sport to many blacks who followed his life through the media. In addition, his passion for the sport led him not only to increase his participation in tournaments, but also to establish his own tournament, the Joe Louis Open, held annually in Detroit during the 1940s and early 1950s. He also employed a number of black professionals at varying times as his personal golf instructors, with the most notable being Clyde Martin and Ted Rhodes. In addition, he encouraged other black entertainers and notable sports figures to follow this lead. He persuaded the popular entertainer Billy Eckstine to hire Charlie Sifford, who later became the first black PGA golfer, as his personal golf instructor and valet (Sifford, 1992). Other black sports stars who sponsored their own tournaments included baseball hero Jackie Robinson and popular boxing champion "Sugar" Ray Robinson who hired well-known golfer Joe Roach as his personal golf tutor. Although Louis was often invited to play golf on an interracial basis because of his boxing fame, he was well aware of the racial restrictions that prevented others from playing on courses and in tournaments reserved for whites. Consequently, he became a champion of African American golfers in their struggle to remove Jim Crow restrictions.

JOE LOUIS'S INTRODUCTION TO GOLF: PRO BOXING CHAMPION AS AMATEUR GOLFER

Louis moved to Detroit from Alabama with his family in 1926 when he was twelve years old. He did not develop a serious interest in golf until the early stages of his professional boxing career after he turned pro in 1934. After becoming world heavyweight boxing champion in 1937, his desire to pursue competitive golf gained public notice. Chester Washington, sports writer of the *Pittsburgh Courier*, presented the observations of Bermuda golf pro, Louis Rafael Corbin, one of Louis's earliest golf instructors, who noted that Louis "hopes to be a links champion some day . . . [and although] one doesn't become a first-class golfer overnight, Joe's intense eagerness and his dead seriousness about becoming a good golfer has helped immeasurably" (*Pittsburgh Courier*, March 23, 1940, p. 16). With little previous exposure to golf, Corbin felt that Louis learned quickly, accomplishing in a few months what many first-class golfers took years to learn. Although he could rarely break 100 before 1939, after only a month of instruction under Corbin, he shot a 77 on the Martin Hill golf course in Stevensville, Michigan, and after seven months could consistently shoot between 77 and 84 on some of the toughest courses in America, leading Corbin to predict that, as a potentially brilliant golfer, Louis might startle the whole world in the next three years by his ability to become a double sports competitor, excelling in both sports (*Pittsburgh Courier*, March 23, 1940, p. 16).

He was an invited guest at many clubs and played at courses throughout the country where his appearance lured many, especially African Americans, to watch him play. Despite being a novice, the public attention he received gave black golf a tremendous boost in popularity. He played regularly at Rackham, the public golf course in Detroit, also home to such well-known black pros as Bob Seymour, Eddie Jackson, and Ben Davis. In 1940, Louis hired another famous pro, Clyde Martin, of Washington, D.C., as his personal instructor. The thirty-one-year-old Martin, who began playing golf while caddying at the Congressional Country Club, was a member of the Royal Golf Club and the first pro at Washington's Langston golf course when it opened in 1939. When Joe Louis visited Langston in 1940 to participate in the EGA annual championship tournament (the Eastern Open), he saw Martin play and immediately hired him as his private tutor, taking him to Detroit to spend most of his time teaching golf and playing on some of the country's best courses (*Pittsburgh Courier*, August 30, 1941, p. 17).

Louis's appearance at the Eastern Open in July 1940 marked his first major tournament. The EGA was a regional affiliate of the UGA and his participation in that region's tournament was a highpoint for the fourteen-year-old UGA. Although his performance was far from spectacular (97, 95, and 90 for a 282 three-round total), he attracted the largest gallery of spectators. An unusually large crowd for an EGA tournament, estimated by park police to be between 2,000 and 3,000 people, followed him around the course. He was described by the *Pittsburgh Courier* as a "better fighter than golfer" (*Pittsburgh Courier*, July 13, 1940, p. 16). The *Richmond Afro-American* noted that "Joe Louis took all the glory away from the real golfers. . . . The better golfers were neglected in the rush to see the Brown Bomber" (*Richmond Afro-American*, July 13, 1940, p. 20). However, because of his participation, the tournament was a rousing success, which provided greater visibility than in previous years for the EGA, the tournament champion, Dave Wilson of Pittsburgh, and for some of the lesser known black golfers who performed well, such as Pleasant Goodwin, locker room attendant at the Chevy Chase Club, who finished tied for second place with Cecil Shamwell of Washington's Royal Golf Club.

Despite the poor showing in this first tournament appearance, Louis entered the 1940 UGA National Open tournament held in Chicago during August, only one month after the EGA championship. UGA officials were delighted by the decision, announcing that "Joe Louis, heavyweight king, will enter the tournament this year, which will be the first time the Bomber has made an attempt to compete against the cream of the sepia golf world" (*Pittsburgh Courier*, 1940, August 17, p. 18). The enthusiasm generated by his participation in the UGA National Open was even stronger than his EGA tournament appearance, and, despite an equally dismal performance, he continued to be determined and excited about golf. The following year (1941) would prove a banner year for black golf as Louis not only continued to play on courses throughout the country, but also initiated his own tournament, which provided a second major showcase, along with the UGA National Open, to propel golf to new national heights in the African American community.

THE JOE LOUIS TOURNAMENT: BLACK GOLF'S SPRINGBOARD TO VISIBILITY AND RACIAL CROSSOVER

Joe Louis's mass appeal as a national boxing hero, following his victories over Jim Braddock for the heavyweight title in 1937 and Max Schmeling in a return match in 1938, received wide press coverage by the white popular media (cf. *New York Times*, June 23, 1938, p. 14; *Look*, May 7, 1940, p. 50; *Life*, June 17, 1940, pp. 48–56; *Time*, September 29, 1941, pp. 60–64). However, it was only in the black press that his rising popularity as boxing champion *and* novice golfer receive significant coverage. While national black newspapers such as the *Pittsburgh Courier, Chicago Defender*, and *Baltimore Afro-American*, along with local and regional papers (cf. *Carolina Times*, June 26, 1937, p. 1; *Richmond Afro-American*, December 20, 1941, p. 22), provide detailed accounts of his boxing career, they also covered Louis's growing recognition as a serious golf enthusiast. During the 1940s, he rose to "hero" status in the world of black golf as he initiated his own tournament, which became a major event in black sports. Between 1941 and 1951, eight Joe Louis Open tournaments were held in Detroit and attracted the top black golfers around the country, providing greater exposure for them. According to Bernard O'Dell, who served as tournament director for five of the six tournaments between 1941 and 1949, the idea for them came from his friend, Detroit pro golfer, Bob Seymour, and

Joe Louis enthusiastically lent his name to the event (personal interview, 1998). The first of these six tournaments deserves special attention because it significantly increased the public visibility of black golfers and raised their hopes of gaining acceptance as legitimate pros by the white establishment.

He was a major participant in planning all stages of the first Joe Louis Open and saw his tournament as an opportunity to showcase the talents of African American golfers as serious competitors. In putting up the $1,000 prize money, he observed that "I think this tournament will prove conclusively to our white friends that we have some [Walter] Hagens and [Gene] Sarazens in our group" (*Baltimore Afro-American*, March 15, 1941, p. 21); He also noted that "It is my aim in giving this tournament to promote and introduce our leading Negro golfers into the golfing world. We have a number of golf pros playing 'par' and 'below par' golf who are not known to the general public . . . [and] have a right to their place in the world of sports" (*Pittsburgh Courier*, July 12, 1941, p. 17). As previously mentioned, the first annual Joe Louis Open Golf Tournament was planned for Detroit's Rackham golf course on August 12, 13, and 14, the weekend before the annual UGA national championship, already scheduled for August 19 through the 22 in Boston. Louis's tournament was strategically planned to lure the best black golfers throughout the nation, who would normally attend the UGA championship but could now attend the Joe Louis Open, first, and then go directly to the UGA championship the following weekend. Anticipating more than 250 entrants, the black press gave extensive coverage to the event, with the *Baltimore Afro-American* calling it "the largest of its kind ever sponsored by colored people" (*Baltimore Afro-American*, March 15, 1941, p. 21) and "the richest tournament among colored golfers" (*Baltimore Afro-American*, July 19, 1941, p. 20). The lure of Joe Louis's name created the greatest amount of attention that had ever been given to black amateurs and professionals throughout the nation as they planned to be a part of this history-making, double-dose of black golf extravaganza. This was probably best illustrated by Ric Roberts's article accompanied by a sports cartoon appearing in the *Richmond Afro-American* with the heading "Louis Lures Golfers" (*Richmond Afro-American*, August 16, 1941, p. 21).

As the August 12 date for the Joe Louis tournament approached, preceding the August 19 start of the UGA championship, Louis participated in a regional tournament in July (the Eastern Pennsylvania Open) to sharpen his game, while promoting interest in both national tournaments. The *Pittsburgh Courier* reported that Louis "attracted the largest crowds to ever witness a tournament in Smoketown [Pittsburgh] with 4,000 spectators following him around the course" (*Pittsburgh Courier*, 1941, July 12, p. 18). Louis played horribly through the first 27 holes of the Eastern Pennsylvania Open, but the crowds nevertheless continued to follow him through the remaining holes "as he trudged along the course, playing with-

After his introduction to golf at the height of his popularity in the 1930s, world heavyweight boxing champion Joe Louis attracted many African Americans to the sport (*Richmond Afro-American*, August 16, 1941, p. 21). Courtesy of the Baltimore Afro-American Newspapers.

out keeping score" (*Baltimore Afro-American*, 1941, July 12, p. 21). Despite his poor performance at the Eastern Open, Louis made plans to play in both of the upcoming national tournaments. The enticement of the $500 top prize for the winner in the professional division and greater visibility than in any previous year were, no doubt, factors that also generated interest in his tournament among the leading black stars, including past UGA national champions Robert "Pat" Ball, John Dendy, Howard Wheeler, Edison Marshall, and local (Detroit) professionals, Clyde Martin, Bob Seymour, Ben Davis, and Eddie Jackson. Another local golfer, Dr. Remus Robinson, who was the reigning national amateur champion, was among the favorites to capture the Joe Louis Open amateur crown (*Pittsburgh Courier*, August 2, 1941, p. 17). Among the challengers for the professional championship title, Chicago pro Pat Ball was given the inside track by some observers who expected him to win because he had won the UGA National Open championship when last held at Detroit's Rackham course in 1934. Others felt that Clyde Martin, who was Joe Louis's personal golf instructor, was the favorite (*Pittsburgh Courier*, August 9, 1941, p. 16). In recent practice rounds on the Rackham course, Martin shot a 69, two under par, and was continuing to blister the course (*Pittsburgh Courier*, August 26, 1941, p. 16). However, tournament director Bernard O'Dell noted that the large field of challengers included long shots among professional and amateur golfers from the Far West, the Atlantic Seaboard, and the Deep South (*Baltimore Afro-American*, August 2, 1941, p. 21). Many of the 68 pros and 118 amateurs scheduled to play were less known, but still considered good golfers. These included Jerry Hood (Chicago), Alfred "Tup" Holmes and Hugh Smith (Atlanta), Landy Taylor and Walter Stewart (Norfolk), Joe Roach (New York), Lonnie Shields (Seattle), Pleasant Goodwin (Washington, D.C.), Sam Shephard (St. Louis), and Mac Dalton (Milwaukee), just to name a few (*Pittsburgh Courier*, August 16, 1941, p. 17).

As added features, a select group of caddies was hired for the tournament, an insurance policy was taken out for protection against injury, and an exhibition match between two well-known black pros and two white pro golfers was planned. Local professional Eddie Jackson, himself a former caddie at exclusive white country clubs in Detroit, was placed in charge of the selection process. Jackson carefully chose 157 caddies among those employed at the Detroit Golf Club to be caddies at the Joe Louis Open. New blue-and-white jerseys were purchased with a monogrammed front reading "Joe Louis Open"; the back of the jersey carried the name of Joe Louis's dude ranch "Springhill Farms," which served as the tournament's headquarters. A $10,000 insurance policy on the tournament was written to protect participants and spectators against injury. Walter A. Lewis, whose insurance agency wrote the policy, was also an amateur golfer and the first entrant to file for the tournament (*Baltimore Afro-American*, August 2, 1941, p. 21). The exhibition match, which was expected to draw a large gallery, pitted two white pros, brothers Emerick and Chuck Kocsis, against two of the outstanding black pros, Clyde Martin and Howard Wheeler.

The competitive action in the three-day event lived up to its pre-tournament publicity, as the winner in the pro division was not decided until the last few holes. Clyde Martin started the final 18 holes with a one stroke lead over a surprising challenger, young (twenty-one-year-old) Calvin Searles, originally from New Orleans but playing as an Atlanta pro at the time of this event. However, early in the round Searles claimed the lead and tried unsuccessfully to maintain it. As approximately 1,000 spectators followed the stars around the course, a play-by-play account of the action demonstrates the high level of competitiveness that typified much of the tournament play: Martin was two down going into the seventh hole. Searles took seven on the par-5 seventh hole, while Martin had a birdie to recapture the lead. Although Martin appeared to be in the driver's seat, up by three going into the last nine holes, Searles had evened it up again by the twelfth and jumped out in front on the par-3 thirteenth hole when he scored a birdie. However, Martin evened it up again on the fourteenth hole, when he took a five and Searles a six. Martin shot par from the fifteenth through the eighteenth holes to close with a two-stroke margin (292 total for the 72-hole event) over Searles (294), who finished one over par on the fifteenth and eighteenth holes (*Pittsburgh Courier*, August 23, 1941, p. 17). Although Searles finished second, he was tied by Zeke Hartsfield of Atlanta, who came on with two rounds of 69, the best two rounds in the tournament, on the final day. Four golfers finished at 301, including Theodore "Teddy" Rhodes, a rising star out of Nashville who would become the next pro to tutor Louis, Ben Greene of New Orleans, along with Ben Davis and Bob Seymour of Detroit. Davis and Seymour, like Martin, were local favorites. Seymour had joined the U.S. Army and played in the tournament while on furlough from Fort Custer, Michigan. Popular pro Howard Wheeler, who was living in California at that time, finished in eighth place at 302, while Solomon Hughes of Gadsden, Alabama, and Eddie Jackson of Detroit shared ninth place with 303 totals (*Chicago Defender*, August 23, 1941, p. 25).

A highlight of the tournament was the exhibition match, which many saw as a demonstration of how well African Americans performed in direct competition with white pro golfers. The match pitted Howard Wheeler and Clyde Martin against Emerick and Chuck Kocsis. Emerick was the current state PGA champion, and Chuck was a former American Walker Cup star and leading pro. Martin and Wheeler were logical choices for Louis to select to represent black pros. Louis thought very highly of Martin, who was his personal golf instructor, and Wheeler was a three-time UGA National Open champion. Wheeler was also a gallery favorite, known for his colorful play, such as an unorthodox, cross-handed grip that produced long drives from a tee made of paper matchboxes. The exhibition match became even more of an attraction when a friendly side bet of $400 on the white pros against "Joe's pros" was put up by a group of white golf enthusiasts in attendance. The thrilling match was clinched by Wheeler and Martin (3–2), with the deciding shot made by Wheeler as he exploded from a trap for a birdie on the 380-yard fifteenth hole. Veteran golfers who witnessed the shot called it "one of the best of the season" (*Baltimore Afro-American*, August 23, 1941, p. 22). The Kocsis brothers were gracious in defeat, stating that "it was the first time that they had played against colored golfers, but they had enjoyed the match and would like to play again . . . [further noting that] the colored golfers should be real proud of Joe Louis who was the finest sport they had ever met" (*Baltimore Afro-American*, August 16, 1941, p. 22).

Although Joe Louis played in the amateur division of the tournament on the first day and qualified to compete in the final 36 holes, he decided to withdraw after injuring his finger on the eighth hole (*Pittsburgh Courier*, August 23, 1941, p. 17). He did not want to risk further injury, which could jeopardize an upcoming boxing match in defense of his world heavyweight championship scheduled a little over a month after the tournament. The amateur title was won by Leroy Smith, a nineteen-year-old florist from Norfolk, Virginia (*Pittsburgh Courier*, August 23, 1941, p. 17), followed by Oscar J. Clisby of Pasadena, California, and Dr. Remus Robinson of Detroit (*Baltimore Afro-American*, August 23, 1941, p. 22). Given his failure to win the amateur title, Louis's performance in the tournament could have been viewed as anticlimatic in a year filled with record-setting boxing feats. In 1941, he successfully defended his boxing championship five times from January to May in what some called the "bum-a-month" campaign, before a historic sixth fight in June against Billy Conn and eventually a record-setting seventh defense against Lou Nova in September (Capeci & Wilkerson, 1983). However, his uncharacteristic display of emotion after witnessing the victory of his personal golf tutor, Clyde Martin, who won the championship in a dramatic finish, clearly showed that the tournament's success was a significant highlight in a year of his other accomplishments. Louis and Martin were so overcome with joy after Martin held off Searles to win the championship that, according to the *Baltimore Afro-American*, "they were about to kiss each other just before the crowd of about two thousand swept Clyde off his feet, placing him on their shoulders and carrying him to the club house" (*Baltimore Afro-American*, August 23, 1941, p. 22). The tournament was also historic for Louis in that the success of the interracial exhibition match, which placed African American golfers in the limelight as pros who could hold their own against good white pros, also placed him in the spotlight as an ambassador of goodwill and an advocate for the creation of opportunities for African American golf pros to join the ranks of their white counterparts. *Richmond Afro-American* sportswriter Nat Rayburg reported that the two white pros (the Kocsis brothers) who participated in the Joe Louis tournament stated that "Clyde [Martin] would be among the first twenty [golfers] in the country if given a chance in big-time company . . . [and] more mixed benefit matches should be held" (*Richmond Afro-American*, August 30, 1941, p. 22). The successful performance of black golfers from the South in the Joe Louis Open was particularly notable given the more strictly enforced Jim Crow practices they faced that limited regular playing opportunities and continued to relegate many to the roles of caddies, shop-boys, and greenkeepers. Many of the best golfers had roots in the South or were currently living there in states such as Georgia, Florida, Louisiana, Tennessee, North Carolina, Virginia, and others. As one example, the *Atlanta Daily World* highlighted the success at the first Joe Louis Open of golfers with Atlanta connections: Calvin Searles from New Orleans, who was runner-up in the Joe Louis tournament, drove his truck from New Orleans to Atlanta to participate in the annual Southern Open tournaments and called Atlanta his second home; Zeke Hartsfield, who became co-runner-up after completing the best two rounds on the final day of the tournament, was a member of Atlanta's Lincoln Country Club; Howard Wheeler, who finished third, formerly lived in Atlanta; and A.D.V. Crosby, who finished fourth, was also an active member of Lincoln's Golf and Country Club when he lived in Atlanta (*Atlanta Daily World*, August 15, 1941).

After an elaborate closing ceremony with the awarding of monetary prizes and trophies, the enthusiasm generated by the Joe Louis Open continued into the following weekend as the scene for that eventful year in black golf switched to Boston where the annual UGA Negro National Open was held. As discussed in the previous chapter, the UGA National Open of 1941 was one of the biggest and most successful, owing in large part to the momentum and enthusiasm that had developed during the previous week in Detroit at the Joe Louis Open. However, plans were cut short for the 1942 staging of what were now regarded as the premier "twin" events in black golf, the Joe Louis Open in Detroit and the UGA National Open scheduled for Washington, D.C., as the United States entered World War II after the bombing of Pearl Harbor in December 1941. Joe Louis himself joined the military and both tournaments were canceled until the end of the war in 1945.

The resumption of the Joe Louis Open tournament in 1945 did not generate the kind of excitement produced by the first one. Many golfers, including Joe Louis himself, were still serving in the military, and some had been lost in the war. Probably the best known among the casualties was Calvin Searles, who had provided the most excitement with a battle down to the wire against Clyde Martin to finish second in the 1941 event. Due to illness, Clyde Martin could not return to defend his title, while Leroy Smith, the amateur champion in 1941, was in the military and serving a tour of duty in Japan (*Pittsburgh Courier*, June 23, 1945, p. 16). Despite wartime restrictions, a somewhat abbreviated tournament was held in 1945, with Solomon Hughes of Indianapolis winning the pro division championship (*Pittsburgh Courier*, September 29, 1945, p. 16). In the following year (1946), the tournament regained its earlier attraction as one of the two premier events in black golf. Although many of the earlier stars such as Clyde Martin, Pat Ball, John Dendy, Howard Wheeler, Zeke Hartsfield, Ben Davis, and the 1945 winner, Solomon Hughes, were among the favorites to win the professional division championship, Theodore Rhodes of Nashville had ascended to the top as the most highly regarded black golfer nationally. He had become the most consistent winner in the tournaments he entered and was Louis's current private teaching pro. Louis, in turn, supported his career as one of the best black hopes to break the PGA racial barrier. Rhodes not only won in 1946, but dominated the following years, winning four consecutive Joe Louis Open championship titles from 1946 to 1949.

Other subsequent highlights included the emergence of golf stars from the western region of the country, expansion of the tournament format to include women, Joe Louis's first championship win in his own tournament, development of Charles Sifford as a future "star" performer, and continuing efforts by Louis to promote interracial golf competition as a goodwill ambassador. By 1946, the wide array of talented African American golfers from the Midwest, East, and South had begun to give way to the rise of West Coast golfers, especially in the Los Angeles area. Although some well-known easterners led by Howard Wheeler had moved out west, the Cosmopolitan Golf Club of Los Angeles was a primary source of golf activity on the West Coast. One of Cosmopolitan's star performers was Cliff Strickland, who won the UGA pro championship in 1939, the only year it was held in Los Angeles. Another member of the Cosmopolitan Club, William "Bill" Spiller, won the Joe Louis Open amateur championship in 1946 (*Pittsburgh Courier*, August 3, 1946, p. 28). When he began playing as a professional in 1947, Spiller became one of the most forceful black golfers to push for PGA entry. The modification of the tournament format in 1946 to include a women's division brought expectations of the same kind of excitement that had become a part of the UGA National Open since a women's amateur championship was added in 1930 (*Pittsburgh Courier*, July 6, 1946, p. 25). Lucy Williams Mitchum, three-time UGA national champion, won the Joe Louis Open first women's championship in 1946, with strong competition from contenders such as Julia Siler, also a former UGA national champ from St. Louis, and Detroit's Theresa Howell (*Pittsburgh Courier*, August 17, 1946, p. 25). A personal triumph for Louis came in 1948 as he captured, for the first time, the amateur championship in his own tournament. Although this victory was special, Louis had actually begun to improve before 1948 and was no longer regarded as a one-dimensional player who could only excel at making long drives from the tee. His first victory, before winning the 1948 Joe Louis Open title, had come in 1947 as he won the EGA Eastern Open amateur title in Pittsburgh (*Chicago Defender*, August 16, 1947, p. 11). His steady improvement would lead later to a UGA national amateur championship title in 1951. Another participant in the Joe Louis Open of 1947 whose recognition was continuing to grow was twenty-six-year-old Philadelphia pro, Charles "Charlie" Sifford. Originally from Charlotte, North Carolina, Sifford came up through the caddying ranks and moved to Philadelphia, where he was influenced by Howard Wheeler and other established golfers. In 1948, he was rated by his peers as the most improved pro golfer on the tournament circuit and the main reason for the success of Teddy Rhodes who had to go all out to top him. Sifford's short game was described as being very good with iron shots true to the pin and a putting touch that was equally true, leading tournament director Bernard O'Dell to predict that "with more experience, [in] about two years, Sifford may become Negro golf's top man" (*Pittsburgh Courier*, July 31, 1948, p. 15).

The 1949 Joe Louis Open tournament was probably the most significant since the inaugural event in 1941. Both of the major black golf championships, the Joe Louis and UGA National Opens, were held in the same city (Detroit), with the Joe Louis tournament proceeding the UGA National Open by about a week. This marked the first time these two major black golf events were held in the same city. Louis attempted to promote greater interracial participation, although both tournaments always welcomed whites and usually provided an exhibition match between two of the accomplished black pros and two white pros who were invited as special guests. However, in that year's Joe Louis tournament, white golfers were extended an invitation to enter as regular participants. Louis also increased his monetary support of the event. Already touted as the richest black golf tournament, the cash prize of $4,000 provided by Louis for his tournament in 1949 was the largest amount ever offered by a private individual sponsor, even surpassing the $3,000 that Bing Crosby annually provided for his Hollywood Open tournament. These modifications brought major press coverage to black golf and ensured that a national audience would view the performances of black golfers in direct competition with their white counterparts. A press conference announcing the coming of the 1949 UGA and Joe Louis tournaments to Detroit was made by the governor of Michigan, G. Mennen Williams, who also donated trophies for the two events. The press gathering was held at Detroit's Gotham Hotel and became a major media event attended by many of the state's leading dignitaries, along with renowned pro golfer, Walter Hagen. Hagen, one of America's professional golf pioneers who held many championship titles, including a record four PGA championships in a row from 1924 to 1927, was on hand to lend his support to the two tournaments. In addition, both tournaments were scheduled to be aired over the recently instituted medium of television (*Pittsburgh Courier*, August 20, 1949, p. 24). The pre-tournament publicity was especially significant for the black professional golfers, such as Ted Rhodes, Howard Wheeler, Bill Spiller, and Charlie Sifford, who continued to be rebuffed by the PGA in their attempt to break the sport's racial barrier. The pro division championship for the Joe Louis tournament in 1949 was once again won by Ted Rhodes, as he had done in the three previous years, but he set a record by also winning the UGA title six days earlier (*Pittsburgh Courier*, September 3, 1949, p. 22) to become the only golfer to win both titles in the same year (*Pittsburgh Courier*, September 10, 1949a, p. 18). Rhodes turned in his usual sterling performance, and the 1949 tournament took on added significance as the runner-up in the Joe Louis Open was the white Michigan PGA pro, Mike Dietz, who tied for second with Robert McCockrell of Newark. Dietz was one of several whites invited by Joe Louis to play in the tournament. Another guest, Elmer Priskhorn, shared fifth place by tying with Charlie Sifford (*Pittsburgh Courier*, September 10, 1949a, p. 18). At the closing of the Joe Louis Open tournament, televised interviews were held with Louis, Rhodes, Dietz, and amateur champion, Emmet Hollins, who were all congratulated by Detroit's mayor, Eugene Van Antwerp (*Pittsburgh Courier*, September 10, 1949b, p. 18). Louis's efforts as black golf ambassador finally appeared to be paying off as expectations were rising that the showcase of black talent displayed in the 1949 twin black golf championships provided convincing evidence of the competitiveness of black pros and would surely contribute to the removal of the Jim Crow barriers in professional golf. These expectations were also fueled by an out-of-court settlement reached in 1948 to a suit filed against the PGA by Spiller, Rhodes, and San Francisco golfer Madison Gunter, who were denied entry to the PGA-sponsored Richmond Hills Open in California. In exchange for dropping the suit, the PGA had promised to review its "Caucasian only" provision (McRae, 1991) with an eye toward its removal (*Pittsburgh Courier*, July 24, 1948, p. 9). In addition, the earlier racial breakthrough in baseball, with the signing of Jackie Robinson, signaled that in 1949 the timing was right for a similar breakthrough in golf.

Despite its enormous success in increasing the visibility of black golfing "stars" and raising their hopes of penetrating the rigid racial barrier to PGA participation, the 1949 Joe Louis tournament did little to change golf's status quo. However, Louis, himself, became more popular in golfing circles even as his retirement from boxing moved him out of the limelight of that sport. By 1950, he was also regarded as a serious amateur contender in the many tournaments he entered. In 1950, he won amateur championship titles in the annual Fairway golf tournament in Dayton, Ohio (*Chicago Defender*, July 15, 1950, p. 14) and the highly competitive annual Central States Golf Association tournament in Omaha, Nebraska (*Chicago*

Defender, July 29, 1950, p. 14). However, he did not attempt to match the monetary support he provided for the previous year's Joe Louis tournament, as the cash prize for the 1950 tournament was sliced from $4,000 to $1,500 (*Chicago Defender*, August 12, 1950, p. 13) and Louis's brief appearance as a participant in the tournament was cut short because he decided to end his boxing retirement and had to return to training camp at West Baden, Indiana, where he was preparing for a match at the end of September (*Chicago Defender*, August 19, 1950, p. 13). Although he devoted full time to golf in his retirement from the ring, except for an assignment with a circus when he toured Canada and staged exhibition boxing matches, he was lured out of retirement to fight reigning champion Ezzard Charles and attempted to become the first heavyweight champion to regain his title. Since his decision to come out of retirement was driven, in part, by a need to settle a delinquent tax problem with the federal government, he was less able to sponsor his tournament as he had previously done. The reduced purse and his appearance in the amateur division did not detract from the excitement provided by the pros, however, with Detroit golfer, Al Besselink, assistant pro at the Red Run Country Club, staging an upset over Ted Rhodes, who had won the last four Joe Louis tournaments between 1946 and 1949. Rhodes, who collected $300, finished second, six strokes behind Besselink ($500), followed in order by Charlie Sifford ($175), Bill Spiller, who tied for fourth place with white Detroit pro Emerick Kocsis, Howard Wheeler, Ted Maged of Detroit, Bob Alexander of New Orleans, Atlanta's Zeke Hartsfield, and Ray Malain of Detroit. Robert Horton of Chicago won the amateur championship title and Alice Stewart of Detroit defeated Eoline Thornton of Los Angeles for the women's division crown (*Chicago Defender*, August 26, 1950, p. 15).

Louis experienced an embarrassing defeat in the boxing ring at the hands of heavyweight champion Ezzard Charles (*Chicago Defender*, September 30, 1950, p. 1); however, instead of retiring permanently, as many inside and outside the boxing world urged him to do, he spent more time training for a continued resumption of his boxing career, while also maintaining a busy golfing schedule. However, 1951 was the last year the Joe Louis tournament would be played. Howard Wheeler captured his first Joe Louis title in 1951, edging past defending champion Al Besselink who finished second followed in order by Ted Rhodes, Charles Sifford, Bill Spiller, Walter Flahie, Ben Davis, Willie Mosley, George Spencer, and Stan Jagwa. Eoline Thornton won the women's division title, dethroning Alice Stewart. The amateur division title was won by Butler Cooper of Pontiac, Michigan, as James Hughes of Detroit and Leonard Reed, Joe Louis's close friend and secretary for much of his career, finished tied for second (*Chicago Defender*, August 4, 1951, p. 36). However, Louis had failed to defend his title in the Central States Golf Tournament a week earlier because of boxing commitments that took him overseas in his elusive quest to recapture his heavyweight title (*Chicago Defender*, June 30, 1951, p. 12), and for the first time did not participate in the Joe Louis tournament, the last one to be held. Despite his unsuccessful attempt to regain his prowess in the boxing ring, he continued to excel as a golfer by winning the 1951 UGA national amateur championship title (*Chicago Defender*, September 8, 1951, p. 11).

JOE LOUIS AND THE PUSH TO END JIM CROW GOLF

Although Joe Louis was a catalytic force in stimulating greater interest in golf among African Americans and increasing the visibility of black professional golf stars, his efforts as a goodwill ambassador failed to break down the sport's long-standing racial barriers. After the 1940s, he became more directly involved in organized efforts to fight these barriers. As legal suits against cities maintaining segregated public golf courses increased and protests against the racially discriminatory policies of the PGA and other white golfing concerns became louder, Louis joined these efforts to push for an end to Jim Crowism in golf. In 1950, when black golfers were not permitted to enter the Bing Crosby and Long Beach Open tournaments in California, he wrote Mayor Burton Chase of Long Beach blasting the exclusion of blacks from the latter tournament, noting that "prejudice and discrimination have no place in sports" (*Pittsburgh Courier*, June 28, 1950, p. 21). The mayor's response, which became a typical answer to such charges during this period, was that the Long Beach Open was cosponsored with the PGA, which set all the rules and regulations. Therefore, the matter was out of his hands or those of the local sponsor, the Long Beach Lions Club (*Pittsburgh Courier*, June 28, 1950, p. 21). Louis felt that his "goodwill" efforts in promoting interracial golf during the previous decade through his own tournament and other activities were being undermined by the PGA, which continued to maintain its exclusionary "Caucasian only" policy, despite advances made in baseball and other sports. By demonstrating their competitiveness against white golfers in the few tournaments in which they were permitted to enter, most notably the Los Angeles Open and George May's All American and World Championship tournaments at the Tam O'Shanter Country Club in Chicago, some black golfers, including Ted Rhodes, Bill Spiller, Howard Wheeler, and the young Charlie Sifford, were primed for PGA entry in 1950 and, along with many other black golfers, would certainly continue to elevate their game if opportunities for expanded competitive play were made available. The recalcitrant PGA, however, kept using race as one of its criteria in qualifications for PGA membership and participation in its events. Louis was determined, as Chester Washington of the *Pittsburgh Courier* noted, "to keep punching until old Jim Crow is counted out in golfing circles" (*Pittsburgh Courier*, January 28, 1950, p. 21). The opportunity for a "return match" with the

PGA came in 1952 in a well-publicized confrontation between Joe Louis and the PGA co-sponsored, San Diego Open golf tournament. Joe Louis and pro golfers Bill Spiller and Eural Clark applied for entry to the $10,000 San Diego Open. The local sponsors of the tournament, San Diego Chevrolet dealers, at first welcomed their application and invited them to compete but then told them that the invitation had to be rescinded because of a PGA ruling that did not allow blacks to participate in PGA-sponsored events. Strong public protest came in the form of telegrams, letters, and calls to the PGA, and the ensuing battle became national headline news, receiving coverage in the country's leading newspapers. The *New York Times* carried a blow-by-blow account of the golf fight leading up to and during the week of the tournament (January 15–20, 1952). Louis's initial response to the PGA-invoked ban on their participation was that this battle was the most significant challenge he had ever faced and, in making an analogy between the PGA and its president, Horton Smith, and the Nazis at the time of his 1938 boxing match with Max Schmeling, he "want[ed] the people to know . . . we got another Hitler to get by" (*New York Times*, January 15, 1952, p. 31). Along with its story about the San Diego "affair," the *New York Times* included a photo of Louis, who was now retired from boxing after a defeat by Rocky Marciano, in full golf attire holding a raised golf club in his hand with the caption "The Brown Bomber Fights Again." Realizing that Louis was galvanizing national support for his fight against the discriminatory PGA policy, Smith immediately called a meeting of the seven-member PGA tournament committee and the co-sponsors to seek a face-saving resolution to the ordeal. In the meantime, Bill Spiller and Eural Clark as pros were allowed to play qualifying rounds, in which Clark fell short of qualifying by two strokes (79–77 for a 156 total), while Spiller just made it with a 152 total. Since Louis was an amateur, he did not have to play a qualifying round. The PGA tournament committee decided to approve the invitation for Joe Louis to play as an invited amateur under a rule that permitted local sponsors to invite ten amateurs, exempting them from qualifying. However, despite his performance in the qualifying rounds, the PGA committee declared that as a professional golfer "the PGA bylaws and other qualification rules could not be waived in the case of Spiller except through changes in the PGA constitution" (*New York Times*, January 16, 1952, p. 30). This action drew criticism from some groups that saw the PGA as attempting to maintain its historic practice of racial bias. The top national officers of the Congress of Industrial Organizations (CIO) adopted a resolution that called for the PGA to end its ban on black players entering its professional tournaments and said that admitting Joe Louis to participate while excluding Bill Spiller served only to emphasize the discriminatory PGA policy (*New York Times*, January 19, 1952, p. 19). Since Horton Smith predicted that the PGA would take up the non-Caucasian rule at its next annual meeting with an eye toward its removal, Louis reluctantly agreed to play in the tournament, but maintained his goal "to eliminate racial prejudice from golf, the last sport in which it now exists" (*New York Times*, January 16, 1952, p. 30). Louis, therefore, became the first African American to play in a PGA co-sponsored tournament. However, expressing dissatisfaction with the decision by the PGA tournament committee to continue the ban on black professional golfers, Bill Spiller re-appealed for an explanation of his ineligibility and threatened to sue the PGA, as he had done four years earlier before agreeing to an out-of-court settlement when the PGA promised to review its "Caucasian only" policy in 1948. A truce was reached on the issue when Smith said that he would seek PGA tournament committee approval for an "approved entry clause" that would permit the tournament committee to circumvent the PGA constitutional restriction by devising a supplemental list of players to compete in a PGA tournament provided the names were approved by the local sponsor and the host club of a city (*New York Times*, January 18, 1952, p. 31). Under the plan, a special committee of black golfers would screen their own players with the aim of selecting *one* professional and *one* amateur to play in each PGA-sponsored tournament. The proposed screening committee would be co-chaired by Joe Louis and Ted Rhodes with Eural Clark, Bill Spiller, and Howard Wheeler as other members (*New York Times*, January 19, 1952, p. 19). Black sports fans were particularly critical of the proposed plan, pointing out that "no committee was named to pick Jackie Robinson to play with the Brooklyn Dodgers, nor Marion Motley to play [football] with the Cleveland Browns. Each was judged on his ability" (*Chicago Defender*, January 26, 1952, p. 27). As the San Diego Open reached its final day, the fate of the proposed plan rather than the golf action itself received top billing by the *New York Times*, which carried an article with the heading "P.G.A. Committee Votes to Ease Tourney Ban on Negro Players" followed by the subheading "Action to Help Admit Them to Co-Sponsored Events Effective at Once, Smith Says" and finally a second subheading "[Ted] Kroll's 206 Leads in San Diego Open" (*New York Times*, January 20, 1952, pp. S1–S2.). Kroll eventually won the San Diego Open, his first major golf tournament victory, after holding off the pressure applied by veteran Jimmy Demaret (*Miami Herald*, January 21, 1952, p. 1-D). Hardly noticed was Louis's elimination earlier in the week as he finished the first 36 holes with a score of 158, eight strokes over the 150 needed to qualify for the final 36 holes of the tournament (*New York Times*, January 19, 1952, p. 19). While the historic plan was characterized as a lifting of the PGA tournament ban on black golfers, the door to participation could still be closed at the discretion of local sponsors or clubs. PGA president Horton Smith expressed the desire that these groups would invite blacks, but was careful to note in describing the details of the plan that the "P.G.A. actually is a guest at wherever tournaments are played and must necessarily be governed by rights of local sponsors, and clubs"

(*New York Times*, January 20, 1952, pp. S1–S2). Co-sponsors of PGA tournaments held in the South, or, for that matter, any place that wanted to maintain its traditional practices of racial discrimination could do so without facing pressure from the PGA or sponsors in other cities. The immediate effect of the new policy was that black golfers were permitted to participate in ten PGA tournaments in 1952 and fifteen in 1953; however, none of these tournaments was held in the South (McRae, 1991). Although the confrontation in San Diego initiated by Joe Louis (and Bill Spiller) drew national attention to the ongoing battle to end the PGA's Jim Crow policies, the results of these efforts represented a crack in rather than the destruction of the racial barrier to full black participation in PGA events. Nevertheless, Joe Louis can be seen as a major catalyst who paved the way for the final assault on the PGA "Caucasian only" rule (covered in Chapter 9), a fight that started to produce successful results toward the end of the 1950s.

CONCLUSION

In this chapter we have examined the role of world heavyweight champion boxer Joe Louis in stimulating greater interest in golf among African Americans and fighting to end racial discrimination in the sport during the period of his national prominence, especially in the 1940s and early 1950s. Unlike many early black golfers whose initial exposure to golf came through caddying at exclusive white country clubs, Louis was attracted to the sport after excelling in boxing. However, his enthusiasm and passion for golf matched those of blacks who rose from the caddying ranks to become recognized pros. At the height of his recognition as the king of the boxing world, he became a serious golfer who not only pursued an amateur career but also supported the careers of other black golfers while expanding opportunities for playing by creating his own tournament that became an instant national success. The Joe Louis Open tournament was a showcase for displaying the talents of African American golf stars, increasing interest in golf among blacks generally and providing a staging ground for the promotion of interracial contact and cooperation in golf. Louis became an "ambassador" of black golf, a role that was expected to break the long-standing racial barrier to greater access to playing opportunities for blacks. Failing to produce these results, however, he took a more aggressive approach, using his fame to draw national attention to the PGA's denial of black access to PGA-sponsored events. Although his militant stance produced limited initial results, these efforts coincided with the rise in direct attacks on racial exclusion growing out of the civil rights movement of the 1950s. Louis helped to draw attention to golf discrimination and opened up limited opportunities that increased the chances of a few black golfers to play in PGA events as non-touring players. Another consequence of his involvement in golf was increased media coverage of African American golf, especially by the black press. The overwhelmingly greater coverage of baseball by the black press during the heydays of the Negro leagues of the mid-1940s yielded a bit as Louis attracted attention to golf through his travels and involvement in tournaments and informal play. However, except for the most notable players, black golfers of the Jim Crow era remained relatively obscure, which has resulted in limited references to them in current biographical sources on black sports.

In the next chapter, we will take a closer look at the level of black participation in golf during the Jim Crow era as reported in the black press and identify some of the participants both from the rank and file and star players.

PART THREE

THE NATURE OF BLACK GOLF

CHAPTER 6

Jim Crow Era Golfers in the Black Press

Black newspapers were the primary means by which African American golfers were exposed to the public during the Jim Crow era. Except for the attention given to black efforts to remove racial barriers restricting access to sports facilities, the white press provided less coverage of their activities and few opportunities for them to gain general recognition for their accomplishments. As a result, coverage of African American players was largely restricted to the readership of black newspapers and their predominantly black audiences. Despite the wide coverage of sports such as baseball, football, and basketball by the black press, golf became increasingly featured as the UGA and other organizations established local, regional, and national tournaments and "star" players emerged. Black media coverage of the sport likewise increased significantly as other African American athletes from more popular activities, as well as entertainers and celebrities, were drawn to the sport. Consequently, the black press, particularly newspapers, can be seen as an important gauge of black golfing interest and an important, but relatively unexplored, means of documenting their accomplishments. As previously demonstrated, and contrary to the current misconception that black interest in the sport of golf is fairly recent, they were active in it almost from the beginning of its introduction to the white elite in the late nineteenth century. Although initially largely relegated to the marginal caddie role, blacks emerged as extremely successful players, established their own organizations, and produced many fine golfers. Much of what is known about the experiences of those who played during the Jim Crow era is either buried in the sports pages of black newspapers or

Table 6.1
Headlines of Golf News Articles Appearing in Two Leading Black Newspapers
(*Pittsburgh Courier* and *Chicago Defender*) During the Jim Crow Era

	Decades		
Major Headline Themes	**1920s**	**1930s**	**1940s (through 1952)**
Club news and golf instructions	33.3	15.2	5.2
Tournament news	27.5	54.3	28.4
Golfers recognized	33.3	29.3	63.9
Interracial golf news	5.9	1.1	2.6
Percent* Number of articles (298)	100.0 (51)	100.0 (92)	100.0 (155)

*May not equal 100.0 percent due to rounding

retained in the memories of a few living golfers of the earliest Jim Crow eras, most of whom have never had the opportunity to tell their own stories. In the current chapter and the following one, we will provide insight into the experiences of black golfers, both major and minor players, through the lens of black newspapers and personal interviews with a few of them, all of whom are now over eighty years old. We are particularly interested in providing profiles of well- and lesser known players.

DOCUMENTING GOLF ON THE SPORTS PAGE OF BLACK NEWSPAPERS

Among early twentieth-century black newspapers that provided national coverage of African American sports for a black audience were the *Chicago Defender, Afro-American, Pittsburgh Courier, New York Age, Amsterdam News*, and *Atlanta Daily World*. Articles by well-known sportswriters such as Sam Lacy of the *Afro-American*, Frank A. (Fay) Young of the *Chicago Defender*, Wendell (Smitty) Smith and Chester L. (Ches) Washington of the *Pittsburgh Courier*, and Eric (Ric) Roberts of the *Atlanta Daily World*, described these activities some of which received little or no coverage in the white press (Wolseley, 1971). In addition to national papers, many local outlets gave substantial coverage to golf activities, especially when an organization of black golfers or a course existed in the community and nationally known golf stars played there. Despite the generally positive portrayal of golf projected by the black press, the restricted role of blacks as caddies was for many years the only image held by white America of their involvement in the sport. Given this pervasive image, the black press sought to counteract this stereotypical view by presenting golfers in a positive light, encouraging greater participation in the sport. This was difficult because, unlike sports such as the segregated Negro baseball leagues in

John D. Rockefeller at Ormond Beach, Florida, where he played his regular daily round during the winter. Courtesy of the Ralph W. Miller Golf Library.

which spectators could view their stars in action firsthand, news coverage of black golfers often provided the sole source of documentation for many readers unlikely to venture to a course as a spectator. As the sport became more widely covered, black "stars" emerged, but were largely confined to black audiences throughout most of the Jim Crow era. Except for a few players such as Bill Spiller, Ted Rhodes, Joe Louis, and Charlie Sifford, who engaged in struggles to fight Jim Crow policies at various times during this period, the white press did not give extensive coverage to the black golfer as *performer*, maintaining the stereotypical view of the past and relegating black experiences to limited and restricted roles.

Black press attempts to counteract negative images of the sport can be assessed through an examination of the major themes presented in the headlines of leading newspapers. As an illustration, a content analysis of golf-related headlines appearing on the sports pages of two leading black newspapers, the *Pittsburgh Courier* and the *Chicago Defender* between 1921 and 1952, was conducted to examine this topic. The results are presented in Table 6.1. Four major themes emerged: (1) general information such as club news and instructions on playing the sport; (2) announcements of coming events and reports of tournaments in progress or completed: (3) golfers receiving recognition for their successful performance or impending participation in tournaments; and (4) interracial golf contact, particularly efforts to desegregate this activity. The frequency of articles with these kinds of headlines was tabulated across four decades (1920s, 1930s, 1940s, and early 1950s). Although most reports included information on more

Old Bruce Jones transported members of the Los Angeles Country Club from the end of the Pico Street carline to the Club House at the corner of Pico and Western. He charged 5¢, and it was customary for the passengers to match one another until one paid the fare for all the passengers. Courtesy of the Ralph W. Miller Library.

than one item, the headlines usually called attention to one major theme. A sample of typical headlines for each type of theme is presented below:

1. CLUB NEWS AND GOLF INSTRUCTIONS—"Golf [by E. L. Renip]" (*Chicago Defender*, April 16, 1921, p. 10), "Fairview golf club" (*Pittsburgh Courier*, May 25, 1929, p. 5), "How to play golf" (*Chicago Defender*, June 4, 1931, p. 9), "Lincoln country club course [Jacksonville] one of best," (*Pittsburgh Courier*, January 10, 1941, p. 16), "L.A. golf club awards trophies" (*Pittsburgh Courier*, December 15, 1945, p. 24).

2. TOURNAMENT NEWS—"National golf tournament in Chicago during September" (*Chicago Defender*, August 19, 1922, p. 10), "500 golfers will vie in big Cleveland links tourney for nat'l title" (*Pittsburgh Courier*, August 7, 1937, p. 18), "Golfdom's best to compete in Joe Louis open tourney" (*Pittsburgh Courier*, August 2, 1941, p. 17), "United golf association arranges summer tournament swing" (*Pittsburgh Courier*, May 27, 1950, p. 23), "Texas tourney offers $1,500 to pros" (*Chicago Defender*, August 30, 1952, p. 14).

3. GOLFERS RECOGNIZED—"Shippen wins Shady Rest golf club tournament" (*Pittsburgh Courier*, July 10, 1926, p. 15), "Dawkins wins Florida golf title" (*Chicago Defender*, September 22, 1928, p. 10), "Dendy and Miss Williams win golf titles" (*Chicago Defender*, September 5, 1936, p. 13), "Golfers expect Charles Sifford, Bill Spiller to grab 1950 titles" (*Chicago Defender*, June 17, 1950, p. 14), "Rhodes, Roach win titles" (*Chicago Defender*, August 23, 1952, p. 14).

Edison Marshall, who won his second consecutive UGA Negro National Open Golf Championship in 1931, prepares to defend his title at the annual UGA event in 1932 at the Douglass Park Golf Course in Indianapolis (*Chicago Defender*, September 3, 1932, p. 8). Courtesy of the *Chicago Defender*.

4. INTERRACIAL GOLF NEWS—"St. Louis golf star barred from tourney" (*Pittsburgh Courier*, May 5, 1938, p. 16), "Judge orders Baltimore golf course open" (*Pittsburgh Courier*, July 3, 1948, p. 17), "How Louis upset PGA race barrier," (*Chicago Defender*, January 26, 1952, p. 10).

Golf news coverage in these two leading papers was lowest during the 1920s, with only fifty-one articles appearing. This number nearly doubled (92) during the next decade, increasing to 155 (more than 50%) between 1940 and 1952. This increase in golf news sports page coverage by the *Chicago Defender* and *Pittsburgh Courier* was accompanied by major headline shifts across these decades. During the 1920s, except for a relatively low percentage (5.9%) of headlines highlighting interracial news, coverage was largely balanced, with a third reflecting club news and golf instructions, a second third recognizing particular players, and a little over one-fourth (27.5%) focusing on tournaments. As black golf became more firmly established in the 1930s, with the UGA leading the way in promoting its annual national championship tournament, articles that carried tournament headlines increased to more than half (54%) of all the articles

Sanders Mason was a four time winner of the Tampa (Florida) city championship and founder of the Tampa Golf Association (*Chicago Defender*, July 16, 1932, p. 9). Courtesy of the *Chicago Defender*.

reporting golf news during this decade. While the percentage of headlines emphasizing club news and golf instructions represented only 15 percent of the articles reporting golf news in the 1930s (compared to 33.3% in the 1920s), there continued to be substantial recognition of individual players with about 30 percent (29.3%) reflecting themes recognizing successful players. In the period from 1940 to 1952, recognition of star performers became the most prevalent headline as nearly two-thirds (63.9%) of the articles during this time named specific individuals whose accomplishments merited coverage. It should be noted that this increase did not signal a decrease in tournament coverage because headlines recognizing golfers by name usually noted their accomplishments in the context of outstanding tournament play. More than fifty different individuals were included in headlines in one of the two newspapers since 1921, with both widely and lesser known golfers appearing. However, such players as Bill Spiller, Ted Rhodes, Howard Wheeler, Charles Sifford, and Joe Louis were especially popular and appeared more frequently in headlines between 1940 and 1952. The relatively small percentage of club news and golf instruction headlines (5.2%) during this period continued their decline during the two

John Dendy, as he wins the coveted UGA Negro National Open championship tournament played at Philadelphia's Cobb Creek Golf Course in 1936 after previously holding the title in 1932 (*Chicago Defender*, September 5, 1936, p. 13). Courtesy of the *Chicago Defender*.

previous decades (33.3% in the 1920s and 15.2% in the 1930s). Headlines dealing with interracial golf news appeared much less frequently than other themes between 1920 and the early 1950s. However, this did not necessarily mean that positive racial experiences or protests against Jim Crow restrictions were less newsworthy, as such actions were usually covered more widely in other sections of the paper such as editorials and front-page lead stories. Many local papers in cities in which racial incidents occurred followed the progress of efforts to address these disputes.

Although the black press increased general interest in star performers, it is important to note that many rank-and-file golfers who played as amateurs in local tournaments were also featured in news stories. However, their activities were less frequently covered. Nevertheless, some items appeared reporting participation by amateurs, many of whom were from the business and professional elite, playing primarily out of love for the game. The Tawawa Golf Club, for example, organized at Wilberforce College in 1926, included among its member golfers, Dr. J. Aubrey Lane, veterinary surgeon, J. L. Simms, secretary to the college president, R. B. Hickman, postmaster, and other college personnel (*Pittsburgh Courier*, August 14, 1926). Another example includes a headline announcing the establishment

George Roddy, 1930 UGA National Open golf championship titleholder in the amateur division and current golf instructor at A & T College in North Carolina, prepares for an invitational tournament in 1936 (*Chicago Defender*, September 19, 1936, p. 14). Courtesy of the *Chicago Defender*.

of the Central States Golf Association in 1931, containing a listing of newly installed businessmen and professional officers and also avid golfers, including Des Moines attorney Charles P. Howard, president, and Kansas City doctors L. T. Montgomery, Eugene Rummons, and J. R. Williams, who served as secretary, chairman of the constitution committee, and tournament chairman, respectively, among other prominent members (*Chicago Defender*, August 29, 1931, p. 8). This kind of participation was stimulated by the success of star performers regularly covered by the black press. Finally, professional athletes who demonstrated excellent potential as golfers also attracted media attention. During the early 1940s, for example, black papers covered an unusually gifted golfer named J. C. Hamilton, a professional baseball player for the Negro League's Homestead Grays who played golf as an aside. Hamilton, who formerly caddied for major league star pitcher Dizzy Dean, was reportedly one of the greatest golf hitters, known for his long drives off the tee (*Pittsburgh Courier*, May 11, 1940, p. 16; *Pittsburgh Courier*, July 5, 1941, p. 17).

Sarah Smith of Washington, D.C.'s Wake Robin Golf Club and 1940 winner of the Eastern Open women's championship, which was held at Philadelphia's Cobb's Creek course (*Richmond Afro-American*, August 17, 1940, p. 19). Courtesy of the Baltimore Afro-American Newspapers.

PHOTOGRAPHIC NEWSPAPER CLIPPINGS AS POSITIVE IMAGERY

Another indication of the effectiveness of the African American press in counteracting negative player images is contained in photographs of black performers. These were, perhaps, the most graphic portrayals of athletic performers, second only to films showing them in action. A golfer's pose in the classic follow-through swing offers a powerful image. Whether assessing the technical merits of the player's swing or determining the circumstances that resulted in the photo's publication, there is little question that the holder of the club is *playing* the sport rather than *carrying* the equipment for someone else as a caddie for wealthy white players or transporting them to the clubhouse and course. Consequently, the portrayal of black golfers as players during the Jim Crow era was an effective means of counteracting the caddying stereotype of blacks. This belief, widely shared by whites during this era, was used to explain why so few blacks pursued

Clyde Martin is shown here at the UGA National Open championship in 1941, after finishing runner-up in the pro division for the second consecutive year (*Richmond Afro-American*, August 30, 1941, p. 22). Courtesy of the Baltimore Afro-American Newspapers.

professional golf—a myth that has persisted to recent times. In 1994, for example, well-known professional Jack Nicklaus sparked a controversy by attributing the low number of current African American professional players to the belief that "blacks have different muscles that react in different ways" (Hatfield, 1996). Clearly, the stereotype that African Americans lacked proper muscle development and other physiological requirements began during the Jim Crow era and was sustained by their relative invisibility to the white public audience, despite their accomplishments "behind the veil" and visibility to the black public.

The frequency and variety of media images depicting blacks as golf *performers* during the Jim Crow era counteracted restrictive roles projected by the white media, presenting golf as a legitimate participatory sport for African Americans. To illustrate this, a sample of newspaper photographs of black golfers as they actually appeared during the Jim Crow era in two black newspapers (*Chicago Defender* and *Richmond Afro-American*) provides documentary evidence of the positive role played by the black press in this regard. These photos, a fraction of the many that appeared during the Jim Crow era, illustrate a range of poses. These black golfers thus

Judson Grant is shown here putting on the ninth hole of the qualifying round at the Chicago Open tournament played at the Kankakee Shores golf course, as other members of the foursome watch, including (from left to right) Alvin James, Joe Louis, and Clarence Chandler (*Chicago Defender*, September 13, 1947, p. 11). Courtesy of the *Chicago Defender*.

served as role models for many aspiring caddies who hoped to join their ranks as tournament players at the coveted UGA Nationals and other tournaments staged by African Americans. These *action* poses were often supplemented by scenes from award ceremonies and banquets at the closing of tournaments and major organizational meetings. These images indicate that Jim Crow era golfers were indebted to the black media for the sport's spread of golf and rise in popularity despite institutionalized racism that kept their activities hidden from the larger public.

CONCLUSION

The popular image of blacks in subservient golfing roles prevailing since the sport's earliest appearance was countered by the African American press that portrayed blacks as members of elite country clubs, tournament organizers, and accomplished golfers. These were advanced by coverage of black golf in a manner that largely mirrored the activities of white America. A brief content analysis of articles in two leading black newspapers published during three decades revealed that the largely black readership was exposed to a very different view of the sport than that which prevailed outside their own communities. Headlines highlighted club activity, golf instructions, tournaments, recognized stars, and, to a lesser extent, interracial incidents. Decade emphases shifted from a more balanced reporting of events during the 1920s, to greater emphasis on tournaments in the 1930s, and more emphasis placed on the recognition of individual star performers after 1940. Photographs portrayed black golfers positively, resulting in greater general interest in this activity. However, whites continued to experience little exposure to black golf in their own media, maintaining the stereotypic image of blacks as "golf course servants" or caddies. Because these papers were read by few whites, these positive images did not reach many of them. Institutionalized racism perpetuated the assumed inferiority of blacks as golfers, despite evidence to the contrary. Although a more extensive analysis of black newspapers is required to fully document the extent of black golf, it is clear from this illustrative evidence that popular beliefs claiming African Americans were uninterested in golf until recently are unfounded.

Although media sources offer information largely unavailable in the existing golf literature, even more powerful evidence of the experiences of black golfers can be obtained from the actual experiences of African Americans who played as serious golfers during this era. We turn to such data in the next chapter, focusing on personal interviews with a few of the remaining players who can trace their experiences to the earliest generations of African American golfers.

CHAPTER 7

Jim Crow Era Golfers
Speak in Their Own Words

Early African American golfers began their careers in various ways: many of them began playing while caddying at white, segregated country clubs and public courses; others became involved in the sport through associations established by the black elite. As this activity became more accessible at black public and private courses, African Americans, ranging from prominent professionals to members of the laboring and service classes, were attracted to the game. Golf was one of the few black activities in which love of the sport transcended socioeconomic distinctions: participants ranged from prominent physicians, lawyers, and educators to government employees, janitors, service workers, and the unemployed. Adding to this variety were those who engaged in unlawful but widely accepted practices such as number runners, friendly betters, and heavy gamblers on and off the course. Furthermore, some considered themselves strictly professional or amateur, while others played without regard to these classifications, resisting attempts to categorize them by skill level. Regardless of how these players defined themselves or were viewed by others, their strong love for the sport and desire to play was common to them all.

In this chapter we examine some of their personal experiences during the Jim Crow era, as told in their own unique voices. Our intent was to learn about the rewards and frustrations of the game, the richness of their experiences, and the kinds of discrimination they experienced both on and off the course. Except for brief anecdotal information (cf. *Black Enterprise*, 1997) and the only detailed account of experiences playing golf "behind the veil" of segregation provided by Charles Sifford in his autobiography

(Sifford, 1992), virtually no personal accounts of the experiences of black golfers during the Jim Crow era are available. The need to document and preserve the life experiences of African Americans during this period through oral history interviews has been recognized as a major means of addressing the dearth of information detailing black life between the period of the *Plessy* decision of 1896 and the civil rights movement of the 1950s and 1960s (*Chronicle of Higher Education*, 1995). Despite limited availability, we were able to select a number of individuals by their accessibility, longevity, and involvement in the sport during this particular era. We were fortunate to interview people who ranged in age from eighty to eighty-nine years old with vivid memories and rich golfing experiences. Their responses provide valuable insight into the activities of past black golfers, particularly the relatively unexplored decades of the 1920s through the 1940s.

INTERVIEWS

The participants include Joe "Roach" Delancey (80), Ralph Dawkins (89), Everett Payne (85), Timothy Thomas (86), and Clarence Boyce (89). Brief profiles of each player are followed by a series of topical questions relating to their experiences. These questions covered: (1) their introduction to the game and their earliest experiences, which usually involved caddying at segregated white golf courses and learning to play through this exposure to the game; (2) interaction with other black golfers, especially by participating in tournaments and black golf club events; (3) contact with white golfers and perceptions of segregation in the sport generally; and (4) direct or indirect racial discrimination experienced during these situations.

Joe "Roach" Delancey

Joe "Roach" Delancey is originally from Miami (Coconut Grove), Florida, but later played out of New York, St. Louis, and Los Angeles. He won numerous tournaments at the local, regional, and national levels, including back-to-back UGA National Open amateur championship titles (1953, 1954, and 1955). As one of the most highly respected black golfers nationally, he was the personal golf instructor for boxing champion Sugar Ray Robinson and others. Joe Roach played regularly with all the great black golfers of this period (Ball, Wheeler, Rhodes, Spiller, Sifford, and others) and was truly one of the outstanding golfers of his generation. Joe Roach continues to play and also conducts a youth instructional golf program through the Joe Roach Junior Minority Golf Foundation in Miami, Florida.

Joe "Roach" Delancey

Earliest Experiences as a Caddie and Beginning Golfer

I started in golf about 1928 by caddying at the Biltmore Country Club in Coral Gables, Florida, at the age of ten years old. I just followed the bigger boys who liked to play golf between times that they were not caddying and I just took it up from there. When you were waiting to caddie we called that caddie pen days because while you were trying to get a bag you were in the caddie pen chipping the golf ball with other caddies and you developed from there.

The first person I caddied for was a white guy named Joe Roach. He took me to the golf course and showed me how to caddie and everything. Every time he'd come to the golf course, they would call out "Joe Roach" and I would come out to caddie for him. That's the way everybody started calling me Roach. That's how I got my nickname. And all my brothers took up the same name. My older brother was Big Roach; the younger one was Little Roach; and I was Joe Roach. If you ask somebody my name, Joe Delancey, they won't know who you are talking about. But everybody knows me by Joe Roach.

There were both black and white caddies. Some of the guys I knew as caddies here in Miami became golfers; guys like Preston Knowles, Benny Sands, and others who I only knew by nicknames. The earliest competitions were between caddies in caddie tournaments. The earliest caddie tournament I can remember was in 1929 at the Biltmore Golf Course. When the Depression came, the number of holes at the Biltmore course was reduced. Although caddies were usually only allowed to play on Mondays up to twelve noon, a man named Harley Russell who was in charge of the course during this time would let you play more often. He would send us out to work on the traps and different things and you could also play golf. He would let you play in the summertime on Monday, Tuesday, Wednesday, and Friday. But you couldn't play on Thursday, Saturday, and Sunday, which were big days for players. Any of the other days were times that the caddies could play up until twelve noon, as long as you kept the traps rigged and different things like that. Actually, that's the way I really got started in golf. Although none of the caddies owned any golf clubs, one of the club members (usually someone who you caddied for) would loan you a set or you would just get a set from the clubhouse and put them back when you finished. You would then go right out there and play.

I left Florida about 1934 and started caddying in the New York area. I kept progressing as a player and around 1937 there was no caddie around that could touch me. We placed bets of fifty cents to one dollar, which I usually won. I played on a caddie team in 1938 and 1939. We went all around the New York area on Long Island and in New Jersey competing against other caddie teams. We played all the caddie teams in the metropolitan area during the summer months. This was a treat for us to know that you could get on the bus and go to play golf. The first caddie tournament I won was in New York, which was called the Metropolitan tournament put on by people out of a club in Scarsdale. There were 36 holes and I think I was one over par, which was good enough to beat out all of the caddies in the metropolitan New York district.

The first tournament where I played beyond the times set aside by whites for caddies was at a popular black-owned country club called Shady Rest in Westfield, New Jersey. Mr. Shippen was the club pro when I played there in 1939. So I went over there and on the first trip around the golf course I broke the course record.

Experiences as a Player and Interaction with Other Black Golfers

I became known as a good golfer and when that happens people start wanting to play with you. I met a lot of the good golfers at that time. One of the earliest I can recall who stands out is Cliff Taylor. I also met John Shippen, who was the club pro at Shady Rest when I played my first tournament there in 1939. He was a real nice guy who was always trying to be helpful. When he'd see a youngster, he would try to help him along. Shippen played in maybe the second U.S. Open and finished fifth. I'm not sure about the year. Later on when Teddy Rhodes came to New York, he came looking for me. We became just like brothers. Charlie (Sifford), Teddy, Howard Wheeler, you just name them, we played the same type of stick. When I started hanging out with them, everybody wanted to hang out with me cause I could play. They wanted to see who I was and what made me tick. When a guy coming from the South would come to New York, my name was the first one to pop up—Joe Roach.

I always kept a job and played golf on my *leisure time*, I'll put it that way. I owned dry good stores, confectionary stores, and between that I played golf. If I was going into any kind of business, I would always have it fixed so that I could have my leisure time to go play golf. Before I left the South, I use to hear from other golfers about caddie tournaments when they returned from the North after leaving to play golf in the summertime. They would talk about how they could play at different golf courses, which we could not do around Miami. This gave me a little enthusiasm to go North and be with them. So, I left. Most of my prizes at that time were trophies because I played as an amateur. I just had a love for playing. The cash prizes were really not that big during my time. The total for the tournament would be $500 to $1,000. I think the Joe Louis tournament was $1,000 and the biggest black tournament, the UGA National Open, was $500. You would go to a lot of tournaments where the total amount for awards was $200 or maybe $250, but then the entry fee wasn't that much.

In 1948, I was associated with Sugar Ray Robinson, teaching him how to play golf. Celebrities were your biggest hope of getting to a golf tour because of the financial support they could provide. Billy Eckstine financed Charlie Sifford; Sugar Ray Robinson financed me; Joe Louis financed Ted Rhodes and also Clyde Martin. With Teddy and Joe it was a little bit different from the rest of us. Teddy didn't do nothing but travel and play golf. That's why Teddy was so good and ahead of us for so long. Twenty-four hours a day Teddy was golfing. That's all Joe wanted him to do: play golf and teach him. In fact, Joe use to help a lot of guys, such as Solomon Hughes, Zeke Hartsfield, you name them, Joe helped them all. I played in the Joe Louis Open Tournament in 1941 which was held at the Rackham Golf Course (Detroit) just before the UGA championship in Massachusetts. That's where I think I first met Ralph [Dawkins]. Joe held one tournament before the war (World War II) and then had another one in 1945 and maybe in 1946, 1947, or 1948. A lot of tournaments were canceled during the war years, then started back again maybe in the middle of 1945.

I knew and played with many good golfers. I'll name a few of them. I knew John Dendy from Asheville, North Carolina, who was a real good golfer. I played with John in the 1930s and also in the early 1940s. Solomon Hughes from Gaston, Alabama, was our stylist who was one of the best swingers in golf we had. Bill Spiller was a good golfer who could hold his own. Spiller was a great guy who believed in equal rights. That's what he fought for and helped out by making it possible for blacks out there today to play. I take my hat off to him. Calvin Searles and I were good buddies. We first met in 1940. Calvin Searles got lost in the war. I played with Edison Marshall, who I think was out of Indianapolis. Teddy Rhodes and I were also buddies and we played many a round together. I would've matched Teddy with anybody. I don't care who, white, black, blue, or brown. I'd say from 1946 up until maybe 1958 they [whites] couldn't beat him. They were just lucky at the time he wasn't playing. And a black player couldn't touch him. He won every tournament he teed up in. Everywhere Teddy Rhodes went he was the man to beat. Hugh Smith was from Thomaston, Georgia; I played with him. Zeke Hartsfield was another good buddy. As a matter of fact, Zeke took me under his wings. He was a little bit older than I was and any time he had to prepare for a big match, he'd come looking for me. I played a lot with Howard Wheeler. Starting from around 1938, Wheeler earned a living from waiting on Eddie Mallory, who was married to Ethel Waters. He was a winner. Wheeler was long and cross-handed. He knew how to handle himself and had his own way of doing things. Like he'd tee the ball up on a scorecard; nobody else could do that during that time; just wrapped a scorecard and put the ball up there and knock it nine miles. I played with Pat Ball when I was in Chicago. I met Charlie Sifford in 1943 before I went overseas during the war and Teddy Rhodes after the war. There are many, many black golfers I played with. I have written down this list which contains probably 100 or more just from sitting down and remembering them.

A lot of black women were involved in golf too. They just started taking up the game and were aggressive with it. You take, for example, Eoline Thornton from California and Ann Gregory of Indiana who were good golfers. You also had Thelma Cowans, Renee Powers, and Althea Gibson, who was our best at that time. Ann Gregory played the same year I played in a tournament in San Diego if my recall is correct. Cleo Ball was another one. I don't know if you also have the name of a woman who was a good player out of St. Louis. My wife was also a pretty fair sticker. Her first golf tournament was in 1956 in Philadelphia. My wife's golf instructor was a black pro named Jimmy DeVoe.

I saw playing in the UGA as a stepping-stone to competition that included playing among a broader field of players. However, without the UGA there might not have been as many black players. Because of the UGA, black golfers had some place to go to have competition among themselves. I played in all of their tournaments up until 1956. I was a winner in the UGA National Open championship in 1953, 1954, 1955, and 1956, then I didn't play no more with them for awhile. I played in one tournament again with them in San Diego in 1976. But when you would go there, everybody was there. You would see everybody from everywhere at the UGA tournament.

Contact with White Golfers and Perceptions of Segregation in Golf

I competed against whites during my time in the U.S. military and in public links tournaments. After the war (World War II) when I was in France, I played golf in Paris. I played in the big military championship tournament in June of 1945. The first day there I opened up with a 69 on a par 75 course. I finished about maybe eighth, but this was an experience. I played throughout Europe—in Germany, Switzerland, and in England at the Saint Andrews Golf Course. I played my share of golf courses throughout the world. In the United States there was a whole lot of contact between black and white golfers in liberal states. I've seen some of the best white golfers call to you and say let's go [to play golf] around New York, in California, and even in Illinois when you hit the town center, that is, Chicago. They saw you as a golfer in certain places. They won't even mix with you in the South. But in the North it was a different thing. Sometimes the same white golfer would treat you different in the South. Just like one white pro I know. He would be in California and say let's go Teddy, you got a game. But if he's in Mississippi or Florida or any other place that wasn't right, he's not going to say nothing to Teddy, and Teddy understood it. Although you experienced segregation, you felt like you were paving the way for somebody if you could stay out there and continue playing.

I played in a lot of tournaments the same as Charlie, the ones that they would let you play in. For example, I played in five L.A. Opens and the San Diego Open. I also played in few tournaments round St. Louis. I felt that I should have the opportunity to enjoy some of the attention that some of the white golfers got. I felt that I was the cream of the crop. I felt that way when I played in San Francisco and Chicago or the public links tournaments (which were integrated). I didn't feel that anybody could beat me. It was a surprise to me when I lost and I didn't feel that my opponent beat me. It was the mistakes that I made. I didn't keep up with the controversy involving blacks being denied the chance to play in tournaments on the PGA tour. At the time, I just played amateur golf and I knew where I could go. I could play in the public links championship, so the rest of it didn't get much attention from me until Charlie and the others wanted to play in the L.A. and San Diego Opens. They wouldn't let them go any further than Tucson. I remember all of that. And then Charlie should have been in the Masters at least by 1965. But he never played in the Masters, which was a dirty blow because they kept changing things around. You'll win a tournament and they'll change it [the policy] to something else.

Direct and Indirect Experiences of Racial Discrimination in Golf

I was behind the plans to sue the PGA because of the "Caucasian cause" in their constitution. Spiller and the others were trying to sue them for a few thousand or a few million dollars or whatever the amount. So then they started letting you play in liberal states. For instance, you could play on the West Coast all the way to Tucson [Arizona] and then the next stop was Texas. You couldn't go into Texas. When they played the [pro] tour they would not let you play there. But it didn't bother me too much because at that time I was playing amateur golf and I was certified there with the USGA, which made a big difference. I could send in an entry and they had to accept me if I had a certified three handicap, so that made a big difference.

As far as discrimination is concerned, the way I would put it, everything happened with me before my time. When things started moving a bit my age is passed. When they start letting you play golf, then you talking about you're forty; Just like Charlie who was about thirty-seven or thirty-eight. Why couldn't it happen when he was eighteen, or during World War II? Now they opened up a senior tour, but I was too late for that. Then there was a super senior and I was too late for that also. So you can forget it. But now here's Jim Thorpe, who is coming right into the seniors, he's got some place to go. Me, I didn't have nowhere to go. Charlie was lucky enough to come into the seniors and made a little money. Charlie Sifford went through the mills. You've got to give it to him. He took all they had and then some. I use to look at Charlie and I didn't know how he could take this stuff. He just didn't know what he was made out of. He'd say, I'm going down to Texas, man, they said I could play. He should be given all the credit. If he had given up, blacks probably still wouldn't be out there today. You had a lot of black golfers who could have developed if there was not discrimination. See, I dreamed about going out to the Biltmore and teeing off number one, you know. And it

Ralph Dawkins, Sr.

could have happened in 1928, but it didn't. You had to slip out there and play. Now you go out there and its just like it never happened. If you want a room in the hotel, you go out there and get it; all they want is money. But, boy, you best not head that way with a golf club during my time when I was a kid.

Ralph Dawkins, Sr.

Ralph Dawkins, Sr., was formerly teaching pro at the Lincoln Golf and Country Club (1941–1949) in Jacksonville, Florida. Dawkins won the first Florida state junior golf tournament in 1928 and participated in the 1941 UGA National Open Championship. Although he did not make another appearance at the UGA Nationals, he participated regularly in tournaments in the southeast, especially in Florida, where he was one of the local pros competing in Jacksonville's Southeastern Open and Gate City Open tournaments during the late 1940s through the 1950s against many of the major black golfers nationally, including Wheeler, Rhodes, Sifford, and others. Before physical ailments ended his playing days, Ralph devoted most of his time as a golf instructor in Jacksonville, while attempting to stimulate interest in golf, especially among African American youth.

Earliest Experiences as a Caddie and Beginning Golfer

When I was about ten years old, in 1919, I can remember caddying my first round and seeing the other caddies play golf in a yard on a hill where they would be waiting for work. I caddied at a golf course in Jacksonville called the Florida Country Club, where only the well-to-do-whites played golf. Although I earned one dollar and twenty-five cents my first time out, there was a sign that read "After September 30, 1919, caddie fees will be as follows: class A caddies will receive 25 cents per hour; class B caddies will receive 20 cents per hour." However, it was usually up to the person you caddied for to decide exactly how much you were paid. The average tip was a quarter. Since I started in September at the end of the summer, I returned to school, where I was in the second grade, and continued to caddie after school let out each day. The schools were double sessions and ended each day at twelve noon and you could ride the streetcar to the golf course for ten cents. After the first year, I realized how much it was helping my mother with buying food so when summer returned I went to the golf course to caddie every day. Being a family of seven, I could usually give my mother at least a dollar a day and take a quarter for lunch. When schools closed in the latter part of the year we had the whole summer and would sometimes make double that amount. So I became involved as a caddie originally because it was an honor to make money to help my family and also have a lot of fun. I would ride the streetcar trolley, go to movies, and still save money to give my mother and be right back there the next day to earn some more money. A number of caddies were doing the same thing so we would hang out together.

Some of the caddies would sit on a hill outside of the golf course waiting for work, while others played golf. I joined in right away with hitting the golf balls in short holes. This became a routine affair every day during the summer and even when I was in school. I would play until dark after working caddie. I was fascinated by the game. I noticed that some of the boys would hit balls and place bets. So I learned how to protect my tip money by outplaying all the other boys. Some guys would lose their tip money about the day after they started betting and would quit playing. I became the best player among the caddies and would take the tip money of other caddies who went up against me. This was another reason I was motivated to go out to the golf course every day. Pretty soon I had enough money to buy a club. In those days they had hickory shaft clubs and we could make our own clubs by buying a shaft and putting together a head. That's the way I developed an interest in golf.

You could play golf at the course where you caddied because the caddies were given a day, Mondays, to play on the course. They would also give a tournament for the caddies, which usually took place on a Sunday. There would be about 100 or more caddies from all over the state playing in the caddie tournament. They were being watched by whites because there were a number of low scores being shot below par. When I started caddying, all the caddies were black. There were no white caddies because in those days they could go to school and then sell papers after the schoolday ended. There were some black kids who sold papers. If the paper cost a nickel you could earn a dime by selling two papers, but selling papers was rough. I chose the other route, caddying. By 1925, when the Municipal golf course opened up, there were a few white caddies, but most caddies were still the blacks. White boys always had jobs. Although most sold newspapers, some would shine shoes or do other things. Very few chose caddying as a way of making extra money.

When I got to be in high school, the time for golf was limited. More time was spent on other sports—baseball and football. I turned to other sports because there was no golf program in high school and I couldn't go on to caddying after school because it would be too late—after 3:45 P.M. I was only able to caddie on Saturdays and Sundays during the school term. However, I continued to play golf along with football and baseball. In 1928, when I was eighteen years old, I won the first state junior golf championship and had hopes that this could win a scholarship for me to play golf in college. Golf was just getting started in college. However, I became sick with an ulcerated stomach and was put on a special diet where I could only eat certain foods. I was bedridden off and on for the next couple of years so I was not able to go to college even though I already had a football scholarship waiting for me.

I took to caddying again during the Great Depression. Although I was in bed with the stomach ulcer during most of 1931, I got up in 1932 and started playing golf again. There were no jobs available during this time but I could caddie every day and look forward to traveling over the state to different caddie tournaments that were being given by whites. There were a lot of grown caddies like myself during the Depression and the prizes that were awarded made it worthwhile to enter. It amazed the white golfers to see us play. Some caddies played around even par. I remember one caddie tournament that was staged by a white professional baseball player, a pitcher for the New York Giants, who was the owner of this country club in Daytona [Beach]. He was giving us the opportunity to play and looking up black talent in golf. I guess he was thinking someday that blacks would be allowed to play golf; that there would be integration. I don't know what his reason was, but every year he would give this

statewide affair open to all the caddies which were mostly grown men
who could play golf. As I traveled over the state, it was the same
thing in other cities; grown blacks, just as I was, taking time out to
play golf. There was even a caddie tournament we gave among our-
selves. We played on a regulated course and I won finishing the last
round with a 73.

Experiences as a Player and Interaction with Other Black Golfers

I became interested in pursuing golf at the professional level during
the Depression after winning the state golf tournament at the Lincoln
Golf Club in 1928. I caddied at the Florida Golf Club before it closed
down in 1934 and I use to watch the professionals play. I would
watch some of the best golfers: people like Walter Hagan, Gene Sar-
azen, and Bobby Jones. And after playing the course (Lincoln) for
about two weeks practicing, I realized I could consistently shoot below par golf. And being one of the only blacks in the country who
could shoot par golf or below, I saw then I could create a job playing
golf. So, I started touring the state. I went to Tampa and a friend of
mine, Sanders Mason, was staging a black tournament there, the
Southern Open. A branch of it would be held in Atlanta every 4th of
July at the Lincoln Country Club there. So, he was given permission
to give a tournament. I wanted to see some of the great black golfers
that I had read about like Howard Wheeler, Edison Marshall, and
Pat Ball. I heard that they were going to be there, so I went there.
But, they didn't show up. So, I got back to Jacksonville and invited
some of the boys to come over from Daytona. We would play there
every year at the caddie tournament that the pros would give them
for all the caddies in the state. We would go there every year—made
it an annual affair.

After seeing that I could create a job for myself playing golf, I
realized that except for the opportunity to play in caddie tournaments
there was nowhere here I could play in tournaments on a regular
basis. However, an opportunity came in 1939 for me to stage my
own tournaments when I was invited to take over the 9-hole Lincoln
Golf Course in Jacksonville as greenkeeper. I accepted the job. My
salary would be whatever I could accumulate from tournament fees
after expenses. So, after successfully staging a tournament out there,
I took a trip to Atlanta in 1940, before I got married, to enter the
Southern Open Golf Tournament. But after getting there this time (I
had been there once before in 1936), they had canceled the professional money pot and it was just for the amateur businessmen to play.
The businessmen lacked the passion for golf to put up money for the
professionals to play. But they said they would take up a sweepstakes

when they played that weekend. I didn't stay because I didn't have enough money to pay for expenses that long. So I came back to Jacksonville and we organized a club of our own to sponsor these type of affairs and send representatives to the Southern Open and other tournaments. This was the beginning of the Jacksonville Negro Golf Association in 1940. About six months later the Jacksonville Amateur Golfers Bureau was formed.

I was selected to be the first club professional at the Lincoln Golf and Country Club in 1941. Interest in golf was high. I gave over 100 golf lessons over a quarter of a year until the war came out. I held a pro and amateur tournament every month. There were 35 teams. The professionals played for money and the amateurs were the businessmen. We gave away prizes; they were very small but the interest was high. President Roosevelt's WPA set up a project, a work project, for six months out at Lincoln remodeling the 9-hole course and it became a regulated 9-hole golf course. They built up greens, put in grass on the greens, a watering system and everything. Then, after the war, J. D. Brooks staged the first tournament known as the Southern Golf Tournament. After the tournament in 1945, the Lincoln golf course was leased by a businessman named James Burris, known as "Jimmy" Burris, for five years. And he staged a tournament every year up until 1951. The first three years, 1946 through 1948, the tournament was won by Richard Lewis of Bartow, Florida. He's in the ministry now. As I traveled to different cities, I saw that other black golfers had the same idea. For example, fellows like Zeke Hartsfield, a well-known black professional at Atlanta's Lincoln Country Club, did the same thing. So then we became representative of the black professional group. As more tournaments were staged, businessmen would put up as high as $1,000 for us to shoot at. We had tournaments in places like West Palm Beach, where we would all come together. We stayed together and played together, hoping that the day would open that we would have a chance to compete in the PGA or other tournaments, which is why some of us held out. But I saw that when I got married there wasn't enough money. So after I went to the UGA national tournament in 1941 I came back and got a job. Although I started working as the club pro at Lincoln, I also started working in all sorts of jobs as a laborer at the naval air stations in Jacksonville. After the war I learned the trade of carpet-laying and soft-tile-laying (linoleum, vinyl) and then the family came on. The tournaments among blacks began to pay a little more but it wasn't enough to attract my attention from my family. When I was finally offered a chance to join the tour I was not interested in it because I was forty-nine years old. There was no senior tournaments; they were twenty years away, and no super senior tournaments like today. I look at the situation and have no regrets of what happened and seeing my opportunities pass away during the time. It's just one of those things that happened.

Many of the well-known golfers in Florida like James Carr and James Everett participated in the Southeastern Tournament. Other well-known black golfers outside of Florida also came down. Zeke Hartsfield, Teddy Rhodes, and Joe Louis came down. All of the celebrities had the privilege of playing at the Lincoln Golf Course. I met many black golfers during my day: Zeke Hartsfield from Atlanta, Porter Washington from Boston, and Clyde Martin from Washington, D.C. I met Pat Ball in 1936 at the Southern Open in Atlanta. Ball was a professional from Chicago's Palos Park Golf Course for many years before he died. He was nationally known among both blacks and whites as a good golfer. Pat Ball won the National UGA tournament the year I went there in 1941, finishing with a 302. I remember meeting him there. He was forty-two and I was thirty-one years old. I also met Edison Marshall, a former UGA champion, at the UGA National in 1941. Marshall was from Indianapolis, originally from New Orleans, and considered one of the best black golfers in the country during his time, which was from about 1928 up until the early 1940s. I played with him my first 9 holes at the 1941 UGA Open, but play was called off that first day due to a big rainstorm. Some of the other golfers I remember from that tournament included Solomon Hughes, who was UGA champion in 1935 and finished fourth, Hugh Smith, the 1934 UGA champion from Thomaston, Georgia, who finished eighth, and Clyde Martin from Washington, D.C.

I also met John Brooks Dendy from Asheville, North Carolina, the UGA champion in 1936 and 1938. He won in Cleveland, Ohio. By the way, he had a total of 288 on a regulated golf course, which was a good score at that time. I knew Calvin Searles from New Orleans. He was always invited to the Mideast Golf Tournament and the Tam O'Shanter in Chicago every year. I was also invited every year to the Tam O'Shanter, being the pro at the Lincoln Golf and Country Club. I would receive a letter that read "greetings and invitation to the Tam O'Shanter Golf Tournament." But as I said, family and money considerations meant it wasn't possible for me to go. I met Teddy Rhodes during a Southeastern Golf Tournament in the latter part of the 1950s. Teddy was from Nashville, Tennessee, and a teacher of Lee Elder and Cliff Brown, who would later come on the tour.

Contact with White Golfers and Perceptions of Segregation in Golf

During my time they had already ironed out how to deal with contact between blacks and whites. They had made arrangements that it wouldn't happen unless you caddied for them and they invited you to show them how to play in the back of the golf course under the guidance of the club professional. Whites were very precautionary and when integration was allowed it was done gradually. Charlie Sifford was selected first and expected to be humble and to obey their rules. The PGA picked where he could play because they wanted to avoid racial incidents. The words Charlie mentioned to me were "Ralph, every time I get to playing good golf they pull me. I was playing good in Arizona and they told me not to go to Pensacola, neither to New Orleans, but to meet them in Greensboro." So they knew of the situations and they took precaution to keep those things from happening. Therefore, things only flared up on small occasions because they were prepared for what could happen. They didn't want blacks who would cause lawsuits to play in a lot of tournaments. They selected Charlie Sifford because he came along in golf starting as a caddie. Blacks who came up through the caddying ranks knew how to relate to whites. We were obedient and anxious to get the chance knowing what you would have to go through, thinking only that now was the opportunity to make good and not wanting to be the one to spoil it. Whites knew that Charlie could handle himself and that they had made a good selection. They were taking precautions so that the PGA could stay clear of any racial affairs. But some black golfers, like Bill Spiller, couldn't handle it as well as Charlie. Spiller had only started playing golf after he finished college when he was thirty years old. Although he took up golf late, in five years' time he was shooting in the 70s and decided to turn professional. He was a good golfer but couldn't handle the racial pressure like Sifford. Charlie had been playing ever since he was a teenager in Philadelphia where he would go around the city courses, even some that wouldn't allow him to play. Therefore, he had experienced all of that before he went on the pro tour and was able to handle himself successfully. On the tour it would be told that he was riding with white professional golfers and a lot of times he traveled through places where he had to appear as the chauffeur. This hasn't got nothing to do with the PGA, its just during that time this is what he had to go through to make that first year successful. Blacks didn't give him enough credit as they should because of what he had to go through in order to stay clear and to open the door for other blacks. He opened the door and other blacks came in but they couldn't stay in and the competition was so great until they had to turn them away.

One of the reasons that a lot of black golfers didn't move into the professional ranks after Charlie Sifford opened the door to the PGA is because the black golfer was not prepared for it. It came in a way that they had given up hope and weren't prepared for it. The game had gotten sour for most of them. They didn't have enough time to work on the game; they didn't have any training ground and when the time did come where things opened up only a few could get sponsors. And with these few, only about a dozen, the limitations imposed by the PGA called for requirements which made it tougher and tougher to meet every year; not just every year, every three months there were new rules until finally after a few years in order for blacks to make it they had to shoot a new brand of golf and go to school for training in order to come out of this group to be sure that they were prepared for television. So, therefore, because they lacked the resources to pay for the expenses of the schooling and other costs and the sponsorship to support them if they made it to the tour, blacks found other sports rather than pursue golf to make a living. Blacks were discouraged, as they are now, from going out for golf as a professional way of life. So they went into baseball and basketball. Golf is a sport you can't learn to play overnight. You have got to grow up with it from youth. Because of changing conditions there were not many blacks getting into golf in their youth. The caddying days were over with when riding carts came. It was just a matter of a blessing that I came along at the right time when you had the chance to learn. But as the time went on, it got to the place where the competition got keener and my wife and I devoted more time to the children and preparing them for more promising opportunities, encouraging all of them to stay in school with the help of scholarships. My opportunities passed away during the time but I never have regrets of what happened.

Direct and Indirect Experiences of Racial Discrimination in Golf

I remember my friend Sanders Mason began sponsoring golf tournaments around 1934 in Tampa, Florida, in an open field that was made into a 9-hole course. Now it's a city municipal course. He had the forethinking, like I did, that one day we could be recognized by the PGA. He went out to apply to enter the PGA and discovered that there was a Caucasian clause saying that only Caucasians were admitted to the PGA. After Joe Louis became indoctrinated by black golfers, he became a lover of the sport and a golf bug himself. He put up money to support a lawsuit to fight the PGA and lift the ban on black golfers. Joe's influence on PGA president Horton Smith was also a factor. Joe Louis and Horton Smith, who was the 1934 Masters champion, were golf companions and had played together. Black golfers fought for years to lift this ban and finally Horton Smith, being the president of the PGA, promised that it would be lifted.

There was also a long struggle in Jacksonville to desegregate the municipal golf courses. Most of the ones that participated in the fight lost their jobs. Joseph D. Brooks, a graduate of Morehouse College in Atlanta, came to Jacksonville in the 1940s to open the Durkeeville Housing project working for the government. He saw what I was doing in promoting golf and he joined in. Then we began to fight for integration. He lost his government job because he fought so hard for integration of the golf course. He went on to another job and still fought. Then finally there was Frank Hampton who came along at the time that most of the leaders that had fought against segregated golf courses had passed and gone. There were other leaders who had the opportunity to fight but wouldn't because they were doing all right. It took quite a bit of money to fight the case because of lawyers and things. So finally the Lincoln Country Club got together as a body to fight. Money was also brought in by organizations and political leaders in the black community. The suits were successful and the early 1960s was the beginning of the integration of the golf courses and the clubhouse. The Brentwood Golf Course was closed down for one year and finally opened up again as an integrated course.

Everett Payne

Everett Payne was a member of the famed Royal Golf Club of Washington, D.C., and recognized as a pro for many years at the Langston Golf Course. He was a highly successful player, winning the Eastern Golf Association's Pennsylvania Open in 1941 and finishing among the top scorers in UGA National Open and other tournaments throughout the 1940s and 1950s. Although currently unable to play due to physical restrictions, Everett maintains detailed documentation of his accomplishments as well as the achievements of other black golfers of his generation in a scrapbook that is his prized possession.

Earliest Experiences as a Caddie and Beginning Golfer

I first started in golf by caddying, which is the way I learned how to play. I caddied for fifteen years and was very fortunate because I learned to play quickly by caddying for many top-ranked white golfers. For example, I caddied for John Short, who was an intercollegiate golf champ; George Warden, who was ranked number five in the amateurs at that time; Thelma Hawthorne, who was ranked number ten, and others. I also caddied for Tony Sylvester, the pro at the club where I caddied in Glen Echo, Maryland. Sylvester gave golf lessons

Everett Payne

to Tommy Armour, who went on to become one of the great golfers of his generation. I learned how to play by listening and watching Sylvester give lessons and then adopting the style of Armour. Tommy Armour had the smoothest strokes I had seen among the golfers taught by Sylvester. I would listen to literally everything that Tony would tell Tommy and then I watched Tommy swing. I said to myself, now if I'm going to play golf, I'm going to swing like Tommy. I used to watch every move he made. I used to practice that move by swinging the club while I was out there caddying and then when I got a chance to hit the ball, I would do everything that he did. I could not apply what I observed and heard until I got to play on the course on Mondays, which were the only days caddies were officially allowed on the golf course. When I started playing in the tournaments with the other boys who caddied, they use to nickname me the "black" Tommy Armour. The caddies played at the Congressional golf course in Washington, D.C., on Mondays and you learned on your own unless you went to another caddie and he would tell you what you were doing wrong if he was more advanced than you; but the (white) players or club members told you nothing.

When I attended high school I was an all-around athlete lettering in four sports (football, baseball, basketball, and track). Although I was a serious golfer, having been around the game since I was a kid,

I did not participate in golf as a student at Armstrong High School in Washington. Since I had been playing for quite some time while I was in high school, I decided to go out for golf so that I could get a golf letter and become one of the few student athletes who lettered in five sports. I went to the golf coach to ask him about joining the golf team. Mr. Westmoreland was not really a coach but a teacher who played golf and was asked to coach the golf team. He asked me, "Just because you are good in baseball, basketball, football, and track what makes you think you can also play golf?" He did not know that I had been playing golf since I was ten or eleven years old. So I told him the two of us can go out to the golf course and play a match. I challenged him by saying if I win then you let me join the team, but if I lose I'll go away. I played the match against the golf coach and beat him. He was so mad about losing to me, thinking I was this football, baseball, basketball, and track star but nongolfer, that he reneged on his part of the bargain and still didn't let me join the golf team. Therefore, I did not letter in golf as a high school athlete, despite my all around athletic achievements.

Experiences as a Player and Interaction with Other Black Golfers

I played in tournaments along with the other caddies. Although I was poor and never had much in my life, I was also proud. I had a ladies golf bag, an old white bag and an old set of clubs. I bought my golf balls from the other caddies. They were used golf balls. Everything I had was used. I'd been to sixteen or seventeen events and never had a new set of clubs in my life; but I was one of the best golfers in my neighborhood. I'm not going to brag but let you see for yourself. [Everett Payne then handed his scrapbook to the interviewer who read some of the articles that Mr. Payne clipped from newspapers to document his performance in various tournaments he entered during his playing days: The first article pointed out that Payne won the Pennsylvania Open golf honors in Philadelphia. Although he was hampered by an unusual electric storm that made for a slow course, Payne won with a score of 117 at the Cobb's Creek Golf Course against the largest field to play in the East. The scores of Payne, playing as an amateur, were identical to J. Skelton of Philadelphia who won the professional class. The article noted that Payne shot below par for the last two holes to cop the coveted trophy. Another article described Everett Payne's triumph in winning the Washington, D.C., city championship. Noting that a new district amateur golf champion was crowned for the first time in four years, the article describes Everett Payne as a D.C. policeman who defeated three-time champion Leroy Harris. Payne and Harris were even after eighteen holes but Payne

won on the nineteenth hole in a sudden death play-off at Langston
Golf Course. A third article focused on team competition, with Payne
and his partner outshooting their rivals by one stroke in a match
described as one of the most hotly contested tournaments of the season. Everett Payne teamed with William Jones of the Royal Golf Club
of Washington, D.C., to capture the best ball open championship
tournament held by the Carroll Park course under the auspices of the
Monumental Golf Club. Play was for 36 holes, with the victorious
team turning in a count of 135 for the three rounds. The Payne–Jones
duo emerged the victors by the scant margin of a single stroke in
what was described as torrid competition for three teams that were
deadlocked for runner-up honors that were decided on the thirty-
seventh hole."] Everybody tells me I turned pro, but I didn't turn pro.
In one amateur tournament, I remember playing against Joe Louis
and he beat me. He not only beat me but won the medal [lowest
score]. I lost to him in the first round. [Everett Payne again hands his
scrapbook to the interviewer for him to read one of the newspaper
clippings: The headlines read "Louis Ousts Payne in United Golf"
and described how medalist Joe Louis scored a come-from-behind
three-in-one triumph over Everett Payne in the first round of the UGA
annual tournament at East Potomac. The article went into details
pointing out that the "Brown Bomber" was three down to the D.C.
policeman after eight holes but starting at nine, Louis won five
straight holes, the eleventh and thirteenth with birdies. Payne then
halved the next three holes, but Louis's par on the seventeenth ended
it.] There were only a few people who would follow me around in
the galleries, but when Joe Louis played you know it was crowded
then. In the tournaments neither men nor ladies wanted to play with
me because I threw my sticks. When I missed a putt I was supposed
to make, my temper just got the best of me and I threw my sticks.
Sometimes on the edge of the green, if a guy says, hey man, hold my
sticks, I'm not going to because they won't hold mine since they know
I will throw golf sticks around.

    I can recall some of the other golfers of the past, but my memory
is not too good; so if you have a group of the Negro players go ahead
and just call the names out. [Interviewer calls the names of selected
players beginning with John Shippen.] John Shippen was from here
[Washington, D.C.], but he was way ahead of me. I didn't know what
golf was when they were playing. When I started playing I knew
about John Shippen, Beltram Barker, Harry Jackson, and John
Thompson. [Teddy Rhodes] Oh, I played with Teddy, Charlie Sifford,
and Joe Roach. There was also Clyde Martin. See, he was with Joe
Louis. Joe Louis came to Washington and got Clyde to help him with
his game. Clyde did, giving him some lessons, and when Joe left he

took Clyde with him and hired Clyde full-time. Clyde was not from Washington but from Maryland. He lived about walking distance from the Congressional Country Club. Clyde, along with his father and brothers, caddied up there at Congressional. [Howard Wheeler] I played with Howard Wheeler, who was cross-handed. Oh, what a good golfer he was! He was the best one of any of them at that time. There was no question about that. [Charles Sifford] Well, "Horse" was a good golfer too; of course, he was behind those boys. He was just starting out, but he was starting with the pros. [Zeke Hartsfield] He was the same; a good player. [Pat Ball] Oh, Pat Ball is a hero, a stationary name in golf! [John Dendy] I sure have heard of John Dendy, who was a good golfer. When these guys came through Washington, they came up to hustle; some of them came to hustle. They'd beat everybody at playing. Putting up money [betting] is what hustling is about. They made the money for their team. See, it cost to travel and stay in a place for four days; Thursday through Sunday. You had to be there on Tuesday and Wednesday or just Wednesday to play a practice round. So you would be with a team for almost a week. I was a golfer, not a person who bet. I never bragged about it. Some guys would come and they'd play for twenty dollars. I would never play for twenty dollars in my life. Twenty dollars would add up to a whole month; and plus I had four kids, three boys and a girl.

Contact with White Golfers and Perceptions of Segregation in Golf

This white fella came on the green where I was giving a lesson to a white lady. I could tell he didn't like me teaching this lady how to play golf. But I was smart enough to not put my hands on her at all. He said, "What makes you think you know so much about golf?" I had to put on my thinking cap real quick. I said, "Mister, suppose your boss came into your office and asked you to bring a file right away. What would you do?" He said, "I'd get up and go get the file right away." I said, "Well, I'm following orders. These are not my words I'm teaching her. These are the words from the master golfer— Tommy Armour. I have been on the golf course with the master himself giving lessons, you see." I had great tutors. I had caddied for all those guys. All I saw was good golf. I said, "If you worked in the kitchen with all chefs, don't you think you're going to be a good cook?" I said, "If you know something, then you know it. These are not my words at all." That's the part I kept saying. "These are not my words at all. These are Tommy Armour's of the Nationals." You know what? He never did say no more after that.

Direct and Indirect Experiences of Racial Discrimination in Golf

I remember caddying for a fellow who was a club member and played at the club by himself. When we got to know each other, he would say "Come on, Everett, we'll play 'closest to the pin' for a quarter." I said "I don't have no clubs" and he said "Use mine." He opened his bag and handed me a ball and a golf club. He hit his ball first, which landed several feet from the pin and then said, "Everett, bring me a quarter." I laughed and just hit my ball up there near his and it landed in front of his, only three feet from the pin. He laughed and gave me a quarter. So we went through that every day. One day he had a visitor and I was caddying for both of them. When we got to number seven or eight, I don't remember the hole, I was preparing to go in front of them to get ready for their next stroke. The member asked, "Where are you going, Everett?" I said I was going ahead. He said, "Come back so that I can win my quarter." The visiting guy said "You gonna play golf with that nigger?" He didn't answer him but just looked down and then said to me, "Come on, Everett." The visitor asked again, "Are you gonna let that nigger use your clubs?" The regular member then said, "Listen, do you want to play this hole with us? If you don't, then shut up." The visiting guy decided to play but turned to me and said, "You don't know how to play." He then went first hitting his ball well for a good setup about fifteen feet from the cup. Turning to the regular member, he said, "I know you gonna pay a quarter now." That was supposedly a good shot. The regular member hit his ball inside of the other guy's ball about ten feet away. But when I hit my shot, it landed about two feet from the cup, closer than both of them. The regular member turned to the other guy and said, "I told you all along that was going to happen." The visitor didn't open his mouth the rest of the time we were on the course. And, of course, I wouldn't say nothing.

Timothy "Timmy" Thomas

Timothy "Timmy" Thomas was a member of the Royal Golf Club in Washington, D.C., and served as the club's tournament director for over thirty years. He also became heavily involved in the organizational activities of the EGA and the UGA, serving as tournament director for both groups. Although he was regarded as a good golfer, listed among the leaders in the Pittsburgh Courier's *1950 UGA Bulletin Board rankings in the amateur division, Thomas is best known for his organizational work. At the national level, he first assisted UGA tournament director, Mrs. Paris Brown, and eventually served in that ca-*

Timothy Thomas

pacity himself. Timmy Thomas knew and played golf with all the major stars of the Jim Crow era and interacted with them off the course as well. He is regarded as a virtual encyclopedia of knowledge about African Americans in golf and happily shares that knowledge as his contribution to preserving the black golf legacy.

Earliest Experiences as a Caddie and Beginning Golfer

My first experience at caddying came one Saturday morning when Roland Simon, who was the son of a deacon at one of the churches in Danville [Virginia], took me out to caddy at the Danville Golf and Country Club. The bag I carried had to be strapped around my neck twice so that it would be off the ground. I was just that small. I was between nine and ten years old. All the doctors and other people who played were of means because very few people played golf unless they were professionals—doctors, lawyers, or successful businessmen. Only white people played golf at the club because it was all Jim Crow in Danville. All of the caddies were black. The only time you saw a white caddie was with a touring professional who came for an ex-hibition match and would bring his own caddie. They made sure we got good instructions. For example, we were taught to stand so that the shadow from your body would not break across the fellow's putt. These were things that the caddie master was responsible for teaching;

of course, the caddie masters at the clubs where I caddied were white. If a complaint about a caddie related to instructions came in, he had to receive special instructions the next week before being allowed to go back to caddying. Caddies were paid a quarter for 9 holes. Most of us had regular people for whom we caddied. I caddied for Dr. Robinson, one of the outstanding physicians in Danville, who was also a pretty good golfer. It was unknown for black people in Danville to play golf unless you were a caddie. That's where I had my first chance to learn how to play. We were allowed to play at the Danville Club course on Saturday mornings as long as you were off the course by twelve noon. You learned from hitting balls and somewhere during that hitting you hit it right. Once you hit that ball right, it was a feeling you couldn't duplicate. You knew you could probably hit a hundred balls before you hit it right again, but you kept going for that feeling that you got that first time you hit it right. They would give us a caddie tournament at the end of the year. The caddie tournaments were set up by the club pro. At Christmas time we would have the playoffs at a different place. Christmas presents would be given to us and trophies would be passed out to the tournament winners. Christmas presents varied from fifty dollars on down and at that time fifty dollars was a pretty good sum of money. The clubs put up the money by having members contribute whatever they wanted to the till and it was recorded and saved for the Christmas event. I saw guys who would caddy at other clubs but would come to the Danville Club at Christmas time because they would end up with five or six dollars. Caddies would have one of the biggest crap games you've ever seen on Christmas.

The clubhouse was definitely off limits to caddies. We didn't have to go into the clubhouse for anything. We had a place that was sectioned off in the back and a stand with a window where we could go to buy pies, buns, soda water, sandwiches, or things of that sort. You didn't go to the clubhouse for anything unless you went in to carry a golf bag or get a bag out of the locker. The only way you could be in there without carrying a bag was if you'd drop dead in there. But we knew what you could do and what you couldn't do and we didn't have any problem with it. As caddies, you knew how to carry yourself in the proper way. If you were reported as loud, boisterous, cursing, or anything like that, you were sent down the road, no "ifs" and "ands" about it. To come back up that road, you had to get permission from the fellow who was managing the golf course. At the particular golf course where I caddied, the manager was hard on everybody. He would holler the word "nigger" just as if he said good morning. I remember an incident that occurred at the golf course after I started "writing numbers." The numbers racket had just come in to the area and my income from writing numbers was far exceeding what I made at the golf course so I stopped cad- dying. The manager caught me one morning at the golf course writing numbers for caddies and whites too. He said, "You know what, nig- ger, I know what you are doing and it had better stop." I stopped because I knew I needed to caddy, which was the only thing I could legitimately do then. However, I did get a different job at the same place (Danville Golf and Country Club) working in the golf shop. I became one of the first black club makers. Later, I was a club maker for a country club in Arlington, Virginia, one of the biggest in the Washington area.

Experiences as a Player and Interaction with Other Black Golfers

In a typical UGA national tournament during the 1940s and 1950s, the first day was usually devoted to registration and practice. Most of the golfers tried to stay in the hotel where the site of the tourna- ment headquarters was located and where you could find out what different activities would be held the rest of the week. You would go into the dining room and see the different people that you saw there the year before and the year before that; and you felt proud to be there. You didn't have to give prizes for the best dressed because it looked like everybody tried to be the best dressed. I'll never forget this boy from Minneapolis they use to call the mayor of Minneapolis. Some came to have fun and there were a lot of serious people who came to play. We'd send off close to 180 people in the morning and the same in the afternoon. The pros only played in the afternoon; that's when you would find all the guys playing with the celebrities or the guys who were real good golfers, those expected to win. In fact, one of the Mills brothers played every year. We always had some type of celebrities at the nationals. The nightclubs where they were appearing would give you tickets to distribute around the course. It was a picnic atmosphere, but I've seen some good golf come out of that.

[The following impressions of selected golfers were given by Timmy Thomas during the interview]. [Ted Rhodes] i believe that Ted Rhodes could have played with anybody. I've seen Ted Rhodes play every type of shot that could be played. In other words, if you got to slice the ball this way or hook the ball that way he could do it. I look at this kid Tiger Woods, and right now if he continues with the same attitude, he is going to be a standout player. [Clyde Martin] Joe Louis took Clyde Martin away from here, from Baltimore. Well, actually he wasn't in Baltimore. Clyde at that time was in Washington and he left Washington with Joe Louis. Clyde made a big impression on Joe

Louis because I don't believe you have ever seen anybody hit an iron any prettier than Clyde Martin. [Cliff Taylor] He was a hell of a golfer. Cliff won the [UGA] nationals. At that time he was a polished golfer. When he won the nationals, Cliff could beat the average guy who called himself a pro. He played out of one of the New York clubs and was a heck of a player. [Ben Davis] Ben Davis could play and he was a threat any time he went out there to play. He was also sharp because he wore the right clothes. [Harry Jackson and John Shippen] Their names speak for themselves and anything that you hear about them you can bet that most likely it's the truth. Harry was a golfer, you could tell that. But Harry was a gentleman. He was a golfer and a gentleman. [A.D.V. Crosby] Crosby played pro and was on the professional committee, but as far as golf is concerned the pros didn't regard him as a threat. [Joe Roach] I didn't have too much respect for Joe Roach as a player at first because I played him in one of the UGA team matches and was seven down at the turn and took him to the seventeenth hole before he finally beat me. But I found out later that he was an exceptional golfer. He used to be Sugar Ray Robinson's coach. He was Sugar Ray's pro. I remember when Sugar Ray Robinson had this tournament out on Long Island [New York] and Joe finished several strokes behind Ted Rhodes who won the tournament. After that I played him again and found out that I was wrong about him. Joe Roach was a very, very good player. [Gordon Goodson] Gordon always played as an amateur and was one of the best. He played out of Harrisburg, Pennsylvania. I beat Gordon Goodson out there at Swope Park in Kansas City, but of course the ground was just like a brick, hard as rock. You'd hit a ball and it would bounce three or four fairways over. You'd have to be in someone else's territory looking for your ball. [Judson Grant] He's from California. This old man was sixty something years old and participated in championship play. He could hit a ball straight down the fairway 150 yards and bend it either way he wanted. He also had a beautiful short game. I've never seen anybody that was any better. [Joe Louis] We all hustled Joe Louis. At that time money didn't mean nothing to him. I always had a good relationship with Joe because he knew I wasn't going to bet but so much money. I couldn't afford to. I was making a dollar and something an hour and couldn't go out there and bet thirty, forty, or fifty dollars on a match. I'd win two or three bets off Joe and was satisfied.

Contact with White Golfers and Perceptions of Segregation in Golf

The UGA did not have restrictions. Anybody could play in our tournaments if they had a club and paid the entry fee. If you paid the professional fee, you played in the professional division. If you paid the amateur fee, you played in the amateur division. Several white pros would come when regular play of the day was over to play against the top black professionals and you would have a lot of heavy bets out there on the golf course. I remember how Charlie Sifford and Ted Rhodes, two of our outstanding pros, were sitting in the grill with all of us at the UGA nationals one year when these two white boys were also sitting with us. One of them said to Charlie, "I can set them pins tomorrow and I can bet you that you won't break eighty." I wasn't a betting man but when you said Charlie wouldn't break eighty it was like saying there ain't no Lord, there's nobody up there. Well, I couldn't bet like I would have liked to, but I think I bet twenty-five dollars and they covered all the bets. At that time Charlie played a hook and the white guys moved a pin right behind a trap on every green that had a trap. Charlie would try to shoot to bring that hook in there and couldn't do it. In my opinion, Charlie had not perfected every type of shot. He could do it now but at that time Charlie couldn't play the hook. When they put that pin all the way at the end of the green, you had a very small space to shoot before you were dead in the trap. Those white guys knew exactly what they were doing. They beat us so bad I think I lost thirty something dollars because after I lost my twenty-five dollars I had to go back and try to get some of that money back. As far as blacks moving into the professional ranks of the PGA when the color barrier was finally broken by Charlie Sifford, to be frank, we just didn't have any good enough. Howard Wheeler had died. I think Ted Rhodes had passed. Lee Elder was the only one left and he was quite old. The UGA did not produce younger players who were ready to go. You can't win no golf tournaments if you can't get under par. No one seemed to want to put up enough capital to start this thing.

Direct and Indirect Experiences of Racial Discrimination in Golf

We had several little incidents to come up right here in Washington, D.C. They locked the doors on us at the East Potomac Golf Course and we had a free-for-all. The first time they ordered that blacks be allowed to play on any municipal golf course, we went to the East Potomac course. When we would go to these different courses like this we carried enough people with us so that we would have an equal chance with them. We wouldn't go no one or two force but ten or twelve force. That particular day was a little cloudy, but they sold us tickets and we were getting ready to tee off when all of a sudden a big rain squall came up. We rushed to get back in the clubhouse but they had locked the screen door on us. We were pretty belligerent

Clarence Boyce

and someone hit on that screen door and it went flying. We had a real free-for-all down there. I carried marks on my chest as we got to fighting. They called the police, the reserves, and everything else, which didn't stop some of those blows. One of our leaders was Cecil Shamwell, who was a member of the Royal Golf Club and a good golfer. After this incident, Edgar Brown, the husband of Paris Brown, went down there to play. When he tried to tee off they stoned the man off the golf course and he went back to the phone and called Ickes [U.S. Secretary of the Interior who had issued the order to desegregate all municipal golf courses in Washington]. Ickes told him to go back down there and start playing where he stopped and they sent a motorcycle policeman to ride the rest of the holes with him, so he had to have a police escort to ride around the golf course for him to finish playing his eighteen holes. You could easily get hurt if you went down there by yourself.

Clarence Boyce

Clarence Boyce was a member of the Quaker City Golf Club in Philadelphia and actively involved in the early development of the EGA. He played with many of the transplanted southerners like Howard Wheeler and Charlie Sifford and was a close

friend of Frank Gaskin, who won the first UGA National Am-
ateur championship title in 1928.

Earliest Experiences as a Caddie and Beginning Golfer

I can say I started in golf by caddying. I was a caddie at the Philmont Country Club. I was a young kid about twelve or thirteen years
old. That's how I met Frank Gaskin. Frank worked on the golf course
at the White Marsh Country Club. On Mondays they would have
caddies' day, where caddies at different clubs were allowed to play.
He would caddy and help the pros by making and cleaning clubs. Me
and Frank got to be friends as the years passed. Later on, we'd go to
Shady Rest [New Jersey], New York, and all over the rest of the
country. We'd go just to play golf. At the Philmont Country Club,
both white and colored caddies all played on the same golf course on
Mondays. Caddies also included boys around fifteen, sixteen, eighteen, and even twenty years old. If a member of the country club liked
you, he would sometimes loan you the better clubs. You could bor-
row just one club; so you'd go to the golf course swinging one club.
I could do anything with the one club. In those days you had to learn
to hit that ball and that's all you could do. I also caddied during that
time to make a little money to help my family. There were nine of us
in the family. My father worked on the farm. We had a sixty-five
acre farm that we rented. If it hadn't been for the farm, we'd had a
bad day during the Depression here in Pennsylvania. By living on this
farm we had our own vegetables, chickens, and pigs. My aunt from
New York would send down a barrel of flour. We had everything we
wanted during the Depression. However, for his work on the farm in
those days, my father didn't make any money, no more than fifty
dollars a month, which he had to take to the general store. My mother
worked by doing laundry for people to make ends meet. I had to quit
school early, going only to the second year in high school before
getting out to work and help with the family. I was twenty-one years
old and turned all my money in to Pop. He would say "Here," hand-
ing me a dollar, "that's enough for you to throw away." I really didn't
mind. I lived not far from the golf course, which was an adjoining
property to the farm that we rented. The people that we rented from
wanted the Philmont Country Club to buy the property. Since Philmont was on the other side of us, we would sneak onto the course
and play on the back course hitting golf balls when nobody was out
there. That's actually how we got started playing golf. There was also
a field where they played polo, horse polo, at the Philmont Country
Club and the field was leveled off. We would go to the polo field and
hit golf balls when they weren't playing polo. They didn't mind be-

cause I would help them with the horses by bringing the horses up
there for them. Many rich whites played at the Philmont Country
Club. They would have chauffeurs to bring them up so you knew
what car they were coming in and, therefore, waited in the woods
until you saw the car coming and began walking toward the caddy
master who would also know and call out, "Hey Boyce, get 'so-and
so's' bag." That was a five-dollar round, which was a big round in
those days. People wanted the same caddie each time they played.
If you could help them out by telling them which club to use, how
to handle the club, and how to play the hole, they wouldn't forget you.

After my first three or four years of caddying, a fellow named John
McGee, who was one of the old colored golfers, came to the Philmont
Country Club after hearing that there were a lot of caddies who were
good golfers. So, he came up here one day and talked to all of us.
He got three or four of us caddies who were pretty good golfers and
wanted us to go to Cobbs Creek Golf Course and learn to play with
other colored boys out there. We went to Cobbs Creek and all of
those boys could beat us. We had about half a dozen good golfers
who started playing over at Cobbs Creek and they wanted us to join
their club. In those days you had no money to join the club so Mr.
McGee paid our joining fees and then would take us all around from
one course to the other to play golf. We'd put half a dozen guys in
one car and take four or five cars traveling to different places for
team matches. We played on public golf courses in places like Reading, Allentown, and Jersey. We also played at the Shady Rest Country
Club. Anybody who paid the green fee could play there and both
white and colored played, but they had a lot of tournaments there
sponsored by blacks and all of the people from everywhere came to
Shady Rest to play. When I first started playing with the teams I was
about twenty. John McGee liked me quite a lot and after four or five
years, he did everything he could to keep me there to help him with
the younger boys. When I was about twenty-seven or twenty-eight
years old, I got an old piece of car and would help by driving the
younger golfers to Cobbs Creek and other courses to participate in
team matches.

Experiences as a Player and Interaction with Other Black Golfers

All the clubs from the Eastern coalition [EGA] held team matches.
There were about fourteen or fifteen clubs from different states. We
had two clubs from Philadelphia: the Fairview Golf Club and the
Quaker City Golf Club. Once a year we had a tournament. All of
them would come together in one place. We had the A-team, B-team,

and C-team. The A-team was the best, the pros, and had the smallest number of players, about seven, while the B- and C-teams had more men, about nine, ten, or eleven. Just like the nationals, every year the tournament would be played in different places, including Washington, Baltimore, New York, and the Apex Country Club down in Jersey. However, the place where we played the most was Reading [Pennsylvania]. Everybody liked Reading, which is about fifty miles from here [Philadelphia].

I played at Cobbs Creek with Howard Wheeler, Charlie Sifford, and with all the fellows. We all belonged to the Fairview Golf and Country Club and played in team matches. We would also get together and play with each other; like on Thursday most of the fellows would try to be out there in the evening around three or four o'clock and all play skins just to have fun, to play. Howard Wheeler was a tall, slim fellow. He liked to show you different things about how to play golf and was very modest. For example, I took him to Pittsburgh to play in the UGA nationals one year. I said, "Well, Wheeler, what you gonna do?" He said, "Clarence, don't bet on me." I said, "I ain't going to bet; I won't bet too much." So he went out there and won the tournament that year. Teddy Rhodes was out there; Charlie Sifford was out there, and all the rest; and against all of them Wheeler won the national tournament that year and I wouldn't bet on him. He was a good player.

John Shippen and I were good friends. Shippen and my uncle played golf out in Jersey and were good buddies. Every time we'd go out there and play up at Shady Rest, he'd be there always with a smile on his face. He was way older than I was but he could play golf and "clean up." He was the pro at Shady Rest. He tried to play in a white tournament here in Philadelphia. They wouldn't let him play over there. They wouldn't let Shippen or no coloreds play on that course, which was back in early 1925 or 1926. He was a fine gentleman and you loved to play with him because he was a fellow that didn't mind showing you something. Shippen would show you how to play the ball out of traps and everything.

Contact with White Golfers and Perceptions of Segregation in Golf

I worked over fifty years for the family that owned the Pittsburgh Glass Company. There were four sons and I became close to them and the other family members. I'm a couple of years older than the eldest son and he would get me to go out and play golf at the private clubs he belonged to. I could go with him as long as I was his guest. He would say, "Mother, can I have Clarence?" She would say, "What are you going to do, play golf?" He would tell her yes and we'd get in the car and he would take me to these private golf courses. Nobody said nothing. I played with them and I wasn't no caddie! The only colored golfer I knew who got the chance to play at these white private country club golf courses like me was Frank Gaskin. Frank worked as a caddie at the White Marsh Country Club. After people got through playing golf at the club, Frank would help the club pro clean, polish, and buff clubs. Frank and the club pro became good friends. After they put the clubs away, the pro started taking Frank out on the golf course and they would hit balls. Frank hit the ball on the greens like a pro. He was a very good golfer.

Direct and Indirect Experiences of Racial Discrimination in Golf

During the period of the Caucasian clause, we had an awfully hard time playing out there on the main line where all the rich people played. They would tell us that the courses were semiprivate but we tried to find out if we could play out there. I remember me, Frank Gaskin, Bill Crawford, and Ed Brice would go out there to the main line to some of the courses. After arriving at this one golf course we went to the clubhouse where you get the permit and the guy told us we had to go around there to serve dinner or work [thinking we were the waiters]. We said we were there to play golf and the guy told us we couldn't. I went around the clubhouse, found the club pro, and asked him if we could play. He asked, "If you fellows go out there and play, can you break a hundred?" I said, "We can break a hundred all right." He said, "Well, if you go out there and break ninety we'll let you play [again]." I think we all went out there and brought back eighty-four, eighty, eighty-seven, something like that. The pro said, "Well you can come back again." We played two or three times after that. We would try other golf courses in different places. We wanted to "break in" so coloreds could go in there and play. We were not afraid. Sometimes people would pass by in cars and go, "Hey, nigger," or something like that, but out here the cops come quick. In another incident, we were playing on this course and when we reached the number three hole, which you could see from the highway, two white fellows in a car pulled over, parked, and got their [golf] bags and started to tee up there on the number three hole. They tied us up so we could not get off and continue with our round. Frank Gaskin had his ball teed up and ready to play next when this old white guy, who was obviously a cracker from somewhere down South, came up and teed his ball up directly over Frank's ball and started to play. Frank looked at this guy and said, "Where is he going? I know he is not going to tee off there." Frank knocked the guy's ball off the tee and pointing toward the first hole said, "Look, first hole is over there. You're on the third hole." The guy told Frank, "Well, down where I'm from we can play anywhere we want to play." Frank said, "You're not down there, you're up here." I thought the guy was going to hit Frank, but with all these colored guys around I know he wasn't going to hit him.

CONCLUSION

The above interviews illustrate in microscopic detail the themes regarding African American golf we have analyzed in previous chapters. Some of their major points are summarized in Table 7.1. It highlights a number of the following major features:

1. All the interviewees began the sport as caddies, often at a very young age. This experience, particularly opportunities to participate in caddie tournaments, was vital to their learning and practicing the game. As a recruitment vehicle, this role was limited yet important to minority participation. With the invention of the golf cart and the caddy's essential demise, this particular avenue was closed, limiting further African American professional participation.

2. Their golf play with other blacks was frequent and included large numbers of players, stars, and tournaments. In this regard, the UGA and regional associations were particularly important. Again, this serves to correct the distorted image of African Americans as largely uninvolved in the sport.

3. Contact with white players occasionally occurred in more integrated settings such as those in Europe, liberal states, UGA tournaments with white players, and when sponsored by white family employers. However, for the most part, segregation and white discrimination reigned supreme in this activity, as with most others.

4. Finally, players largely experienced white exclusion and resistance to desegregation, on some occasions involving lockouts, overt violence, and need for police protection to implement integrated play. They clearly experienced institutionalized racism in a number of personal, organizational, economic, and physical ways. Whites did not take kindly to black attempts to participate in the sport with them, whether viewed as legitimate or otherwise.

Viewed as a whole, these fascinating interviews illuminate the limited, but important manner in which black golfers began their careers. They also played with significant numbers of other African American participants, many of whom were stars in their own right, in tournaments sponsored and run by their own well-organized associations. Furthermore, a few whites participated in these events and integrated play occurred in Europe and more liberal U.S. states. For the most part, however, whites fiercely resisted formal club desegregation, resorting to violent and extreme mea-

Table 7.1
Interview Summaries

Players	Early Experiences	Interaction With Black Players	Interaction With White Players	Experience of Racial Discrimination
Joe Delancey	caddied at 10 years old, with white and black caddies	black UGA tournaments with extensive play	military experience = played with whites in Europe; played in liberal U.S. states = California, Illinois.	PGA exclusion experience
Ralph Dawkins	caddied at 10 years old for family support money; caddie Monday play; caddie tournaments.	state and own tournaments; Southeast tournament; high number of black players.	black caddie demonstration play for whites; whites selected black caddies; rising PGA requirements.	desegregation battle in Jacksonville; PGA exclusion.
Everett Payne	caddying start; discouraged from high school golf play.	caddie tournaments; black tournament play with black stars.	white resistance to black golfing instruction.	white resistance to black golfing participation.
Timothy Thomas	caddying at 9 years-old; regular caddying for whites; caddie play-offs	UGA tournaments with high numbers of black players	white participation in UGA play.	white lock-outs, violence against black players; need for police escorts.
Clarence Boyce	caddying start; Monday course play; black tournaments.	Eastern Golf Association play; high play with blacks.	played with white employer's son.	white resistance to/interference with black play.

sures on occasion. These results, once again, underline black activity and white resistance in this particular sports arena.

In Part Four of our analysis, we examine the desegregation battle in more detail.

PART FOUR

DESEGREGATION BATTLES

CHAPTER 8

The Push to Desegregate Public Golf Courses

Since racial segregation was a pervasive feature of American society during the Jim Crow era, the fight to eliminate this practice extended to many areas of public life, particularly schools and swimming pools. Whites energetically resisted these attempts. In the case of golf courses, much of the opposition was concentrated in southern cities such as Atlanta, Greensboro, Jacksonville, Miami, Nashville, and New Orleans. However, efforts to restrict public play by blacks also extended to cities in other areas of the country such as Cleveland and Los Angeles (Newby, 1987). Resistance was particularly strong in the period following the landmark 1954 U.S. Supreme Court decision in the case of *Brown v. Board of Education*, as evident in some of the fierce battles addressing the de facto segregation of golf courses. In this chapter, we examine some of the legal battles involved and the consequences of these struggles relating to African American promotion of the sport and removal of further barriers to full black participation.

The legal battle to desegregate public courses occurred from the 1940s through the mid-1960s. However, as early as 1925, the *Baltimore Afro-American* chastised leading black citizens of Washington, D.C., for participating in ceremonies dedicating the black Lincoln Memorial Golf Course while five other local public courses remained segregated. This professional elite was viewed as having willingly adopted "Jim Crow" golf with enthusiasm, sabotaging efforts against other types of discrimination (*Baltimore Afro-American*, June 8, 1925, p. 8).

Outside the Deep South whites maintained racial segregation by building courses designated *exclusively* for African Americans such as the one constructed in Washington, D.C. Under the principle of "separate but equal" that prevailed during the pre-*Brown* period, this response was sufficient to satisfy legal requirements for nondiscrimination despite the clearly unequal facilities involved (McKay, 1954). In the South, whites frequently allocated a period of time (usually one day a week) for exclusive black play rather than building all-black courses. Consequently, white courses remained segregated the rest of the week. This tactic was also used in regions outside the South. After the *Brown* ruling struck down this type of discrimination, blacks continued to experience discriminatory treatment. In response, they accelerated their legal attacks on municipalities that used subterfuge to avoid desegregation. Ironically, these victories produced mixed results: although courses were forcibly opened to minority play, this resulted in a decline of the remaining private black courses and fewer tournaments at most of the previously unaccessible public courses. This was particularly the case in cities like Jacksonville, Florida, which eventually closed its black-owned course (Lincoln Golf Course) after a successful fight to desegregate municipal courses there. Lincoln was once one of the "showcase" courses for black golf tournaments in the South but rapidly declined after the 1961 desegregation victory and was sold to developers who used the land to build homes.

After briefly describing the circumstances surrounding some of the major desegregation cases fought between 1940 and 1960, we shall provide a more detailed examination of two of the cases that eventually reached the U.S. Supreme Court—those filed in Miami and Greensboro.

EARLY CASES

Black legal reactions to the racial segregation of public courses began in the 1940s. One of the earliest occurred in 1942 in Baltimore, Maryland: in *Durkee v. Murphy* (1942), Arnett Murphy sued Baltimore City to remove the limitation of African American players to one city course and admit him to others. A number of appeals and reversals took place, with the case eventually heard by the Maryland Court of Appeals. Background issues included equal protection of the law, segregation under "separate but equal conditions," the city's power to maintain segregation to avoid racial conflict, and the conduct of an earlier judge. The racial history of Baltimore courses involved the alternation of white/black play at specific courses, temporary integration, the negative reaction of white players, and exclusive assignment of one course to African Americans who consequently complained about its inferior facilities relative to white courses. The city argued that provision of an equivalent golf course was not necessary to recreational privileges. The judge emphasized that segregation was normal in this area, was constitutional, need not be relinquished, and might be dealt with by the city in a variety of ways. A new trial was awarded.

An interesting northern case emerged some years later (1947) in connection with the Martha's Vineyard Country Club. Black players were excluded on the grounds that it was a private facility (*Vineyard Gazette*, 1947). Judge Braley, while finding in favor of the defendant, ruled that discrimination had not been proved beyond a reasonable doubt, despite concluding that the course was public rather than private. Interestingly, the defendant's attorney argued that, while discrimination was forbidden by the state prior to 1865, various kinds of racial separation had emerged since that time, depending on the situation involved. This case generally illustrates a differential, situational, legalistic rationalization of continuing segregation, despite previous state laws forbidding it. Although sensitivity to the issue of discrimination was higher, perhaps, than in southern reactions, the legitimation of excluding black golfers, even from public courses, was evident. The North/South distinction is seemingly more apparent than real.

Later that decade in *Law v. Baltimore* (1948), Charles Law sued Baltimore, arguing that equal facilities had not been provided for blacks, as evident in the one of four public courses assigned them. Background issues included civil rights, "separate but equal" facilities, and equal protection of the law. The judge found that the city had made a "good faith" effort to provide adequate facilities for black players, considered the course superior to others in some regards, but concluded that significant inequality in facilities did exist in this case. Nevertheless, he felt the city was not obliged to provide golfing facilities, might discontinue them at any time, and concluded that a "fair solution" could be found in maintaining an exclusively black course by permitting golfers to play elsewhere at restricted hours or on limited days, particularly in view of the very limited numbers of minority players involved. While acknowledging the existence of "separate and unequal," the court allowed the city to maintain and compensate for this arrangement by permitting very restricted black play at white courses. Segregation was maintained and adapted to the "separate but equal" notion in a manner that protected white privileges with minimum inconvenience. Not only is segregation maintained, but the "separate but equal" policy is circumvented.

An interesting exception to this trend occurred the next year in Cleveland, highlighting North/South differences in court reactions. Gillespie and Lucas, officers of the Cleveland NAACP, sued the all-white Lake Shore Golf Club for refusing to admit blacks (*Gillespie v. Lake Shore Golf Club*, 1949). The club responded that, while previously public, the course was leased from a private company by its manager, making it private and open to members only. According to them, race was not an issue. Nonwhites were neither accepted as members nor admitted to play. The judge, however, viewed this "private" arrangement as a "subterfuge" and concluded that the course remained essentially public. Consequently, racial exclusion represented a violation of the "civil rights section of the General Code of Ohio" (*Gillespie v. Lake Shore Golf Club*, 1950). In this particular case, the plaintiffs were victorious. While the circumstances were somewhat unique, the court's decision was clearly significant, given attempts by other municipal courses to avoid integration by leasing their facilities to private companies, thereby making them "private."

The notion that attitudes toward segregation were generally more liberal in the Midwest, however, would be inaccurate. Some 1949 NAACP correspondence, for example, confirms that Kansas City, Missouri, maintained two 18-hole courses, only one of which was available to all players (Carter, R. Letter to D. H. Davis, May 26, 1949). This was implemented despite a lack of official policies requiring racial segregation in public facilities. Clearly, discrimination was maintained through the deception of restricting black players to one of the two courses available. Nevertheless, the Board of Park Commissioners argued they were being "positive" and equitable in their provision of public facilities.

Although southern segregation was adapted to the "separate but equal" principle in a manner that maintained racial inequality, *some* cases in other areas reflected limited victories for black plaintiffs. Others avoided integration by arguing that they were not being deliberately discriminatory, despite maintaining racial separatism. Nevertheless, southern delay and adaptive techniques continued into the 1950s.

PRE-*BROWN* CASES: THE EARLY 1950s

Racial exclusion from Miami's public courses was attacked by Rice in *Rice v. Arnold* during 1950 and 1951. Relevant constitutional issues again included equal protection of the law, the "separate but equal" clause of the Constitution, and differential racial access to facilities. The racial history of the Miami Springs Country Club included segregation, temporary admission of black players, negative white reactions to this event, very small numbers of African American golfers, and a policy limiting minority play to one day a week. Rice's request was initially denied by the Circuit Court, with the state Supreme Court initially affirming that a one-day allotment for black players did not constitute discrimination. An appeal to the U.S. Supreme Court resulted in an order that the case be reconsidered. The Florida Supreme Court concluded that this "one day allotment" did not amount to discrimination and found for the city, affirming the differential play allotment rules based on race, and accepting the defendant's justification of these discriminatory allocations. Accordingly, "separate and unequal" rather than "separate but equal" was reinforced.

A second major case occurred in Houston in *Beal v. Holcombe* (1950). In this action, Beal and others sued the city to play golf on public courses restricted exclusively to whites. In 1950, the U.S. District Court examined

Houston's system of twenty one parks, four of which were reserved for the use of blacks and contained no golf courses. The court emphasized the policy of racial separation and concluded that the city had conformed to the "separate but equal" doctrine despite not providing golfing facilities for blacks. The latter situation was viewed as nondiscriminatory. A year later (1951) the U.S. Court of Appeals reversed this judgment (*Beal v. Holcombe*, 1951), arguing that the above arrangement denying equal access to playing facilities in fact constituted discrimination and must be stopped. However, the city was to be awarded "reasonable opportunity" to conform to the "separate but equal" provision. In all of this, an emphasis on *delayed* "separate but equal" segregation is clearly evident.

Another suit was filed in Nashville a couple of years later (1952)—*Hayes v. Crutcher*—in which the plaintiffs demanded "separate but equal" city golf privileges. The U.S. District Court held that segregation was constitutional in the context of equal facilities "apportioned to need." The judge reaffirmed the "separate but equal" doctrine, rejected the motion for a summary judgment, and concluded that this policy would be implemented by the defendants, based on proof of the extent of demand for black play. He argued that segregation was both constitutional and natural, emphasizing that government and law should not intrude into our private and social "affairs"; instead, we should attempt to effect change through education and "religious inspiration." Segregation was thereby justified on natural, private, and political grounds, to be implemented on the basis of demonstrated demand.

The year 1953 witnessed the beginning of a groundbreaking case in Atlanta. Alfred (Tup), Oliver W., and Dr. Hamilton M. Holmes, along with family friend Charles T. Bell, sued the city for denying them golfing privileges at city courses, all of which were exclusively assigned to white players (*Holmes v. Atlanta*, 1954). The U.S. District Court granted an injunction against their exclusion, arguing that they were denied equal protection of constitutional law, but stressing that the defendants be accorded "reasonable opportunity" to implement the "separate but equal" arrangement fully and fairly. This ruling was further affirmed by the U.S. Court of Appeals (*Holmes v. Atlanta*, 1955), underscoring the importance of ensuring its full and prompt implementation. Once again, the "separate but equal" notion was used to justify the continuation of racial segregation—a decision upheld by an appellate court in New Orleans. Eventually, the case reached the U.S. Supreme Court, which ruled against the city on November 7, 1955. Consequently, the Holmes family players became the first black golfers to play on an Atlanta course that year, the day before Christmas (*Black Enterprise*, 1996). In this case, full integration was achieved after decades of denial and exclusion on a "separate but equal" basis, often implemented in a racist manner. However, this did *not* mean that white attempts to avoid integration had come to an end. The mid-1950s and early 1960s reveal further integration delays and municipal attempts to sell their courses to private organizations to avoid desegregation.

POST-*BROWN* SUITS

In 1957, the city of Portsmouth, Virginia, was sued by a group of blacks who sought an injunction against their exclusion from city recreational facilities on racial grounds, particularly the golf course (*Holley v. Portsmouth*, 1957). The court granted a temporary injunction initially; however, they later denied a permanent injunction, continuing the motion for a year, based on the conclusion that the city was in compliance with the initial ruling and that many of the case's related problems would probably work themselves out over time. The problem of discrimination was acknowledged, yet it was dealt with in a temporary, adaptive manner in favor of the defendants rather than the plaintiffs.

A particularly interesting incident occurred the same year in Greensboro, North Carolina: six African Americans were convicted of criminal trespass for attempting to use the Gillespie Park Golf Course without permission (*Simkins v. Greensboro*, 1957, 1958, 1960). They appealed to the federal district court, which issued a decree against discrimination, a decision affirmed by the Court of Appeals for the Fourth Circuit. The convicted players then appealed to the North Carolina Supreme Court, which again affirmed the anti-discrimination ruling and found that the original warrants were defective. The defendants were then convicted a second time in municipal court. This was affirmed by the superior court and the state supreme court, again ruling against racial discrimination. Finally, an appeal to the U.S. Supreme Court was dismissed based on the argument that the case's issues did not raise any federal questions. Particularly significant here was the *criminalization* of attempted desegregation, despite rulings confirming the latter's illegality, thereby maintaining strict control of the status quo and permitting social change largely through the legal system alone. Despite the *Brown* ruling, attempts to enforce integration were defined as "trespassing" and treated as crimes rather than legitimate social change in light of major court rulings. Consequently, changes in racial policy remained under the control of the white majority. The potentially intimidating effects of such an approach on potential protestors cannot be overestimated.

On a more positive note, in 1957, the Attorney General of Michigan ruled that golf courses that were licensed to sell liquor were essentially "public accommodations" (Kavanagh, 1957). Consequently, they were subject to the Michigan statute prohibiting racial or religious discrimination in such locations. In his opinion, such negative treatment probably warranted license revocation and civil penalties under the law. Interesting here is the emerging view of discriminatory *public* facilities as essentially discriminatory under the law, requiring significant legal action. Disturbing,

however, is the continuing view, implicit or otherwise, that private estab-
lishments have the right to exclude anyone they desire, reaffirming discrimination to a limited degree.

Continuing in this positive direction, in 1958, the U.S. Court of Appeals
affirmed a U.S. District Court's judgment for the plaintiffs in a suit against
the City of New Orleans for denying their use of its park facilities on racial
grounds (*Detiege v. New Orleans*, 1958). Both courts concluded, particularly in light of the *Brown* decision, that racial exclusion from public facilities was erroneous and previous decisions affirming such an arrangement
should be reversed. In this case, at least, implementation of the *Brown*
ruling was clear. However, this was not always the case, as evident in
municipal avoidance of integration through the sale of their courses. This
occurred both in Fort Lauderdale and Jacksonville. In the former case,
black plaintiffs sued in county circuit court to prevent the city from selling
its course to a private association (*Griffis v. Fort Lauderdale*, 1958). The
court denied an injunction and this decision was upheld by the state supreme court, which ruled the city could sell its property, given its evident
adherence to proper procedures. In Jacksonville, blacks filed a federal class
action suit against the city's policy of excluding them from its two golf
courses (*Hampton v. Jacksonville*, 1959, 1961). The court supported their
case and ruled against these discriminatory policies. The city then closed
these facilities, arguing that integration would severely reduce revenues,
making them impossible to operate. Suits were consequently filed in circuit
and district courts, seeking injunctions against the city's attempts to sell
these facilities. The courts decided against the plaintiffs, affirming the city's
right to sell, despite a price lower than appraised value, and gave the new
private owners the right to "undisturbed" use and possession. Both major
cities were thereby permitted to avoid integrating their courses by selling
them to private parties. Clearly, power of ownership surmounted the public's right to unrestricted use of taxpayer-funded facilities.

Court-sanctioned delay is again evident in 1960 in Charleston, South
Carolina. In this case, the court ruled for the plaintiffs in their suit against
a segregated municipal course (*Cummings v. Charleston*, 1960), but
granted the city an eight-month delay in light of difficulties in adjusting to
an integrated facility. In contrast, the California Attorney General the same
year notified municipalities that the PGA's racial membership restriction
precluded all state agencies from cooperating with such an association or
any of its members (Mosk, 1960). He particularly emphasized that the state
is determined to do whatever it can to bring an end to such discrimination.

In the early 1960s, a strong stand against discriminatory golf courses
was also taken by Colorado. Reacting to the exclusion of a black judge
from a state golf tournament, the Denver Commission of Community Relations urged a city policy of nondiscrimination relating to facility access
and golf tournaments. Later, the Denver City Council adopted a policy

forbidding city tournament permits being granted to groups with discriminatory practices (Denver City Council, 1961). Reacting to the exclusion of four blacks from a private course open to public play in 1962, the Colorado Anti-Discrimination Commission ruled that this was a violation of state law and must stop (Colorado Anti-Discrimination Commission, 1962). Clearly, reaction to discrimination in this state was firm and generally consistent in these cases.

Undue optimism on this matter, however, would be premature: as late as 1969, several African Americans were denied admission to a tournament held on a municipal course in Savannah, Georgia, and brought suit in federal district court seeking relief in the matter (*Wesley v. Savannah*, 1969). Although the course had been desegregated in 1961, a private association limited to white members held a city tournament each year. The court ruled that private organizations may hold discriminatory events but not at a public facility and found for the plaintiffs. Even in the late 1960s, public facilities were being used for private, racially exclusive events, requiring court intervention to ensure desegregation but in a manner affirming the right to discrimination on private locations.

The years immediately following the *Brown* decision consequently involved avoidance tactics such as temporary rather than permanent anti-discriminatory injunctions, arrest of African Americans who attempted to play on white courses as trespassers, approved city sales of courses to avoid integration, court-sanctioned delays in implementing desegregation, and attempts to maintain private discrimination on public facilities. While some nonsouthern cities rejected discrimination outright, the former's racist tradition was extremely slow to change, involving a variety of avoidance and delay tactics in the wake of the Supreme Court decision. We turn to examine two such cases in greater detail.

TWO CASE STUDIES: MIAMI AND GREENSBORO

Miami

African American golfers in Miami became involved in the first golf course discrimination case to reach the U.S. Supreme Court. The suit galvanized the entire black community, including civil rights groups, churches, and other social and civic organizations. The fight had an inauspicious beginning as Joseph Rice, an ex-caddie, along with a small group of black golfers, went to the Miami Springs Municipal Golf Course demanding the right to play. The management, taken by surprise, called the city manager asking what they should do. The city manager, H. H. Arnold, was instructed to tell the delegation they could not play that day because they did not have the proper equipment. The delegation returned another day suitably equipped and began using the course. However, this privilege was only temporary because the city enacted a rule restricting black play to Mondays only, while white golfers were allotted the rest of the week (*Miami Times*, September 30, 1950, p. 17). Challenging this rule, a lawsuit was filed in the local Circuit Court on April 24, 1949, by Rice as plaintiff and Arnold as the defendant (*Miami Times*, October 21, 1950, p. 1). *Rice v. Arnold* represented more than a fight by a black golfer to win the right to use this public course—the case mobilized blacks to fight a highly visible symbol of white control and domination in which blacks customarily occupied subservient roles such as caddie and porter. The *Rice* case promoted greater involvement in golf by blacks in Miami generally.

Rice was represented by G. E. Graves and John Johnson, local NAACP attorneys, while the city's lawyers included John W. Watson, Jr., and John D. Marsh. The Cosmopolitan Golf Association, a newly established black golf club organized to assist Rice in his lawsuit, also supported the suit. After the Dade County Circuit Court ruled that restricting black play to one day a week did not constitute discrimination (*Miami Times*, April 1, 1950, p. 1), the black community vowed to fight to the highest court in the land if necessary. The next step involved the Florida Supreme Court. Graves and Johnson requested unlimited use of the course, arguing that the time set aside for members of their race was not adequate and that Monday was the most undesirable day of the week for golf. Watson and Marsh countered that if the city opened the course to blacks seven days a week it would have to close because of lack of funds (*Miami Times*, February 18, 1950, p. 1). The Supreme Court of Florida agreed and upheld the lower court's decision by ruling that the restricted use of the golf facility based on physical and social differences was justified under the principle of "separate but equal" since total black revenues were insufficient to support the links (*Miami Times*, April 1, 1950, p. 1). The court's decision was strongly influenced by a test week of unrestricted black play, with fifty-two the highest number playing on any one day. The city was willing to permit more black play if numbers increased enough to warrant it (*Miami Times*, April 1, 1950, p. 1).

After the ruling, the Cosmopolitan Association, which had supported Rice and other black golfers from the outset, mobilized the black community to raise funds for an appeal to the U.S. Supreme Court, and encouraged play at the Miami Springs course to challenge the claim that one day a week was sufficient to meet their needs. The association included many of Miami's black community's leading citizens. A legal redress committee was appointed by the president, Bernard O'Dell, and was chaired by Elmer Ward, apparently the real force behind the association's success in mobilizing community action. He personally paid the costs for the original filing of the suit and lent his organizing skills and contacts to the organization. Women were also prominently involved: Mitzi Coleman and Maria Mackey co-chaired the benefit dance committee and Ann Lindsey, a wealthy socialite, became actively involved in fund-raising efforts. Successful businessmen such as Garth Reeves and Jack O'Dell also led the drive to raise funds. Rice's attorneys received very little for their legal services and had already expended approximately $700 in court costs and travel. Since they required an additional $2,000 in court costs, the association appealed to other organizations to donate at least $100 or more toward this important cause (*Miami Times*, September 30, 1950, p. 17). Activities designed to enlist financial contributions and introduce golf to the local black citizenry were also held. These included a benefit dance, with all asked to purchase a ticket, whether or not they planned to attend (*Miami Times*, July 22, 1950, p. 15). The regular appearance of "golf news" items in the local black newspaper also encouraged golfing, particularly among out-of-town guests, teachers, and local high schools (*Miami Times*, June 17, 1950, p. 5). Advertisements for golf equipment also began to appear in the local black newspaper (see, e.g., *Miami Times*, March 11, 1950, p. 2).

The *Rice v. Arnold* case reached the U.S. Supreme Court in October 1951. By that time the justices had already ruled on two 1950 cases (*Sweatt v. Painter* and *McLaurin v. Oklahoma State Regents*) involving segregation of law schools in Texas and Oklahoma. In the Sweatt decision the Supreme Court ruled that a new state law school for blacks, created to avoid integration of the all-white law school, could not be regarded as equal to the white school since it lacked the prestige and tradition that took time to develop. In the *McLaurin* decision, the Supreme Court ruled that a graduate school that segregated black students in the classroom, library, or cafeteria denied their right to an equal education (Levine, 1996). Under these principles, the states were required to provide facilities to both racial groups with no restrictions on either. It did not make illegal the "separate but equal" doctrine, but it made it almost impossible. Based on these rulings, the U.S. Supreme Court ordered the *Rice* case back to the Florida courts for action. Black Miamians expected that, in light of these actions, the Florida Supreme Court would force the city to give Negroes full use of the Miami Springs Club (*Miami Times*, October 28, 1950, p. 10). However, to their astonishment the court stood by its previous ruling, maintaining that segregation did not violate the constitutional rights of African Americans under the existing principle of "separate but equal." This opinion was based on the assumption that since its previous ruling on the *Rice* case had not been reversed by the U.S. Supreme Court, Miami had a right to enforce racial segregation. This decision highlighted the difference between educational and golf course facilities, facilitating an argument that was to be employed extensively but unsuccessfully later in the 1950s. In the Texas and Oklahoma university cases (i.e., *Sweatt* and *McLaurin*), the benefits of debate and discussion with other students were taken into consideration. In contrast, on a golf course there is little contact among players except by group members and no clear benefit in clubhouse meetings. Accordingly, the actual facilities offered to Negroes on the golf course were deemed to be precisely equal (*Miami Times*, September 8, 1951, p. 1). Black golfers and civil rights advocates felt betrayed by the U.S. Supreme Court, which they expected to extend desegregation to recreational as well as educational facilities. Nevertheless, they vowed to continue the fight. Attorneys Graves and Johnson immediately petitioned the Florida Supreme Court for a rehearing, vowing to go back to the U.S. Supreme Court if necessary. Their interpretation was based on the assumption that since the high court did not rule that Miami was right in its discriminatory practices and cited the rulings in the *Sweatt* and *McLaurin* cases in sending the *Rice* case back, the State Supreme Court of Florida would not repeat its earlier ruling. However, despite some justices supporting a hearing of the case, the Supreme Court refused to review the Florida Supreme Court decision that upheld limited black play (*Miami Times*, March 8, 1952, p. 1).

This was a blow to many black golfers, especially those who had supported the *Rice* suit through the Cosmopolitan Golf Association. However, black leaders vowed to continue the fight and the fund-raising. Former heavyweight champion Joe Louis was invited to Miami to address members of the Cosmopolitan Golf Association and expressed his desire to help the local organization press for equal golfing rights (*Miami Times*, May 5, 1952, p. 4). In addition, growing golfing enthusiasm did not decline: in 1953, Thomas Graham, Jr., a local black golfer, became the first African American to compete in a Miami qualifying contest for the national public links golf championship. His entry marked the first time in Florida's history that a Negro had competed in the sectional qualifying for such a championship (*Miami Times*, July 11, 1953, p. 1).

By 1954, the optimism of Miami's black golfers was renewed by the U.S. Supreme Court's decision in the *Brown v. Board of Education of Topeka* ruling that the principle of "separate but equal" was unconstitutional, thus striking down practices such as the city's exclusionary public golf course policy. However, this optimism was premature as the city joined a "massive resistance" response among southern cities and states who defied any attempt to change prevailing segregation practices. Despite the valiant 1949 lawsuit, black golfers did not achieve their goal until 1957, when the city gave up the kinds of delaying tactics typical of post-*Brown* responses to court-ordered desegregation of public facilities. Those included the following: (1) leasing golf courses to private individuals and groups who operated them as "nonpublic" facilities to avoid desegregation; (2) arresting blacks who attempted to play at traditionally segregated courses, treating these "trespassers" as law-violating criminals who should be prosecuted, (3) closing all public facilities rather than permitting blacks to play; and (4) requesting additional time for the gradual implementation of desegregation. The determination of Miami's African American golfers to seek legal redress of discrimination during the pre-*Brown* period inspired blacks in other cities to fight these kinds of resistance. Another notable case that captured considerable attention occurred in the city of Greensboro, North Carolina.

Greensboro

In 1940, the city of Greensboro, North Carolina, constructed a golf course in cooperation with the Works Progress Administration (WPA), one of President Roosevelt's New Deal programs. The federal government provided 65 percent of the construction cost of this course that was to be opened as a public facility on land originally owned by the school board (the Gillespie school property) and leased to the city at a modest cost. Between 1941 and 1949, the course was operated directly by the city as a public facility exclusively for whites until blacks demanded their right to use the course and were formally denied by a resolution of the Greensboro City Commission. However, at the urging of Negro citizens and in an effort to comply with the "separate but equal" doctrine, the city agreed to build a golf course for blacks. The resolution also expressed the opinion that it would be in the best interest of the city to discontinue operating the municipal golf course directly and lease it to a private golf club. In 1949, the city of Greensboro leased the course to the Gillespie Park Golf Club, a nonprofit corporation, which continued to operate it on a segregated basis. The following year (1950), a 9-hole course, known as Nocho Park Golf Course, was constructed for blacks. The Gillespie Park course was expanded to 18 holes and provided vastly superior facilities to the Nocho Park course. The typical separate and unequal accommodations in the facilitation of public golf in Greensboro was, nevertheless, an improvement over the pre-1950s when African Americans had no access to golf courses in the city of Greensboro.

In 1955, during the post-*Brown* climate of challenges to segregation by African Americans, six black citizens, led by Dr. George Simkins, a prominent dentist and community activist, decided to challenge the city council's segregation rule by going to the Gillespie Park course to play (Dr. George Simkins Papers, 1998). On December 7, 1955, the same week the Montgomery bus boycott was launched following Rosa Park's bold defiance of Montgomery's bus segregation ordinance, he and others went to the Gillespie Park course where they presented green fees but were not given permission to play. They were told they could not do so because the Gillespie Park Golf Course was a private course for members of the Gillespie Park Golf Club and their guests only. Instead of leaving, each of the men placed seventy-five cents (green fee) on the counter and proceeded to the course after insisting on their right to play. When they reached the third hole, the manager came out and ordered them to leave. They refused and said they would continue to play unless an officer arrested them. The manager swore out warrants and later that night the men were arrested and charged with trespassing. In January 1956, the six men were tried and convicted on February 6, 1956, of simple trespass on the property of the Gillespie Park Golf Course and fined fifteen dollars and court costs. They appealed to the Superior Court; a technical dispute arose and was resolved by permitting the original warrants to be amended so as to charge the trespass as having been committed on the property of "Gillespie Park Golf Club, Inc." instead of "Gillespie Park Golf Course" as formerly charged. The golfers were then tried by a jury in the Superior Court that returned a guilty verdict in December 1956. The men appealed to the North Carolina State Supreme Court, which found a "fatal variance" between the actual name of the corporation (Gillespie Park Golf Club) and the name that appeared on the arrest warrants when they were issued (Gillespie Park Golf Course). Therefore, in June 1957, the convictions in the criminal trespass charges were thrown out by the North Carolina State Supreme Court.

In October 1956, while this criminal trespass case was still in process, Dr. Simkins filed a suit in federal court (U.S. District Court for the Middle District of North Carolina) against the City of Greensboro and the School Board for racial discrimination in attempting to maintain the public golf course for white citizens only. This case (*Simkins et al. v. Greensboro*) was a class action suit with Simkins, who was president of the local chapter of the NAACP, joined by nine others, including the five black golfers who had accompanied him to the Gillespie course in 1955, and members of the delegation of blacks who initially requested the city council to open the course to blacks in 1949. This case was different from similar suits in cities such as Atlanta (*Holmes v. Atlanta*) and Portsmouth (*Holley v. Portsmouth*), where whites leased public courses to private clubs, in that the city of Greensboro contended the lease agreement existed *before* the suit was brought. The city argued that the lease was not entered into for the purpose of denying blacks the right to play in defiance of the *Brown* decision but was a long-standing, valid lease under North Carolina law and could not be invalidated by the courts. On March 20, 1957, the judge ruled in favor of Simkins, issuing an opinion that the city of Greensboro, as the course owner, by leasing it could not escape its legal duties to provide equal privileges to all citizens to enjoy city functions (*Greensboro Record*, March 21, 1957, p. A8). The case was immediately appealed to the Circuit Court of Appeals for the Fourth Circuit. On June 28, 1957, the appeals court affirmed the earlier decision and the city was ordered to discontinue operating the facility on a segregated basis.

The city continued to discourage African Americans from playing golf at the course by permanently closing it. Shortly after the appeals court ruling in June, a mysterious fire severely damaged the clubhouse facility and the course was temporarily closed due to the damage. During the next month and a half, the City Council debated whether the city's interests would be best served by reopening the golf course or permanently closing it. On August 20, 1957, by a unanimous vote, a resolution was passed by the council to close the Gillespie Park Course, citing lack of operating funds. The official position of the council was that the city could not afford to spend money on golf course improvements without jeopardizing other recreation projects (*Greensboro Record*, August 20, 1957, p. B12). However, it was clear that the council's resolution revolved around the recent judicial decisions, as individuals and groups attending the meeting spoke for or against the resolution: one white resident of the Gillespie Park neighborhood who supported closing the course objected to black children running through that area, while a prominent black minister objected that the resolution represented a "step backward" during an era of interracial progress (*Greensboro Daily News*, August 20, 1957, p. B2).

Another tactic involved reopening the criminal charges against Dr. Simkins and the other arrested golfers. On December 2, 1957, almost two years after the black golfers were first arrested and six months after the State Supreme Court set aside the trespass convictions, the golfers were again indicted on new warrants issued by the Greensboro Municipal-County Court on criminal trespass charges. They were found guilty in Municipal Court and appealed to the Superior Court of Guilford County where on February 3, 1958, they were once again found guilty. They appealed to the State Supreme Court, which this time found no error in the lower court decision and, therefore, let the convictions stand. The black golfers were convinced that the city's intention in reopening the case was to discourage other African Americans from attempting to integrate public facilities despite the illegality of segregation. These convictions also presented an interesting legal dilemma since Simkins and the other golfers were convicted in 1958 of actions that were clearly lawful (i.e., playing golf on a public golf course), upheld by the State Supreme Court in 1957, and for which other blacks who took the same course of action in 1958 could not be arrested. As president of the local chapter of the NAACP and a veteran fighter in other cases involving civil rights violations in Greensboro, Simkins appealed to the U.S. Supreme Court. After reviewing the case in 1959, the U.S. Supreme Court decided to let the lower court convictions stand, declining to hear the case on the grounds that no federal question was at issue. Although this represented a victory for the city, it was purely symbolic since it could no longer deny blacks equal recreational privileges. The governor of North Carolina eventually commuted the group's thirty-day sentence.

CONCLUSION

This chapter has delineated the manner in which blacks have consistently opposed their exclusion, restricted access, lack of facilities, and discrimi-

Table 8.1
Selected Golf Course Court Desegregation Decisions

Year	Location	Ruling
Early Cases		
1942	Baltimore	Segregation is normal and city can deal with it in its own way
1947	Martha's Vineyard	Discrimination not proved beyond a reasonable doubt
1948	Baltimore	Maintain black courses and restricted black hours on white courses
1949	Cleveland	Course not private and cannot discriminate
Pre-Brown Cases		
1950	Miami	Differential play hours based on race not viewed as discrimination
1950	Houston	Given "reasonable opportunity" to conform to "separate but equal"
1952	Nashville	"Separate but equal" based on demand for black play affirmed
1954	Atlanta	Initially "separate but equal" ruling but full integration finally effected
Post-Brown Situations		
1957	Portsmouth	Temporary but no permanent injunction against racial exclusion
1957	Greensboro	Black trespassing convictions affirmed at every level
1957	Detroit	Courses with liquor licenses are public and cannot discriminate
1958	New Orleans	Racial exclusion from public facilities is illegal
1958	Fort Lauderdale	City sale of course to private association is approved
1959	Jacksonville	City sale of courses to private associations is approved
1960	Charleston	Granted delay to implement desegregation
1960	Berkeley	State restriction against cooperating with discriminatory PGA
1961	Denver	Policy of non-discrimination in all public facilities
1962	Colorado	Racial exclusion from private course open to public is forbidden
1969	Savannah	Discriminatory tournaments forbidden on public courses

natory treatment by golf courses controlled and operated by whites, from the 1940s through the present. In response, whites consistently opposed these efforts at integration, proceeding through a number of distinct historical and legal stages: in the 1940s, courts viewed segregation as constitutional and normal, implementing the "separate but equal" doctrine in a manner that largely maintained racial inequality. During the early 1950s, this doctrine continued to dominate decisions, permitting blacks restricted access to courses but on a very limited basis, supposedly based on their very limited interest and numbers of players. Remarkable during this period was the 1955 U.S. Supreme Court decision integrating Atlanta public courses. Third, rulings during the late 1950s and after the *Brown* decision reveal delays, trespass arrests, and court-approved sales of city courses, permitting whites to avoid racial integration completely. Only during the 1960s were rulings more consistently integrationist and even then whites attempted to continue private discrimination on public courses. White resistance ranged from attempted segregation, through the unequal enforcement of the "separate but equal" doctrine and tactics designed to deliberately avoid integration, to the recent and more consistent enforcement of integrated public facilities but with continuing private resistance. These historical stages are summarized in Table 8.1 and it is evident that early rulings largely affirmed the normality of segregation, moving through pre-*Brown* cases emphasizing the maintenance of the "separate but equal" doctrine, to post-*Brown* situations in the 1950s and 1960s, indicating a

gradual shift toward policies of full nondiscrimination in the case of public facilities—decisions avoided in some cities through the sale of public
courses to private concerns. These reactions vividly illustrate the continuing
and devious operation of *institutionalized racism* (cf. Kinloch, 1974): restricted access, unequal resources under segregation, differential activities
by race (e.g., exclusion from professional tournaments), and stereotypes
rationalizing such discrimination (e.g., low numbers of black players, lack
of play as indicating low interest in the sport). The lengths to which whites
will go to avoid integration is also remarkable, highlighting their fear and
rejection of social contact with minorities and desire to protect their soci-
ocultural homogeneity. Furthermore, although significant integration of
public facilities has occurred, economic inequities continue to restrict the
degree to which minorities can afford to join country clubs and/or play on
courses, both public and private, with increasingly high green fees. Golf is
a particularly expensive sport, accentuating the interactive effects of both
race and class on integration in this particular social arena. African American players may also choose to play on courses previously designed for or
assigned to their exclusive use and more part of their neighborhoods, reinforcing the continuing trends of the past. Whites may choose to play these
courses also, but de facto segregation largely continues in such contexts,
despite the history of public desegregation.

CHAPTER 9

Barrier Breakers and White Resistance

Throughout its history, golf, with its country club atmosphere and often secluded golf courses, physically and socially removed from the life experiences of most African Americans, has maintained its white elitist image. Despite this, the game permeated the black community during the Jim Crow era, first, through the introduction of black youth to the sport by caddying for whites at exclusive country clubs and later through the attraction of the black elite to golf as they established their own organizations and activities.

African American golfers who aspired to play at the professional level, however, found that channels of participation and mobility open to whites were closed to them. They were relegated instead to playing primarily in settings and tournaments that they established. Meanwhile, the PGA became the major organization that conferred professional status on white pros and provided prize money at tournaments that it co-sponsored. As the PGA developed, career-minded golfers had little hope of earning a living from the sport without access to its lucrative tournaments and other opportunities associated with PGA affiliation. The PGA maintained a racially exclusionary posture from its inception in 1916 throughout its early history. In 1943, the PGA amended its constitution to institute a formal policy of excluding "non-Caucasians" from becoming members. This amendment, Section 1, Article III, which became known as the "Caucasian only" clause, limited membership to "Professional golfers of the Caucasian Race, over the age of eighteen years, residing in North or South America" (PGA Constitution, 1948).

In this chapter, we examine the circumstances and actors involved in forcing the removal of the "Caucasian only" clause from the PGA constitution in 1961 along with the major sources of white resistance that continued after its eradication.

CHALLENGES TO THE PGA

Although black players fought unsuccessfully during the 1940s for termination of this clause, the PGA maintained its policy of restricting membership to whites only. However, the assault on the PGA's restrictive policy gained momentum during the late 1940s and early 1950s. A suit was brought against the organization in 1948 by black golfers Ted Rhodes, Bill Spiller, and Madison Gunter, who were excluded from playing in the PGA-backed Richmond (California) Open. The suit was settled out of court, with the organization promising to review its policy of racial bias. Although the PGA did not discuss or take any action removing the clause as promised, the attention generated by the case made the issue more widely recognized during a time when other major sports were experiencing racial breakthroughs.

Four years later, in 1952, the PGA policy of excluding black golfers from its co-sponsored tournaments was again targeted by black golfers as Joe Louis, Bill Spiller, and Eural Clark attempted and were denied entry to the annual San Diego Open Tournament. Under severe public criticism and pressure, the PGA relented by permitting Louis to play in the tournament under a special provision used to enter him as an amateur. However, although professional golfer Bill Spiller successfully completed a qualifying round (Clark was unsuccessful), he was not permitted to play because the PGA refused to grant a waiver of its racially restrictive policy. As the first black golfer to play in a PGA-sponsored tournament, Joe Louis's participation in the San Diego Open was hailed as a significant breakthrough. On the other hand, the decision to deny entry to Spiller as a professional because he was not a PGA member suggested that the PGA did not want to appear to be giving in to pressure to remove its racially restrictive policy. As in 1948, the PGA promised to review the policy at its 1952 annual meeting with an eye toward its removal. Since it appeared that the organization was heading toward a repeat of its inaction of 1948 on this matter, public reaction remained highly critical, pressuring the PGA tournament committee into devising a plan for incorporating black golfers into its activities in some form. In response to continuing social pressure, a plan was created that allowed black golfers to play in selected PGA tour events beginning in 1952. As discussed in greater detail in Chapter 5, the somewhat controversial idea of forming a committee of players, led by Joe Louis, Bill Spiller, Ted Rhodes, Eural Clark, and Howard Wheeler, to screen African Americans for possible participation in selected PGA tournaments produced a mixed response, with many observers remaining highly critical because the PGA was able to respond to criticism without actually removing the "Caucasian only" clause. Nevertheless, it represented a significant breakthrough in terms of African American participation in PGA events. As a result, for the first time invitations were to be extended to a limited number of black pro golfers to enter selected PGA tournaments, provided that local sponsors agreed and the golfers successfully competed in qualifying rounds. Beginning in 1952, black players entered a selected number of tournaments on the PGA tour with hopes of widening their participation in the years to come. However, white resistance to their attaining full PGA membership continued to be strong, even after segregation became a major target of national focus in the civil rights movement, beginning in the mid-1950s. Because the PGA, as a private organization, was largely unaffected by the 1954 U.S. Supreme Court ruling in the *Brown* decision that prohibited segregation in public accommodations, the "Caucasian only" clause could not be targeted directly for legal attack by civil rights advocates. Consequently, institutionalized racism continued to prevent full participation by African Americans in PGA activities. In addition, the experiences of the few black golfers who managed to persist on the tour during the 1950s, often facing white hostility and financial strain, further reflected the nonreceptive posture of the organization toward them.

Only a few Jim Crow era players could muster the resources and endurance needed to seek entry to the selected PGA events made available for possible participation during the 1950s. Successful participants included Ted Rhodes, Howard Wheeler, Zeke Hartsfield, and a few others who were well past their prime. Charlie Sifford, who was in his early thirties, stands out as the most persistent applicant and participant. Since he emerged in the 1950s as the dominant player among black golfers, winning six UGA national championships between 1952 and 1961, his performance in predominantly white tournaments was closely followed by the black press and he became the hope of a small pool of black golfers with aspirations of one day entering the PGA tournament circuit. His autobiography (Sifford, 1992) provides details of his experiences and the persistence of his efforts to enter and successfully perform in PGA-sponsored tournaments during this period. However, his role as "trailblazer" should be placed in the larger context of the struggle of black golfers throughout the Jim Crow period to compete in the sport on an equal basis. His efforts during the late 1950s represented the final assault on the "Caucasian only" clause and a significant pursuit of social justice during the larger civil rights movement that was sweeping the South. Sifford was a central figure in removing the "Caucasian only" clause from the PGA constitution in 1961 but, along with the few black golfers who proceeded him in gaining PGA membership, he faced additional obstacles to full participation in the white golf world. Eradication of the "Caucasian only" clause was more symbolic than real, as formal nonracial barriers and a racial climate that fostered exclusion remained. Despite making progress toward gaining access to tournaments on the PGA tour after 1961, black golfers continued to face institutionalized barriers that ensured that no significant increase in the numbers of blacks joining the ranks of the PGA would occur for the foreseeable future.

Before turning to the final assault on the PGA's controversial discriminatory policy, we will first briefly discuss selected racial breakthroughs in golf made by blacks who were trailblazers before Charlie Sifford's encounter with the PGA.

EARLIER RACIAL BREAKTHROUGHS

At various times in the history of golf in the United States, African American golfers gained entry to white golfing circles, sometimes in the face of white resistance and at other times by invitation. John Shippen's participation in selected USGA tournaments in the earliest years of that organization's history between 1896 and 1913 initially met with objections from white entrants but was allowed to proceed without incident. However, despite being recognized by Graffis (1975) and others as one of American golf's pioneering personalities, he neither became a PGA member when it was organized in 1916 nor was invited to participate in its activities in later years. Similarly, Robert "Pat" Ball sought to participate in public links tournaments in Chicago when they were first held in the early 1920s and originally encountered resistance from whites. By the end of the 1920s and early 1930s, however, he had broken through the racial barrier to play in several of these events and actually became a winner of Chicago's public links tournament (Cook County Open) in the late 1920s. However, when he attempted to enter the national public links tournament in Philadelphia in 1932, he was refused entry but was successful in gaining tournament admission by winning an injunction in Common Pleas Court (Afro-American Historical and Cultural Museum, Philadelphia, 1996).

Another significant breakthrough involved the invitation extended to black golfers to play in the All American and World Championship tournaments at the Tam O'Shanter Golf and Country Club organized by its flamboyant president, George May. These tournaments, first played during World War II, provided one of the few settings during the 1940s and 1950s in which the relatively few black golfers who entered had the opportunity to compete directly with some of the best white players in the country. However, these events and their carnival-like atmosphere were not regarded as mainstream and, therefore, did not open avenues for black golfers to be accepted in more established circles of white golf tournaments. Not until the major challenge led by Joe Louis and Bill Spiller at the San Diego Open, as discussed earlier, did African American golfers break through the PGA barrier, achieving a limited victory whereby a few blacks could be "invited" to play in PGA-co-sponsored tournaments provided that other "conditions" were met. Nevertheless, this small triumph led to the emergence of a small cadre of black golfers, headed by Charlie Sifford and Ted Rhodes, who persistently attempted to enter PGA tournaments and earn a living playing professional golf, despite barriers that made it difficult to accomplish either. Although these players continued to participate in black-sponsored events, by the late 1950s Charlie Sifford emerged as the lone representative and holdover of past generations of top Jim Crow era black golfers who persistently pursued the goal of playing professional golf.

THE FINAL ASSAULT ON THE "CAUCASIAN ONLY" CLAUSE AND ITS AFTERMATH

The circumstances surrounding the decision by the PGA to erase the "Caucasian only" clause from its constitution reflects the lengths to which whites will go to maintain racist practices even in the face of considerable pressure. In this regard, Charlie Sifford can be accorded the status of pioneering trailblazer who paved the way for others by overcoming seemingly insurmountable obstacles and continuing resistance *after* the initial breakthrough. In actuality, the trail he paved amounted to a narrow path that only a handful of black golfers from the ranks of professionals on the UGA "tour" were prepared to follow, leading Sifford to reject characterizations of him as the "Jackie Robinson of golf," a label often applied without an informed understanding of the lack of parallel circumstances in the cases of professional golf and major league baseball. In 1959, the PGA granted him the status of "approved tournament player" following social and legal pressure. The latter mounted as his performance at predominantly white tournaments gained public notice. His first-place finish at the Long Beach (California) Open in 1957 earned him the distinction of being the first African American golfer to win a predominantly white tournament (Ashe, 1988b). By comparison, the major sports of baseball, football, and basketball were experiencing considerable increases in the number of black players at the professional level throughout the 1950s, while professional golf was a lone exception to this trend. In his autobiography (Sifford, 1992), he attributed the beginning of the national awareness of his "cause" to the first black major league baseball player, Jackie Robinson, who devoted his column in the *New York Post* to criticizing sponsors of white tournaments for failure to invite black golfers and the PGA specifically for barring him from PGA membership. Legal pressure was also applied at this time by California attorney general Stanley Mosk, who wrote a letter of inquiry to the PGA in 1959 asking them to verify that they practiced open discrimination in their membership bylaws and also questioned Sifford's exclusion from the PGA tour (Sifford, 1992). Mosk's inquiry was responded to by the PGA in the form of an offer to Sifford in December

1959 to join the PGA tour in 1960 as an "approved tournament player."
This offer was hailed by many as a major victory. However, although he
could now officially play on the PGA tour, he was not a full-fledged member of the organization. The "approved tournament player" status could
be perceived, nevertheless, as the first stage of an alternative route leading
to full membership that a number of eventually well-established white PGA
pros took to gaining full membership status; the most frequent route to
PGA membership required serving a period of five years as a pro or assistant pro at a recognized club. However, at its 1960 meeting in November,
the same year Sifford joined the tour as an approved tournament player,
the organization voted to retain the "Caucasian only" clause. He had been
granted invitations to participate in twenty PGA tournaments in 1960. Despite granting him "approved tournament player status," the 1960 decision
to retain the "Caucasian clause" made it clear that the PGA did not intend
to open an avenue for Sifford and other black golfers to become full members. Instead, the organization appeared to be attempting to avoid immediately addressing the issue of its racially restrictive constitution. This
strategy of permitting black golfers access to the PGA tour on a limited
basis, while continuing to ban them from full membership, may have been
intended to avoid public criticism of the organization, but it did not end
further legal threats applied by Mosk, who issued a further warning to the
organization immediately after its decision to retain the "Caucasian only"
clause. Even though this private organization could legally include a restrictive racial clause in its membership criteria, the use of public facilities
by a private organization that was openly discriminatory remained open to
challenge. At least eight tournaments on the PGA circuit were played in
California in 1961, most of them scheduled for public courses. As Attorney
General of California, Mosk not only issued a warning to the PGA that it
would not be allowed to hold its tournaments in the state, but also urged
attorneys general in other states to take similar action (Barkow, 1974). This
pressure meant that the PGA would risk losing millions of dollars derived
from their co-sponsored events in California as well as other states that
decided to take similar action (Barkow, 1974). In light of the legal pressure
led by Mosk and mounting social pressure from the National Association
for the Advancement of Colored People (NAACP) and others, the PGA
Executive Committee at its Mid-Year Meeting in May 1961 passed a resolution voting unanimously to recommend elimination of the "Caucasian
only" clause from the PGA constitution (*Professional Golfer*, July 1961).
A vote of the delegates at the annual meeting in November was still required before removal of the clause could take effect. However, the an-
nouncement of the Executive Committee's action at the mid-year meeting
was an immediate response to the continuing pressure on the organization.
This was the first time in its history that an Executive Committee resolution
to amend its constitution was not kept confidential until the delegates voted

to approve it (*Professional Golfer*, July 1961). The full delegation voting at the November 1961 PGA annual meeting at the Diplomat East Hotel in Hollywood, Florida, unanimously approved the amendment to eliminate the "Caucasian only" clause. There were actually two amendments to membership requirements: the first eliminated the clause "of the Caucasian race" and the second amended the clause "residing in North or South America" (*Professional Golfer*, January 1962). Membership would now be open to "Professional golfers over the age of 18 years, who can qualify under the terms and conditions hereinafter specified . . ." (PGA Constitution, 1962). Accordingly, African Americans became *eligible* for full membership in the PGA. However, the "terms and conditions" that had to be met before full membership could be attained were more difficult for them compared to their white counterparts coming through the approved tournament player route. A five-year apprenticeship rule during which time a player seeking full membership had to play in a minimum of twenty-five PGA tournaments each year, along with other requirements, presented a major challenge to black players given continuing racial exclusion in the sport, especially in the South where black participants had traditionally been distinctly unwelcome at most of the PGA tournaments on the tour. Consequently, Sifford and those black golfers who immediately followed him in pursuing full PGA membership—Richard Thomas, Pete Brown, Rafe Botts, and Lee Elder—faced an uphill battle, even after the elimination of the "Caucasian only" clause in 1961. As the first African American to play on the full PGA tour, he described the experience as only the beginning of the struggle for the black man in golf and "one of the most frightening and dangerous things [he had] ever faced" (Sifford, 1992). His graphic and detailed accounts of the financial, emotional, and sometimes overtly racist hardships he encountered during the apprenticeship period leading to full PGA membership in 1964 were termed "bitter memories" (*Golf*, June 1992), which seemed to suggest that these thoughts were buried in the past. However, the decades following Sifford's historic PGA breakthrough saw only a limited number of black golfers move into the professional ranks and entry to many previously all-white settings, including the prestigious Master's tournament, which continued to be the source of racial controversy.

CONCLUSION

This chapter has focused on actions taken to eliminate the long-standing operation of institutionalized racism in golf, symbolized by the so-called "Caucasian only" clause that the PGA inserted in its constitution as a membership requirement. Although the organization was racially exclusionary from its inception in 1916, the constitutional amendment that created the whites-only clause in 1943 formalized the practice of regarding non-

Table 9.1
Selected Racial Breakthroughs in Golf in the United States, 1896–1997

Year	Breakthrough
1896	John Shippen plays in the second USGA national championship tournament over the initial objections of a delegation of white entrants.
1932	Robert "Pat" Ball files motion and is granted court injunction to play in Philadelphia public links tournament.
1937	Pennsylvania Open is first interracial tournament sponsored by a private organization (Eastern Golf Association).
1938	Pat Ball is appointed golf pro at a public course (Palos Park in Chicago).
1942	Black golfers invited to play in interracial Tam O'Shanter All-American and World Championship tournaments in Chicago.
1952	Joe Louis plays (as amateur) in a PGA sponsored tournament (San Diego Open).
1957	Charles Sifford wins predominantly white Long Beach Open tournament.
1959	Charles Sifford is granted "approved tournament player" status by the PGA.
1961	PGA deletes "Caucasian only" clause from its constitution.
1964	Charles Sifford is granted "full membership" status by the PGA.
1967	Charles Sifford wins PGA-sponsored tournament (Hartford Open).
1975	Lee Elder plays in the Masters tournament.
1997	Tiger Woods wins the Masters tournament.

Caucasians unfit for participation in PGA sponsored tournaments and other membership privileges. The final assault on the PGA "Caucasian only" clause in the late 1950s is better understood in the context of the larger struggle by African American golfers to break through barriers that existed throughout the history of golf in America. Table 9.1 summarizes a century (1896–1997) of racial breakthroughs in the sport, focusing on periods of open resistance to black participation in the sport (i.e., the Jim Crow era) and after this era, highlighting the long road to full PGA membership in the 1960s and later. As we can clearly see, each specific victory was limited, intermittent, and long in coming to pass. Although institutional barriers were targeted by black golfers who sought access *to the golf course*, they also represented white resistance to black involvement *off the course*, requiring battles waged against many private golf clubs that, until as recently as 1990, restricted membership to whites only. If there are "bitter memories" for Jim Crow era black golfers who attempted to play on the PGA tour, they are as equally enduring as the "long memories" of the PGA's restrictive policies.

We turn to draw some general conclusions regarding black golf and white resistance in the final chapter.

PART FIVE

CONCLUSIONS

CHAPTER 10

Black Golf and White Racism

This work represents a study of institutionalized discrimination as it occurred in the case of black golf, particularly during the United States's Jim Crow era. In our opening discussion, we emphasized that sports represent social dramas in which all aspects of society (i.e., its roles, norms, intergroup dynamics, organizational elements, institutional arrangements, social problems, types of inequality, and social change) are "played out" in a manner that reflects power arrangements in the larger social situation. These kinds of activity are important indices of social relations in the broader contexts in which they occur. Furthermore, golf tends to be an elitist, individualistic, and community-based type of activity, taking place in relatively isolated country-club settings with typically restrictive, "members-only" admission rules. These kinds of locales often involve other kinds of social facilities, including swimming pools, banquet rooms, and opportunities for formal rituals such as weddings, all of which have traditionally functioned in a highly segregated manner. Consequently, although this sport may appear to be of limited social significance, it clearly reflects broader race relations in microscopic detail. Such a case study offers potentially relevant insight into the changing dynamics of majority discrimination and minority reaction over time.

This book has revealed a number of major features of black golf during this highly segregated period of U.S. history: the caddie role largely assigned to African American players; their use of this position, in some cases, to become professionals; black elite sponsorship of the sport, enabling participation by individuals from a broad range of socioeconomic backgrounds;

African American organization of the game in the form of the UGA as a major response to white exclusion from the PGA; black sponsors of the sport who organized tournaments and fought segregation, exemplified by Joe Louis; the large number of African American players and tournaments that resulted from this kind of individual and organizational sponsorship; their lifelong experiences; a wide range of legal cases in which African American players challenged their exclusion from the game in the courts; and players such as Charlie Sifford who took a major part in attempts to integrate professional tournaments. These details clearly reveal the extremely widespread, continuous, and active response of black golfers and communities to the kinds of white exclusion, segregation, discrimination, and resistance they experienced over time. As a result, we are offered detailed insight into the changing dynamics of institutionalized racism over time, proceeding through a number of stages in white/black race relations as indicated in this case.

GOLF AND INSTITUTIONALIZED RACISM

This project has clearly revealed a number of stages in white reactions to black golf over time, ranging from outright exclusion, through restricted, subordinate roles, segregation, discrimination, and varying levels and types of resistance to restricted levels of integration. Black players, in turn, have proceeded from participating in their own activities, through limited golfing roles, black sponsorship and organization of the sport, and desegregation lawsuits to limited professional play in the face of continuing white resistance. These major phases in race relations may be delineated as six stages, as outlined in Table 10.1. Stage 1 represents total white *exclusion* of black golfers, with the latter participating in their own activities. The next stage involved *limited minority roles*, in which blacks were permitted to serve white players as caddies, greenkeepers, or pro-shop attendants. Although some used these eventually as routes to professional play, these options were designed to be both subordinate and restrictive. The next stage comprised *enforced segregation* in the context of these subordinate roles, with African American elites sponsoring black players and organizing their own tournaments. Formal *discrimination*, or stage 4, included the "Caucasian only" PGA clause, continuing segregation and subordinate minority roles, along with black establishment of their own golfing organizations (the UGA), and organization of tournaments with significant numbers of black players and emerging stars. *Desegregation battles* predominated next, involving large numbers of black lawsuits seeking equal access to courses and eventually the PGA. Whites resisted integration fiercely, proceeding through the maintenance of segregation, "separate-but-equal" interpretations of the U.S. Constitution, closing their own facilities or leasing them to private organizations, in some cases, to limited public integration combined with

Table 10.1
Race Relations Stages in the Case of Golf

Stages	White Racism	Black Golf
(1) Total Exclusion	Complete exclusion of blacks from white sports	Own activities and sports
(2) Limited Minority Roles	Controlled, limited minority roles	Caddies, greenkeepers, pro-shop attendants
(3) Enforced Segregation	Segregation combined with limited minority roles	Parallel structures: black sponsorship by elites and sports figures
(4) Discrimination	Discrimination: "Caucasian only" PGA clause; continuing segregation and limited minority roles	Organization of UGA, high number of black tournaments, players, and stars
(5) Desegregation Battles	White resistance stages: segregation; "separate but equal"; limited public integration; maintenance of private exclusion	Black lawsuits from the 1940s through the 1960s, suing for integration and equal access to courses and eventually the PGA
(6) Limited Integration	Continuing white resistance in the form of PGA eligibility rules, professional /amateur distinctions, negative effects of declining caddy numbers	Continuing sensitivity to private exclusion, limited social and professional integration Continue to experience white prejudice

the maintenance of exclusion from private courses and tournaments. Recent trends have seen continuing white resistance in the form of highly demanding PGA eligibility criteria, along with the maintenance of professional/amateur distinctions in "resolving" discrimination suits. Blacks, in turn, have continued to experience white prejudice, private exclusion, and very *limited* professional *integration*, with racial incidents on the golf course continuing to occur from time to time. Notable throughout these stages is the high level of black golf activity on *every* level: individual, group, community, and national. African American players were highly involved as workers, players, organizers, sponsors, litigants, and, eventually, professional participants. Whites, on the other hand, worked incessantly to exclude, control, segregate, and discriminate against potential African American participants, either through the courts or their own professional organization, the PGA. From this it is clear that white (institutionalized) racism, in the case of golf, primarily consisted of total exclusion, limited minority roles, segregation, discrimination, resistance to attempted integration, and professional elaboration designed to maintain exclusion. Blacks, on the other hand, were active in their own sports, used their limited golfing roles to achieve professional status, developed their own professional organizations and activities, played extremely well in extensive numbers, occasionally against whites, and attacked discrimination in the courts for many decades. Accordingly, *white resistance* and *black activity* have tended to typify American race relations in the case of twentieth-century golf.

What kinds of conclusions do these trends cause us to draw regarding race relations in this society?

CONCLUSIONS

A number of specific conclusions arise from this study, as follows.

1. Previous studies have tended to neglect or underestimate the significance and extent of black golfing activity at both individual and organizational levels. The data reported throughout this book highlight the large numbers of very successful players and tournaments held constantly during the Jim Crow era. Furthermore, black athletes, in some cases, were professionally successful in more than one sport (e.g., Joe Louis). Also, as is often the case with majority perspectives on minority situations, such neglect may reflect limited, biased views of the latter, defining them as passive and relatively unsuccessful when, in fact, the opposite is actually the case.

2. The above trends also underscore white racism's tenacious attempts to maintain itself in the face of minority challenges: from complete exclusion, through controlled exploitation, segregation, organized discrimination, avoidance, resistance, and professional elaboration, their attempts to maintain racial dominance were varied but clear. Although these techniques may involve force, separation, differential legal interpretations, facility closures, professional modifications, and maintenance of private exclusion, they were *all* designed to protect white privilege in this exclusive-type context.

3. White racism, in this multifaceted reaction to black challenge, attempts to maintain racial dominance at all costs. Its overt policies, forms, modifications, and guises may change over time, but its power position remains relatively stable as the white majority adapts to changing minority reactions to discrimination. Particularly noteworthy are attempts to elaborate and modify eligibility criteria for professional membership and play, reflecting increasingly sophisticated methods of exclusion in the "private" sphere. Such elite adaptations in the colonial context are typical: in the face of subordinate minority nationalism, colonial elites tend to modify their racial rationales in more "acceptable" terms in the face of economic and social change, but in a manner that ensures their continuing dominance of the

situation (cf. Kinloch, 1974). Consequently, what may *appear* to be significant social change may instead represent a form of elite adaptation to a situation's dynamics, resulting in the modified, maintenance of the status quo but in less apparently offensive ways. *Actual* social change may require a great deal more modifications, particularly in power arrangements.

What kinds of implications do these conclusions hold both academically and policywise?

IMPLICATIONS

These conclusions bear a number of specific implications, as follows.

1. First, the relative neglect and/or inaccurate portrayal of minority responses to majority discrimination continue to require much greater attention in the academic world. Far too often, minorities are depicted as largely passive, dependent, or underactive in their reaction to the prejudices, exploitation, and subordination of others. Black golfers have often been ignored, underemphasized, neglected, or represented in inaccurate ways in contrast to their historical reality. Although perhaps symptomatic of institutionalized racism in the academic world, it is vital that such a deficiency is corrected for the sake of intellectual and social integrity.

2. Second, this study highlights the need to expand the analysis of institutionalized racism to take account of its elaborate, multilevel, and dynamic nature, particularly reflected in the dynamics of social change as racial elites adapt to change in a manner that ensures their continuing dominance. Obviously, policies aimed at reducing discrimination and increasing integration to date have been relatively ineffective in ensuring racial equality in the sports world and elsewhere. Much more detailed understanding of the multidimensionality of modern racism is required to ensure its effective demise. Although not a particularly fashionable approach, this framework remains potentially relevant to effecting meaningful social change.

3. Third, this case study accentuates the crucial nature of the continuing private/public distinction made with respect to desegregation and policies relating to racial equality generally. Private groups and organizations may be given the "right" to use their facilities any way they please, including in an exclusionary, discriminatory fashion, yet such a policy only helps maintain modern institutionalized racism, whatever "progress" might be accomplished in the public sphere. When applied to professional organizations, the private/public line becomes blurred and requires clarification in a manner that ensures "equal opportunity under the law." The "private club exemption" also tends to perpetuate social and economic discrimination, subjecting minorities to continuing stereotyping and financial disadvantages, highlighting its *public* impact far beyond the *private* rights of its practitioners (Shropshire, 1996). Consequently, its legal protection needs to be curtailed; although such a view may be unpopular in the context of

current constitutional initiatives reversing policies such as "affirmative action," this should not deter its broader implementation. Otherwise, majority blindness to the enduring and crucial nature of social inequality will continue with damaging and potentially destructive consequences for all involved. While golf may appear to be of relatively minor significance in this regard, this study of the sport has revealed a number of major issues posed by its history. Consequently, what may appear to be a "game" has more serious implications for society generally.

4. Fourth, the insights into the past that this case study provides will be useful in guiding efforts currently under way to facilitate the entry of minorities in golf. For example, by establishing that, contrary to popularly held notions, blacks have a long history (as players) in the sport of golf, programs designed to attract inner-city youth should draw on these historical role models to supplement the images of successful recent black golf stars (e.g., Tiger Woods) that are expected to generate greater minority interest and participation.

5. Fifth, a major impetus for this study was the desire to document life "behind the veil" among African Americans in the United States during the Jim Crow period. This study makes a contribution to an emerging body of literature revealing the richness of experiences of many ordinary black people during segregation whose life stories have often been untold despite the enormous insight they provide into the dynamics of race relations during the Jim Crow period. However, this study falls far short of the thorough and detailed work that remains in documenting, through historical biography, sociological analysis, and other means, the experiences of blacks in golf during the Jim Crow era. We hope that this study will stimulate further research, especially that focusing on biographies of past black "stars" and "rank-and-file" golfers, detailed examination of the UGA, analysis of the role and impact of African American women on the development of black golf, and case studies of notable black-owned, private golf courses.

6. Finally, given its long history of institutionalized racism, golf in America has been successful in creating a public impression that until fairly recent times African Americans neither sought nor achieved notable successes as players. This case study reveals that, in response to exclusion, African Americans successfully created their own golfing activities and despite tremendous white resistance black golfers were sometimes able to demonstrate their effectiveness in interracial golf settings. A recognition of some of the most notable Jim Crow era golfers by the World Golf Hall of Fame would provide an important indicator of the progress and sincerity of such organizations as the PGA, which has assumed a leading role in promoting minority inclusion in a number of its current programs. A model for such inclusion has been provided by baseball's Hall of Fame, which created a category for recognizing the achievements of black players of the Negro baseball leagues, who toiled in relative obscurity during the period (pre-1947) before Jackie Robinson broke through the racial barrier in that sport.

References

Adams, G., Letter to UGA members, October 1, 1945.

African American Historical and Cultural Museum. 1996. Healing the mind and body: The African American sports tradition in Philadelphia, 1890–1970 [Museum exhibit]. Philadelphia, PA.

Alliss, P. & Hobbs, M. 1986. *Peter Alliss's supreme champions of golf.* New York: Scribners & Sons.

Andrews, P. 1991. "Links with history." *American Heritage* (April): 53–63.

Ashe, A.R., Jr. 1988a. *A hard road to glory: A history of the African American athlete, 1919–1945.* New York: Warner Books.

———. 1988b. *A hard road to glory: A history of the African American athlete since 1946.* New York: Warner Books.

Atlanta Daily World. 1934. "Country club to end membership drive." August 12, p. 5.

———. 1934. "National meet eyed by Atlanta golfers." August 19, p. 5.

———. 1934. "Hartsfield features spectacular playing." August 21, p. 5.

———. 1941. "Hartsfield, Searles tie for second place in Louis $1,500 golf tournament." August 15.

———. 1941. "National golf tourney delayed by rainstorm." August 20, p. 5.

———. 1941. "Hartsfield third in national open." August 23, p. 5.

Baltimore Afro-American. 1925. "Two golf clubs in Washington." June 8, p. 8.

———. 1925. "Harry Jackson is leading golfer." July 18, p. 6.

———. 1926. "Golf championship to be held Labor Day at Stow." May 22, p. 8.

———. 1941. "1,000 for pro golf champ, Louis donates prize to winner of tournament." March 15, p. 21.

———. 1941. "Wilson tops field with 222 at Pittsburgh." July 12, p. 21.

———. 1941. "$500 prize big magnet in Louis golf tourney." August 2, p. 21.

———. 1941. "157 caddies signed for Louis open." August 2, p. 21.

———. 1941. "Meddlers make golf costly on district course." August 9, p. 21.

———. 1941. "Two birdies paved way for victor." August 23, p. 22.

———. 1941. "Ex-D.C. pro shoots 292 for $500 prize." August 23, p. 22.

Barkow, A. 1974. *Golf's golden grind, the history of the tour.* New York: Harcourt Brace Jovanovich.

———. 1989. *The history of the PGA tour.* New York: Doubleday.

Beal v. Holcombe, 103 F. Supp. 218, 219 (S.D. Tex. 1950).

Beal v. Holcombe, 193 F.2d 384, 387 (5th Cir. 1951).

Bivens, S. & W. M. Leonard, II. 1994. "Race, centrality, and educational attainment: An NFL perspective." *Journal of Sport Behavior* 17:24–42.

Black Enterprise. 1996. "Breaking par against racism: Holmes vs. Atlanta." September, vol. 27, p. 104.

———. 1997. "Remembering the old UGA tour." September, p. 138.

Blackwell, J. E. 1991. *The Black community: Diversity and unity.* New York: HarperCollins.

Bluford, F. D. Library, North Carolina A & T University. 1998. The Papers of Dr. George Simkins. Greensboro, NC.

Braddock, J. H., II. 1989. "Sports and race relations in American society." *Sociological Spectrum* 9:53–76.

Capeci, D. J., Jr. & M. Wilkerson. 1983. "Multifarious hero: Joe Louis, American society and race relations during world crisis, 1935–1945." *Journal of Sport History* 10:5–25.

Captain, G. 1991. "Enter ladies and gentlemen of color: gender, sport, and the ideal of African American manhood and womanhood during the late nineteenth and early twentieth centuries." *Journal of Sport History* 18:81–102.

Carolina Times. 1937. "Joe Louis winner: Brown bomber scores knockout in 8th to win championship." June 26, p. 1.

Chicago Defender. 1921. "Golf—by E. L. Renip." April 16, p. 10.

———. 1992. "National golf tournament in Chicago during September." August 19, p. 10.

———. 1926. "Windy city golf assn. Is bent on bringing national championship to Chicago." August 28, p. 6.

———. 1926. "Washington man wins the national golf championship." September 11, p. 8.

———. 1928. "Porter Washington wins national golf championship." September 8, p. 7.

———. 1928. "Dawkins wins Florida golf title; Griffin tops Netters." September 22, p. 10.

———. 1931. "How to play golf." June 4, p. 9.

———. 1931. "Nation's golf stars eye Chicago." August 22, p. 11.

———. 1931. "Edison Marshall, golf champ, here September 5th for meet." August 29, p. 9.

———. 1931. "Chicago welcomes golf kings." September 5, p. 8.

———. 1931. "Marshall drubs Ball at golf." September 12, p. 8.

———. 1931. "Marshall and Ball match all even." September 19, p. 8.

———. 1936. "Dendy and Miss Williams win golf titles." September 5, p. 13.

———. 1941. "Boston ready for national golf championships." August 9, p. 21.

———. 1941. "Clyde Martin wins Joe Louis open tourney." August 23, p. 25.

————. 1941a. "The Pat Balls cop two golf championships, a double win for Chicago." August 30, p. 20.

————. 1941b. "The Pat Balls cop two golf championships, Pat wins title for 4th time." August 30, pp. 20–21.

————. 1947. "Joe Louis wins eastern amateur golf tournament." August 16, p. 11.

————. 1950. "Golfers expect Charles Sifford, Bill Spiller to grab 1950 titles." June 17, p. 14.

————. 1950. "Joe captures amateur title in Ohio meet." July 15, p. 14.

————. 1950. "Joe Louis wins central states amateur crown." July 29, p. 14.

————. 1950. "Ted Rhodes favored to win Louis tourney." August 12, p. 13.

————. 1950. "Joe kayoed in his meet when he fires 79." August 19, p. 13.

————. 1950. "Ted Rhodes reign in Joe Louis tourney broken." August 26, p. 15.

————. 1950. "Joe fails in comeback, Ezz keeps crown." September 30, p. 16.

————. 1951. "Expect big entry for central states tourney." June 30, p. 12.

————. 1951. "Wheeler winner of Louis open." August 4, p. 36.

————. 1951. "Joe Louis wins UGA amateur golf title." September 8, p. 11.

————. 1952. "How Louis upset PGA race barrier." January 26, p. 10.

————. 1952. "Rhodes, Roach win titles." August 23, p. 14.

————. 1952. "Texas tourney offers $1,500 to pros." August 30, p. 14.

Chronicle of Higher Education. 1995. "An oral history of Jim Crow: Researchers document the lives of black people in the segregated South." August 18.

Coakley, J. J. 1990. *Sport in society: Issues and controversies.* St. Louis: Times Mirror/Mosby College Publishing.

Colorado Anti-Discrimination Commission, January 31, 1962, No. A-34.

Cummings v. City of Charleston et al. 7048 (DC 1960).

Dawkins, M. P. 1996. "African American golfers in the age of Jim Crow." *Western Journal of Black Studies* 20:39–47.

Denver City Council, Ordinance No. 316, November 30, 1961.

Detiege v. New Orleans City Park Improvement Association. 252 F2d 122 (CA. 1958).

Duberman, M. B. 1988. *Paul Robeson.* New York: Alfred A. Knopf.

Durkee v. Murphy, Maryland Court of Appeals, December 8, 1942.

Editors of *Golf* Magazine. 1970. *America's golf book.* New York: Scribners & Sons.

Edwards, H. 1969. *The revolt of the black athlete.* New York: Free Press.

Eisen, G. & D. K. Wiggens (eds.). 1994. *Ethnicity and sport in North American history and culture.* Westport, CT: Greenwood Press.

Eitzen, D. S. & G. H. Sage. 1986. *Sociology of North American sport.* Dubuque IA: W. C. Brown Publishers.

Florida Star. 1959. "Golf pioneer honored." September 5, p. 7.

Frazier, E. F. 1962. *Black bourgeoisie: The rise of a new middle class in the United States.* New York: Free Press.

Gems, G. R. 1995. "Blocked shot: The development of basketball in the African-American community of Chicago." *Journal of Sport History* 22:135–149.

Gillespie v. Lake Shore Golf Club, Ohio Court of Appeals, #21568, January 23, 1950.

Gillespie v. Lake Shore Golf Club, Ohio Court of Common Pleas, #594–299, February 21, 1949.

Gilmore, A. 1995. "Black athletes in an historical context: The issue of race." *Negro History Bulletin* 58:7–14.

———. 1975. *Bad nigger! The national impact of Jack Johnson.* Port Washington, New York: Kennikat Press.

Golf Magazine. 1992. "Bitter memories: Excerpts from *Just Let Me Play*." June 1992, pp. 106–107.

Graffis, H. 1975. *The PGA: The official history of the Professional Golfers' Association of America.* New York: Crowell.

Greensboro Daily News. 1957. "City golf course ordered closed permanently." August 20, p. B2.

Greensboro Record. 1957. "Integration appears likely for gillespie park golf course." March 21, p. A8.

———. 1957. "Permanent closing is decreed for gillespie park golf course." August 20, p. B12.

Griffis v. City of Fort Lauderdale et al., Supreme Court of Florida, 104 So.2d 33, June 18, 1958.

Grimsley, W. 1996. *Golf, its history, people & events.* Englewood Cliffs, New Jersey: Prentice-Hall.

Hampton v. City of Jacksonville, U.S. District Court, #4073-Civil-J, April 1, 1959.

Hampton v. City of Jacksonville, U.S. District Court, #4073-Civil-J, June 22, 1961.

Hatfield, D. 1996. "The Jack Nicklaus syndrome." *The Humanist* 56:38–39.

Hauser, T. 1991. *Muhammad Ali, his life and times.* New York: (Touchstone) Simon & Schuster.

Hawkins, J. E. 1994. *History of the southern intercollegiate athletic conference 1913–1990.* Butler, GA: Bennis Printing Co.

Hayes v. City of Nashville, U.S. District Court, #1344-Civ, November 21, 1952.

Holley v. City of Portsmouth, U.S. District Court, 150 F.Supp.6, April 10, 1957.

Holmes v. City of Atlanta, U.S. Court of Appeals, 223 F.2d. 93, June 17, 1955.

Holmes v. City of Atlanta, U.S. District Court, 124 F.Supp.290, July 8, 1954.

Jable, J. T. 1994. "Sport in Philadelphia's African-American community, 1865–1900." In Eisen, G. & D.K. Wiggins (eds.), *Ethnicity and sport in North American history and culture.* Westport, CT: Greenwood Press: 157–176.

Jaher, F. C. 1985. "White America views Jack Johnson, Joe Louis, and Muhammad Ali." In Spivey, D. (ed.), *Sport in America: New historical perspectives.* Westport, CT: Greenwood Press: 145–192.

Jordan, W. D. & L. F. Litwack. 1987. *The United States.* Englewood Cliffs, NJ: Prentice-Hall.

Kavanagh, Letter of Opinion, August 16, 1957.

Kinloch, G. C. 1974. *The dynamics of race relations, a sociological analysis.* New York: McGraw-Hill.

Lapchick, R. E. 1991. *Five minutes to midnight: Race and sport in the 1990s.* Lanham, MD: Madison Books.

Law v. City of Baltimore, District Court of Maryland, 78 F.Supp. 346, June 18, 1948.

Leonard, W. M. II & T. Ellman. 1994. "The influence of race/ethnicity in salary arbitration." *Journal of Sport Behavior* 17:166–177.

Levine, M. L. 1996. *African Americans and civil rights: From 1619 to the present.* Phoenix, AZ: Oryx Press.

Life Magazine. 1940. "Joe Louis, the champion idol of his race sets a good example of conduct" [Earl Brown]. June 17, pp. 49–55.

Look Magazine. 1940. "I hate to hurt anybody" [Joe Louis & Gene Kessler]. May 7, p. 50.

Mackenzie, R. 1997. *A wee nip at the 19th hole: A history of the St. Andrews caddie.* Chelsea, MI: Sleeping Bear Press.

McDaniel, P. 1994. "Wake robins forever." *Golf World* (Vintage Issue), V23.

McKay, R. B. 1954. "Segregation and public recreation." *Virginia Law Review* 40: 697–731.

McRae, F. F. 1991. "Hidden traps beneath the placid greens." *American Visions* 6:26–29.

Mead, C. 1985. *Champion: Joe Louis, black hero in white America.* New York: Scribner.

Melnick, M. J. & D. Sabo. 1994. "Sport and social mobility among African-American and Hispanic athletes." In Eisen, G. & D.K. Wiggins (eds.), *Ethnicity and sport in North American history and culture.* Westport, CT: Greenwood Press: 221–241.

Miami Herald. 1952. "Ted Kroll captures coast golf." January 21, p. 1-D.

Miami Times. 1950. "Supreme court upholds golf discrimination policy." April 1, p. 1.

———. 1950. "Golfers seek Fla. Court ruling." February 18, p. 1.

———. 1950. "Golfers!" March 11, p. 2.

———. 1950. "Golf news." June 17, p. 5.

———. 1950. "Golf association to sponsor benefit dance." July 22, p. 15.

———. 1950. "Golf ass'n seeks $2,000 for supreme court fight." September 30, p. 17.

———. 1950. "Negroes win right to golf course-supreme court rules against Jim-crow setup." October 21, p. 1.

———. 1950. "Negroes may win rights to D.C. owned recreation." October 28, p. 10.

———. 1951. "State court upholds golf segregation-rules in face of U.S. supreme court mandate." September 8, p. 1.

———. 1952. "Golfers to file new suit against city of Miami." March 8, p. 1.

———. 1952. "Joe Louis to address golfers." May 5, p. 4.

———. 1953. "Graham competes for nat'l golf championships." July 11, p. 1.

Moorland-Spingarn Research Center, Howard University. 1986. Wake Robin Papers [Ethel Williams was interviewed by Elinor Sinnette on January 22, 1986], tape 1 side A.

Mosk, Letter to municipalities, June 1, 1960.

Newby, F. 1987. "Maggie Hathaway, golf player and civil rights leader." *Essence* 17:26.

New York Age. 1915. "Colored golf players." October 14, p. 6.

———. 1926. "New country club opens at edge hill." August 19, p. 7.

———. 1930. "Tuskegee women golfers join hole-in-one club." September 13, p. 6.

New York Times. 1938. "Street dance in Chicago: Negroes in gay celebration of Louis' triumph." June 23, p. 14.

———. 1948. "Louis top 'disappointer.' " January 17, p. 13.

———. 1948. "Champion, training for exhibition contest, says he has quit golf, will concentrate on being at peak for Walcott in June." January 24, p. 18.

———. 1952. "Joe Louis insists on entry in golf." January 15, p. 31.

———. 1952. "P.G.A. clears way for Louis to play." January 16, p. 30.

———. 1952. "Kroll leads coast golf as P.G.A. promises action in racial issue." January 18, p. 31.

———. 1952. "Kroll captures four-stroke lead in San Diego open golf." January 19, p. 19.

———. 1952. "C.I.O. decries golf bias." January 19, p. 19.

———. 1952. "P.G.A. committee votes to ease tourney ban on Negro players." January 20, p. S1.

O'Dell, B., Personal interview, May 6, 1998.

Perata, D.D. 1996. *Those pullman blues: An oral history of the African-American railroad attendant.* New York: Simon & Schuster.

Peterson, R. 1984. *Only the ball was white.* New York: McGraw-Hill.

Pittsburgh Courier. 1926. "Race golfer to try for NY city championship." June 19, p. 15.

———. 1926. "Shippen wins shady rest golf club tournament." July 10, p. 15.

———. 1926. "Shady rest to hold golf tournament." August 21, p. 14.

———. 1927. "Race caddies expert golf players, said." June 6, p. 4.

———. 1927. "Race caddie slain on course." June 11, p. 1.

———. 1927. "Bunker club is organized by local men." July 16, p. 6.

———. 1927. "Eastern golf course opens." July 30, p. 4.

———. 1927. "Members of shady rest to reorganize." October 29, p. 6.

———. 1927. "Golf grows in favor in east, west." August 13, p. 4.

———. 1927. "Get ready for golf meet." September 3, p. 5.

———. 1927. "Ball wins golf title." September 17, p. 4.

———. 1928. "Fore!" August 4, p. 4.

———. 1928. "Beautiful mapledale club scene of nat'l golf tourney." August 11, p. 4.

———. 1929. "Golf kings risk titles in NJ, nat'l tour begins." August 24, p. 5.

———. 1929. "Bobby Ball sets new record in winning nat'l golf crown." September 7, p. 5.

———. 1930. "Stage set for golf tourney." August 9, p. 4.

———. 1931. "Marshall wins pro golf title." September 12, p. 4.

———. 1934. "Wheeling to defend golf title in dixie." June 16, p. 4.

———. 1934. "Tutor, pupil win golfing titles in Mich." September 15, p. 5.

———. 1937. "500 golfers will vie in big Cleveland links tourney for nat'l title." August 7, p. 18.

———. 1938. "St. Louis golf star barred from tourney." May 5, p. 16.

———. 1940. "Tutor sees rare possibilities in Louis as brilliant golfer" [Chester Washington]. March 23, p. 16.

———. 1940. "Dave Wilson eastern open golf champion." July 13, p. 16.

———. 1940. "UGA meet to draw ranking golfers." August 17, p. 18.

———. 1941. "Lincoln country club course one of best." January 10, p. 16.

———. 1941. "Joe Louis golf meet in Detroit, Aug. 12–13–14." July 12.

———. 1941. "Wilson cops open; 8,000 turn out to see Joe Louis play." July 12, p. 18.

———. 1941. "Golfdom's best to compete in Joe Louis' open tourney." August 2, p. 17.

———. 1941. "Clyde Martin is favored to win Joe's tourney." August 9, 1941, p. 16.

———. 1941. "68 pros and 118 amateurs play in Joe's tournament." August 16, p. 17.

———. 1941. "Hurt! . . . A $1,000,000 hand." August 23, p. 17.

———. 1941. "Martin wins Detroit golf tourney." August 23, p. 17.

———. 1941. "Amateur king." August 23, p. 17.

———. 1941. "Golfdom's best to compete in Joe Louis' open tourney." August 26, p. 16.

———. 1941. "National open in Boston attracted nation's outstanding Negro golfers last week." August 30, p. 17.

———. 1941. "Golf" [Nat Rayburg]. August 30, p. 17.

———. 1945. "Expect top golfers in Louis' meet." June 23, p. 16.

———. 1945. "L.A. golf club awards trophies." December 15, p. 24.

———. 1946. "Nation's ranking golfers to enter Joe Louis open." July 6, p. 25.

———. 1946. "Rhodes favorite in national golf meet." August 17, p. 25.

———. 1946. "Wheeler and Brown pro, amateur golf kings." September 7, p. 27.

———. 1948. "Judge orders Baltimore golf course open." July 3, p. 17.

———. 1948. "PGA damage suit set for September." July 24, p. 9.

———. 1949. "Nation's top golfers set for Joe Louis tournament." August 20, p. 24.

———. 1949. "Ted Rhodes does it again; Captures U.G.A. title." September 3, p. 22.

———. 1949a. "Ted Rhodes' monopoly in Joe Louis open continues." September 10, p. 18.

———. 1949b. "Rhodes the master." September 10, p. 18.

———. 1950. "United golf association arranges summer tournament swing." May 27, p. 23.

———. 1950. "Courier point system will select golf's big 3." June 17, p. 22.

———. 1950. "Pittsburgh Courier UGA bulletin board." July 15, p. 24.

———. 1950. "Pittsburgh Courier UGA bulletin board." July 22, p. 24.

———. 1957. "Sumpter to defend elks' crown." June 8, p. 23. *Professional Golfer.*

———. 1961. "Mid-year meeting keyed." July, pp. 16–17, 53.

———. 1962. "PGA to continue leadership of new 'golden era' in golf." January, pp. 7–8, 58–59, 69.

Professional Golfers' Association of America. Constitution and by-laws, 1948; 1962.

Reed, W. L. 1991. "Blacks in golf." *Trotter Institute Review* 5:19–23.

Rice v. Arnold, Supreme Court of Florida, 45 So.2d 195, March 24, 1950.

Rice v. Arnold, Supreme Court of Florida, 54 So.2d. 114, August 31, 1951.

Richmond Afro-American. 1940. "Scenes at eastern golf championships." July 13, p. 20.

————. 1940. "Louis enters national amateur golf tourney." August 24, p. 8.

————. 1940. "Robinson regains amateur title, takes golf national at palos hills." August 31, p. 21.

————. 1941. "Louis lures golfers." August 16, p. 21.

————. 1941. "Golf by Nat Rayburg." August 30, p. 22.

————. 1941. "Joe Louis voted fighter of the year." December 20, p. 22.

Riess, S. A. 1994. "From pitch to putt: Sport and class in Anglo-American sport." *Journal of Sport History* 24:138–184.

Rust, E. & A. Rust, Jr. 1985. *Art Rust's illustrated history of the black athlete.* Garden City, NY: Doubleday and Co.

Sammons, J. T. 1994. "'Race' and sport: A critical, historical examination." *Journal of Sport History* 21:203–278.

Shapiro, M., Dohn, W. & Berger, L. 1986. *Golf: A turn-of-the-century treasury.* Secaucus, NJ: Castle.

Shropshire, K. L. 1996. "Private race consciousness." *Detroit College of Law at Michigan State University Law Review* 1996:628–652.

Sifford, C. & J. Gullo. 1992. *Just let me play: The story of Charlie Sifford, the first Black PGA golfer.* Latham, NY: British American Publishing.

Simkins v. City of Greensboro, N.C. 485, 103 S.E. 2d 846, 1958.

Simkins v. City of Greensboro, U.S. District Court, 149 F.Supp. 562, March 18, 1957.

Simkins v. State of North Carolina, U.S. Supreme Court, 80 S.Ct. 1482, June 27, 1960.

Sinnette, C. H. 1998. *Forbidden fairways: African Americans and the game of golf.* Chelsea, MI: Sleeping Bear Press.

Smith, R. A. 1979. "The Paul Robeson-Jackie Robinson saga and a political collision." *Journal of Sport History* 6:5–27.

Smith, T. G. 1988. "Outside the pale: The exclusion of Blacks from the National Football League, 1934–1946." *Journal of Sport History* 15:255–281.

Sommers, R. 1996. *The U.S. open, golf's ultimate challenge.* New York: Oxford University Press.

Spivey, D. 1988. " 'End Jim Crow in sports': The protest at New York University, 1940–1941." *Journal of Sport History* 15:282–303.

Spivey, D. (ed.). 1985. *Sport in America: New historical perspectives.* Westport, CT: Greenwood Press.

The Courier. 1952. "T. Rhodes shoots 71 in Phoenix." January 26, p. 20.

————. 1952. "Hawkins, 'father of negro golf,' helped pioneer UGA." February 2, p. 20.

Time Magazine. 1941. "Black Moses." September 29, pp. 60–64.

United Golfer and Other Sports. 1938. "Golfers sue when refused right to preferred course." August, p. 11.

Vineyard Gazette, 1947. Legal Files, 1940–55. Papers of the NAACP.

Washington Post. 1987. "For black women, golf wasn't easy" [Courtland Milloy]. April 26, p. B3.

————. 1997. "Given little choice, black golfers select their club" [Leonard Shapiro]. May 28, A1, A10.

Wesley v. City of Savannah, U.S. District Court, 294 F.Supp. 698, January 9, 1969.

Wiggins, D. K. 1977. "Good times on the old plantation: Popular recreations of the Black slave in Antebellum South, 1810–1860." *Journal of Sport History* 4:260–284.

———. 1980a. "The play of slave children in the plantation communities of the Old South, 1820–1860." *Journal of Sport History* 7:21–39.

———. 1980b. "Sport and popular pastimes: Shadow of the slave quarter." *Canadian Journal of History of Sport and Physical Education* 11:61–88.

———. 1983. "Wendell Smith, the Pittsburgh Courier-Journal and the campaign to include Blacks in organized baseball, 1933–1945." *Journal of Sport History* 10:278–299.

———. 1986. "From plantation to playing field: historical writings on the Black athlete in American sport." *Research Quarterly for Exercise and Sport* 57: 101–116.

———. 1988a. "Boxing's sambo twins: Racial stereotypes in Jack Johnson and Joe Louis newspaper cartoons, 1908–1938." *Journal of Sport History* 15:242–254.

———. 1988b. "The future of college athletics is at stake: Black athletes and racial turmoil on three predominantly white university campuses, 1968–1972." *Journal of Sport History* 15:304–333.

———. 1989. "Great speed but little stamina: The historical debate over Black athletic superiority." *Journal of Sport History* 16:158–185.

———. 1994. "The notion of double-consciousness and the involvement of Black Athletes in American sport." In G. Eisen & D. K. Wiggins (eds.), *Ethnicity and sport in North American history and culture*. Westport, CT: Greenwood Press: 133–155.

Wind, H. W. 1956. *The story of American golf*. New York: Simon and Schuster.

Wolseley, R. 1971. *The black press, U.S.A.* Ames: Iowa State University Press.

Woodward, C. V. 1957. *The strange career of Jim Crow*. New York: Oxford University Press.

Yu, H. 1996. "Taking a swing at stereotypes." Reported in the *Tallahassee Democrat*, December 15, p. 3F.

Zang, D. 1988. "Calvin Hill interview." *Journal of Sport History* 15:334–355.

Index

About the Authors

MARVIN P. DAWKINS is Associate Professor of Sociology, Research Faculty in the Center for Research on Sport in Society and Director of the Caribbean, African and Afro-American Studies Program at the University of Miami. Professor Dawkins has published extensively on aspects of Black life in books and articles.

GRAHAM C. KINLOCH has been engaged in teaching and carrying out research in the areas of sociological theory, race and minority relations and comparative analysis for the past thirty-one years. He has been at Florida State University since 1971 and has published a number of books and papers on these topics. Presently, he serves as Associate Dean of Academic Affairs in the College of Social Sciences and as Professor of Sociology.